C0-DBG-411

In History's Shadow

In History's Shadow

Lee Harvey Oswald, Kerry Thornley & the Garrison Investigation

Joe G. Biles

Writers Club Press
San Jose   New York   Lincoln   Shanghai

In History's Shadow
Lee Harvey Oswald, Kerry Thornley & the Garrison Investigation

All Rights Reserved © 2002 by Joe G. Biles

No part of this book may be reproduced or transmitted in any form or by any means, graphic, electronic, or mechanical, including photocopying, recording, taping, or by any information storage retrieval system, without the permission in writing from the publisher.

Writers Club Press
an imprint of iUniverse, Inc.

For information address:
iUniverse, Inc.
5220 S. 16th St., Suite 200
Lincoln, NE 68512
www.iuniverse.com

Parts of this book have appeared in different forms in *Kennedy Assassination Chronicles* and *JFK Deep Politics Quarterly*.

ISBN: 0-595-22455-5

Printed in the United States of America

For my mother

"The whole thing was very interesting for awhile, the assassination, because—on the surface—there was good reason for the unenlightened SS and F.B.I. to suspect I might've had a hand in it. We had some polite conversations and finally, I guess, I was cleared. No word from them lately. I hope, though, my move to this area scared the piss out of 'em. Whether or not I'll be asked to put my 2¢ in at the Warren hearing, I don't know. Or care. When it is all over, though, I may yet go piss on JFK's grave, RIP."

–**Letter from Kerry Thornley,**
February 1964

Contents

Foreword

The assassination of President John F. Kennedy is now, more then ever before, a historical event that will continue to fade from the living memory of the population, where it could be discussed at the dinner table. Nevertheless it is a monumental occurrence that traumatized this nation and was a major launching point which set in motion a cynicism and disbelief that still plagues our nation. It occurred when this nation was disturbed by a stalemate in Korea and the loss of Cuba right on our doorstep. The Bay of Pigs fiasco and the Cuban missile crisis brought the era of mass destruction to a vivid, riveting reality and Vietnam was looming larger on the horizon. The quick arrest of Lee Harvey Oswald, a Marxist, and his murder seemed to bring an unsettling quiet. The Warren Commission was set up and a top level investigation gave an assurance that this horrible event would have the light shone on it and bring back some sort of tranquility. Everything would be answered. It wasn't and still isn't. The Report and the twenty-six volumes of exhibits were studied. Cracks appeared and doubts arose, questions were left dangling, conclusions of the Report seemed to wildly differ from the evidence presented. Documents were classified and locked away for seventy-five years. A strong outcry of dissatisfaction and disbelief set in motion other Committees such as the Rockefeller and Church Committees, and then a House Select Committee on Assassinations was tasked with shining the light on the Warren Commission Report and the cold blooded murder of the Rev. Martin Luther King Jr.

It must be settled, for better or worse, to restore a confidence in "Our" government and its official agencies as true representatives of "We The People", one nation united in a firm belief that "someone" is standing watch against the evil of individuals and deceit or lies in the tightest, official closets, of our "secret" agencies.

The HSCA had its own staff and a budget that seemed adequate. The Committee had the benefit of years of study and research and it could obtain expert opinions on its own. Its report was written and released in 1979 along with twelve volumes of exhibits. Now at last the truth would be known.

It wasn't to be. The HSCA report did not settle anything and added a shooter from the front and a theory that "the mob" might have done it. Many of its own documents were locked down. It did not get the autopsy and crime scene straightened out and it accepted the "magic bullet theory". It did not explain how "the mob" could have blocked all of this from being done properly in the first place, or how this all could still be locked away from public view. How could this be?

When this nation can not make a believable report on the assassination of its Chief Executive, the President of the United States, then it is necessary for the people to raise such an outcry that their elected officials must act. It is ironic that a simple citizen with an 8mm camera, with color but no sound, could record an event that the best and the brightest that this nation had to offer could not reconcile into a believable report. Oliver Stone's movie, *JFK*, seemed to fire up a renewed outcry. President George Bush in 1992 set up the Assassination Records Review Board that would release the classified documents that pertained to this travesty of events. Not a report, not an investigation, but just release the documents. That speaks volumes of this nation's ability to investigate the murder of its President. There's a reported four million documents in these archives and who has the ability to read that?

Researchers. Historians. Just plain authors.

Citizens are left to attempt to sift out the truth, if it is to be found in the land where the Capital City Band seems to play the Potomac Two-Step, and the public servants dance to it. It is slow, deliberate, and meant not to be broken. In this case, officially, it has not been broken. Official investigations at the highest levels did not break it. How can this be in the land of the free?

L.J. Delsa and I were born and raised in New Orleans and we worked for over twenty years in and around the French Quarter as police detectives. The Quarter is loved by all who fall under its influence but in its one hundred and twenty square blocks were and are some of the most interesting mixes of people that can be found from around the world. Organized crime, bohemians, artists, hustlers, musicians, homosexual and lesbian cultures, writers, thriving neighborhoods of ordinary, everyday, honest citizens, businesses, as well as wealthy and influential people captured by the charm.

It has stories of pirates, duels, slave owners, sellers and haunted houses. It has stories of Lee Harvey Oswald who lived there for many of his formative years, with his mother. Any detective working this area will tell of the strange way the simplest of cases can get caught up and mixed into this "Gumbo". It takes patience and a special understanding to put up with this mix to get at any truth contained in this Quarter. In the early sixties the fight against communism and the upheaval of the nation's racial Civil Rights struggles was mixed into this stew with feelings running strong. Oswald's boyhood friends and new acquaintances were strongly anti-Federal Government over the Castro and racial issues. They were actively supporting the movement to follow up on the Bay of Pigs fiasco, which they were involved in, and hopefully overthrow Castro. Oswald mixed with these friends and the French Quarter and the New Orleans detectives started to follow some crazy sounding leads. They were stopped cold and put into the overall plan that seemed to be organized crime oriented rather than going where the leads were pointing. Organized Crime leads were present but strongly aligned with rogue and possible active intelligence assets. Which was right? Maybe the de-classified documents will reveal the answers. This book gives insight into that area and attempts to show parts of how this could be in the land of the free and the home of the brave.

Oswald, suddenly and publicly, turns pro-Castro and goes on radio as a Marxist. He has excellent credentials but why did he mix easily with the radical right and persons of alleged intelligence connections from his younger days? He moves to Dallas and the assassination occurs. New Orleans District Attorney Jim Garrison, gets and gives the Federal Government information within days of Nov. 22, 1963 of these associates and it is not followed up to its full potential. Years after the Warren report and after years of receiving information Garrison brings charges against Clay Shaw. The "Gumbo" of the French Quarter is mixed into a story right out of a Damon Runyan, "Guys and Dolls" cast of characters. Strange stories, strange characters, and intrigue. It looked ludicrous on the national stage and T.V. and newscasts made a laughing stock of the D.A. Garrison, loses that case and is brick walled and slam dunked for ten years. He had the audacity to try to solve the assassination of the president that he loved and "declassify" a conspiracy that took shape in New Orleans. When the HSCA was convened Garrison is redeemed in the eyes of New Orleans, and is elected to judge of the Louisiana Fifth Circuit Court of Appeals. Judge Garrison never quit, never bowed to pressure—that is seldom seen—against attempts to solve a murder case. He rarely got truthful answers but he surely asked some truthful questions. He brought into focus some people like David Ferrie, organized crime and intelligence connections, Kerry Thornley, a marine buddy of Oswald and possible disinformation agent, and Jack Martin, a private investigator who made a phone call and claimed that all of the investigations came from that call.

If anyone wants an insight into the Assassination without reading four million documents then this book is an excellent source for understanding the "investigations" or the lack thereof. This book gives some of the answers right out of new documents and in a brief form. This author is a young researcher and the future will belong to the careful researchers and the historians. We haven't done too well in the past, but this nation is the home of the brave isn't it? Will the researchers get it right when the government didn't?

Robert C. Buras Jr.
Lieutenant, New Orleans Police Department (retired)
Staff Investigator, House Select Committee on Assassinations
New Orleans, Louisiana
February 2002

Preface

"It may well turn out, in the course of time, that our expanding concept of the fair trial, of the rights of the defendant against the state, may come to be seen as the greatest contribution our country has made to this world...."

–Jim Garrison, 1965[1]

It has been thirty-five years since New Orleans District Attorney Jim Garrison undertook the investigation of the assassination of President John F. Kennedy. That investigation was marred by controversy from nearly the moment it began. Allegations of intimidation tactics, bribery and testimony solicited under drugs and hypnosis all served to discredit Garrison's investigation. For thirty-five years Garrison's discoveries have been seldom written about, often obfuscated and never *ever* looked at through the objective lens of history.

My own involvement in the story of Jim Garrison began three years ago when, after a long night of traveling home from a trip, I caught the last hour or so of Oliver Stone's *JFK* on television. *JFK*, the only instance when Garrison has ever been portrayed positively by a major media organization (Warner Brothers), was itself subject to immense criticism after its 1991 debut. The debate had long since ceased to be front-page news by the time I was old enough to see it. What I gleaned from that hour of celluloid—Garrison's closing summation at the trial of Clay Shaw—was my first quasi-comprehensive understanding of the president's assassination. I had been aware before of the conspiracy theories surrounding the assassination but I had never made an effort to know what those theories were or what the evidence was. And while Stone's *JFK* can only be looked at as historical fiction, the majority surely would agree that Stone's counter-myth is clearly more honest and factual than the Warren Commission's own fable.

From that day on I was consumed by the killing of the president. I bought several of the major books (James DiEugenio's excellent *Destiny Betrayed: JFK, Cuba and the Garrison Case*, Seth Kantor's *The Ruby Cover-Up* and Michael Griffith's modest but incisive monograph *Compelling Evidence* were among the first), searched the web high and low and continued to watch any TV program I saw on the subject. For a solid month that spring I would go to the library at lunch and spend about ninety minutes a day reading the Warren Report. Afterward I found an excellent website, called simply "The John F. Kennedy Assassination Homepage," (now located at www.jfk-assassination.de) maintained by a gentleman called Ralph Schuster that featured much of the testimony from the Warren Commission's hearings. Reading the actual evidence, one has to conclude that the Commission either was deaf or had other motives in mind besides publishing the objective truth about the assassination.

My assassination obsession continued to be fed by various sources. My personal library skyrocketed in volume, and I eventually obtained the published volumes of the Warren Commission and the House Select Committee on Assassinations. I also began my documentary research through the National Archives in College Park, Maryland. All the while, I kept coming back to DA Jim Garrison and his maligned case. During this early period Garrison's probe was still periodically the subject of a news article, and it wasn't hard to figure out he wasn't very well liked.

The Assassination Records Review Board (ARRB) had already shut down by the time I began studying the assassination seriously. William Davy's book *Let Justice Be Done* followed on the heels of this flood of new documents and reinforced my opinion that whatever his faults, Jim Garrison did have *something* and the best way to study it was to study the living documentary history of the investigation. Armed with Peter Vea's index to the Garrison files, the focus of my studies at the National Archives became New Orleans. Reading the actual evidence Garrison unearthed and studying the history of his probe, it became obvious that the harshest criticisms of the district attorney were entirely unfounded. The most serious—that Garrison suborned perjury from star-witness Perry Russo by hypnosis—falls apart completely under realistic examination, and any objective student will find that almost all of the allegations leveled against Garrison today are mere repetitions of the original accusations made during the 1967 propaganda campaign designed to shut down the investigation.

Since Clay Shaw's acquittal in 1969, Garrison has been a pariah to the mainstream media. Whatever the truth is, ABC, CBS and NBC are simply not willing to honestly study the assassination, nor admit that their conclusion in 1967 was wrong.[2] This is highly unfortunate. An honest look at the evidence shows Garrison's case was valid. But the media, and many even in the assassination research community, are unwilling to give Garrison's case that honest look.

Another interesting omission in the study of the Garrison case is the case against Dean Andrews and Kerry Thornley. Garrison charged both with perjury in connection with the assassination probe. Andrews was tried and convicted, and Garrison's successor, DA Harry Connick, Sr., dropped the charges against Thornley before he could go to trial. The Andrews case has always been largely looked at as a mere footnote in the conspiracy case against Clay Shaw, which in some respects it is. I have nevertheless always felt Andrews' August 1967 perjury trial deserved more attention than it has received. The other individual, Thornley, was even more critical.

Kerry Thornley was a Marine who was stationed with Oswald in California. When Oswald was shot by Jack Ruby, the FBI, the Warren Commission and the media used Thornley to paint a horrific picture of Oswald as a lonely, twisted communist capable of killing the president.

Thornley testified before the Orleans Parish Grand Jury five years later, and denied, as he had in 1963, that he had met or seen Oswald since the Marine Corps. This time though, Thornley was arrested and charged with perjury. Anti-Garrison authors, David Lifton being the most vocal, have always portrayed Thornley as the innocent victim of the DA's excesses. Viewing the evidence against Thornley in Garrison's own files leaves the impartial student only one conclusion—David Lifton is wrong. Thornley was certainly not innocent, and if any ex-Marine had a twisted, disaffected psychology, it was he.

This book is a straightforward attempt to relate a more complete history of the Garrison investigation. Its primary focus is not on Clay Shaw, as has been done so often in the past, but on Kerry Thornley—the evidence against him, how Thornley ties to Oswald, and what conclusions we can now make about Lee Harvey Oswald. Much of this evidence ties into Oswald's intelligence connections. All of it reveals the untold story of the life and lies of Kerry W. Thornley. Along the way, I've included a more complete account of the Dean Andrews perjury case. And by necessity, the reader will find complete coverage of Clay Shaw's arrest and trial—including much of the new evidence against him. Finally, at the end of the book, I will attempt an informed speculation on who might have been *the* mastermind of the plot.

Jim Garrison is often criticized for erecting a shoddy case against Clay Shaw. Indeed, *The New York* Times called Garrison's investigation "one of the most disgraceful chapters in the history of American jurisprudence." But investigators for the House Select Committee on Assassinations in charge of probing the New Orleans area, found that, "While the trial of Shaw took two years to bring about and did eventually end in acquittal, the basis for the charges seems sound and the investigation and prosecution thorough, given the extraordinary nature of the charges and the times." I believe the reader will find this to be true, not only of the case against Shaw, but of all of Garrison's defendants.

Joe G. Biles

Mineral Wells, Texas
December 2001

Acknowledgements

This book would not have been possible without the assistance of many in the research community, and the support of my friends and loved ones. Thanks goes to the following researchers who have aided my study of the Garrison case and the assassination: Lisa Pease, Michael Griffith, John Hunt, Tim Smith, Walt Brown, Gary Mack, Debra Conway, Robert Groden, Paris Flammonde, Peter Dale Scott, Stuart Wexler, Rex Bradford, Ed Sherry, Stewart Galanor, Malcolm Blunt, J. Gary Shaw, and John Williams. I am pleased to say my discussions with William Davy, James DiEugenio, Larry Hancock, Joan Mellen, Dave Reitzes, Stephen Roy, Henry Stroud and Stephen Tyler have been particularly insightful and significant. Dr. David Mantik's work on the medical evidence is required reading, and his kind words at the 2001 JFK Lancer Conference were appreciated. In September 2000 I spent about an hour talking on the phone with HSCA investigator L.J. Delsa. It was a highly enjoyable experience, and Mr. Delsa was full of interesting and important information. I was extremely honored to share the head table last year at the Lancer awards banquet with Jim Olivier, a Louisiana television personality, and Dennis David, one of the Navy medical technicians present at JFK's autopsy. Both were fun to talk to, and, as any patriotic American would, I found Mr. David's comments about our country positively inspiring.

Tracking down those hard-to-find books would be impossible were it not for Andrew Winiarczyk's Last Hurrah Bookshop. The Last Hurrah is located at 849 W. Third Street, #1, Williamsport, PA 17701. Their phone number is (570) 321-1150.

For their editorial assistance and numerous insights, I must thank many of my teachers at Mineral Wells High School, among them Coach

Mark Beaty, Mrs. Joyce Ford, Mrs. Leah Sessum, Mr. and Mrs. Mike Dills, Mrs. Wanda Reddell, Mr. Dan Stanford, Coach Steve Smith, and Mme. Antoinette West. I must also think members of the faculty and administration for helping make this work possible: Ms. Jane Dickerson, Mrs. Linda Medlin, Mr. Jerry Dix and Dr. Ben Setliff.

In my Civil Air Patrol career I have been blessed with a number of fine superiors and colleagues, both cadets and senior members, who have contributed to my professional growth. On the cadet side are Cadet Majors Kevin Lawhon and Adam Tyra and Cadet Colonels Jennifer Lamonte and Paul Wilson. On the senior side are First Lieutenants Taylor Cleghorn and John Lavoie, Captain Gene Akins, Majors Brooks Cima and Jose "Jimmy Hernandez," Lieutenant Colonels Michael Crognale, John Paulos and Don Windle, and Brigadier General James C. Bobick. And finally, I have been proud to know and work with Lieutenant Colonels Mark McNair and Waldo Steen, USAFR (Ret).

Friends are what make the world go round and I am pleased to count these individuals as friends: Trey Temple, Lauren Wheat, Sarah Baker, John Upham, Jeremy Glidewell, Hillman Ryan Clark "Skippy" Hayes, Marcus Paulsen, Adam Hull, Andrea Henderson, Yari Nunez, Michael Benavides, Evan Blasor, CiCi Walker, Rebecca Akins, Rance Seay, Terrell Radford, Jamie Tuggle, David Shorter, Seth Hudson, Adam Tyra, Jason Tyra, Frank Chou, Brandon Price, Ty Thomas, Jose Luis Hernandez, Rebecca Davis, Maryssa Szekeres, Kalan Turner, MeLissa Baker and many others.

Allison Fowler has become my greatest asset in my life over this past year. She is friend, confidante, counselor, partner in crime, and so much more. I don't know what I'd do without her.

My family, including my sisters, Sarah, Glenda, Brenda and Laura, and my brothers, Dick and Jimmie Jr., has been especially helpful and supportive in the progress of this book. My mother above anyone else has made this research possible.

Chapter One

Revelations of a "Battling District Attorney"

"I was happily married, the father of three children (with two more to come), and I had a great job. I was quite content with the way my life was going and with the world around me. In retrospect, it would be more accurate to say that I was tranquilized by the very world in which I lived."

–Jim Garrison, 1988[1]

"Those fellows on the Warren Commission were dead wrong. There's no way in the world that one man could have shot up Jack Kennedy that way."[2] The words struck at Jim Garrison like knives. For the last four years, Garrison had been the highly successful District Attorney of New Orleans. At this time, in November of 1966, Garrison had just become the first DA in recent memory to actually be re-elected. A 1968 Ramparts cover story by ex-FBI Agent William Turner describes vividly Garrison's popularity at the time:

For six years now he has been the tough, uncompromising district attorney of New Orleans, a rackets-buster without parallel in a political freebooting state. He was elected on a reform platform and meant it. Turning down a Mob proposition that would have netted him $3000 a week as his share of slot machine proceeds, he proceeded to raid Bourbon Street clip joints, crack down on prostitution, and eliminate bail bond rackets. His track record as the proverbial fighting DA is impressive: his office has never lost a major case, and no convictions have been toppled on appeal because of improper methods.[3]

In September of 1966, Garrison had been invited by Joseph Rault of Rault Petroleum Corporation to attend the annual American Petroleum Institute meeting in New York City. After the meeting, Garrison sat with Rault and U.S. Senator Russell Long (D-Louisiana) onboard his flight back home. When Long aired his dissatisfaction with the methods and conclusions of the Warren Commission, it opened Garrison's mind. Garrison had never before, he felt, had reason to question the Commission's lone-assassin verdict, but now that he saw the increasing public criticism of the Report as justified it brought him back to a series of strange events that occurred in his jurisdiction the weekend of the assassination.

The Tipster, the P.I. and the Getaway Pilot

On the evening of November 22, 1963, Guy Banister (a local Private Investigator formerly with the FBI), went to the Katz and Jammer Bar with his associate Jack Martin.[4] Though Banister was known to drink he consumed an unusually large amount of alcohol on the night in question.[5] Later, he and Martin went back to their office at 531 Lafayette Street where they got into an argument. At one point Martin said, "What are you going to do—kill me like you all did Kennedy?"[6] Banister then retrieved his .357 Magnum and proceeded to beat Martin in the head with it.

That same night, a New Orleans Police Department (NOPD) Intelligence cop called the New Orleans FBI office to report that an anti-Castro adventurer and former airline pilot named David Ferrie "was possibly friendly" with Oswald "in view of his Cuban activities," and that Bill Reed of WWL T.V. was doing a check on Ferrie because Ferrie allegedly "was a friend of LEE HARVEY OSWALD...."[7] The strange thing was while Ferrie was anti-Castro (he had reportedly smuggled people in and out of Cuba, as well as participated in incendiary bombing missions), the media was having a field day that Assassination Friday reporting that Oswald was a dedicated Marxist. In fact, that very night, Dallas DA Henry Wade was planning to indict Oswald for murder "in furtherance of an international Communist conspiracy."[8] Things did not add up.

Jack Martin survived the beating from Banister—though he later said that had Banister's secretary Delphine Roberts not involved herself he would have been killed—and was treated by Charity Hospital.[9] While the beating had loosened Martin's tongue about what went on at Banister's office, he would curiously not implicate Banister, but rather the same David Ferrie whom the FBI had been told of the previous night. Martin refused to file charges against his employer Banister—who he said was "like a father" to him—or mention him in connection with the assassination.[10] He (Martin) had no such qualms about Ferrie. While Martin was once a friend of Ferrie, the pair had a bitter falling out concerning their involvement in fake "ordination mills." Later, Ferrie found out that Martin had been making long-distance phone calls and charging them to the offices of Banister and Ferrie's employer G. Wray Gill. Author Patricia Lambert theorizes that Ferrie may have ratted out Martin to Banister, furthering the pair's feud.[11]

Martin now contacted the FBI, the NOPD and the NODA—in this case through Assistant DA Herman Kohlman who informed Garrison of the lead about Ferrie.[12] During this time, in addition to credible information, Martin also made various claims such as the idea that Ferrie "had flown Oswald to Dallas" and that he had induced a posthypnotic suggestion on Oswald's part that resulted in Oswald's participation in the shooting.[13] This may have been due to Martin's alcoholism, his hatred of Ferrie or his own psychological failings:

> *A States-Item reporter, who has spent more time than most listening to Jack Martin talk, describes him "as one of the most interesting men I ever have met."*

> *"He is as full of that well known waste material as a yule hen. On the other hand, he is many times a very competent investigator who has the friendship and confidence of reputable, well-placed individuals. He drinks, often to excess, but bears no real evidence of being an alcoholic. He desperately wants to be loved, and this is his downfall. Often, he wants to please everyone, everywhere so damn much that he ends by hurting the people who have befriended him. He must be taken with a grain of salt leavened by a grain of confidence. If you listen to him for two hours, often you will receive two minutes of useful information. I suppose, to sum him up, he is like a muddy river. You have to use a very fine filter."[14]*

Despite his problems, many of Martin's allegations against Ferrie were credible and were verified by later evidence. By this time Garrison was quietly looking into the assassination—he had since learned that Oswald had spent the previous summer in New Orleans—and the search began for David Ferrie.

The Houston Trip

When Garrison learned of Martin's accusations, he sent some of his assistants to Ferrie's apartment to question him. Inside were two of "Dave Ferrie's boys," awaiting Ferrie's return. They told Garrison's men that Ferrie had gone to Texas on a trip the night of the assassination and were not back yet. Intriguingly, the DA's investigators retrieved from Ferrie's home three U.S. passports, all of which were stamped but lacked names, pictures and descriptions.[15] When Ferrie did return on November 25, he appeared at Garrison's office for questioning. Garrison found Ferrie's story unbelievable and turned him over for further questioning by the FBI. Ferrie told the FBI that he did not know Oswald and accused Jack Martin of being an "unethical and dangerous person"[16] who was attempting to falsely link him to the Kennedy murder. Ferrie was released. The New Orleans FBI Office now contacted Jack Martin. According to Martin, "They took a few notes, they were more interested in punching at me…They were pretty well fixed in their opinion so I never questioned the FBI to their motives. The minute my wife and I saw those things, we snapped."[17]

Martin now told the FBI that he had been overtaken by a case of "telephonitis," said that the beating by Banister was motivated by the previously mentioned long distance phone bills and not the assassination, and when he saw how quickly Ferrie was cleared by the FBI, "recanted" his statement. Despite what he told the FBI, Martin wrote later that day to Richard Robey of the FAA:

> *Don't your case records on Ferrie show that this guy Oswald was a member of Ferrie's so-called phony CAP squadron?*
>
> *Remember all those large group pictures…Wasn't his picture in these? Perhaps you will also remember Ferrie had a bunch of these foreign rifles that he used to train his cadets with.[18]*

What actually did transpire during Ferrie's trip to Houston is unclear. According to Ferrie, he and companions Melvin Coffee and Alvin Beauboeuf went to Houston to relax after Gill's victory in the Marcello trial that ended that day, as well as do some investigative work for Gill. He also said that the trio departed after dinner and planned on duck hunting and going ice skating.[19] Coffee said the group left around 7:00 PM, but that they left without any guns for the duck hunting expedition Ferrie talked about. Alvin Beauboeuf disagreed with Ferrie and Coffee's recollections about the time—he said they left around 4:00 PM—but agreed with Coffee that they brought no weapons. Coffee also said that the trip had been planned a couple of days in advance and that it was Ferrie's idea, while Beauboeuf remembered that he had proposed the trip, which had been planned in detail a week before.[20]

All three agreed that on Saturday, November 23rd they paid a visit to the Winterland Ice Skating Rink in Houston. Owner Chuck Rolland testified that Ferrie had called ahead, a week or so in advance of their visit (raising doubt as to the veracity of Coffee's statements). While Coffee and Beauboeuf skated, Ferrie made and received several calls at the pay phone, and introduced himself several times to Rolland, an activity Rolland found strange. Later, the group left and Ferrie told Rolland that they would return later that day. They did not, and instead drove on to Galveston. The group began their trip home to New Orleans the next day and on their way back learned that Oswald had been killed in Dallas. While talking on the phone with G. Wray Gill, Ferrie learned that he was being sought by the DA's Office for questioning. After leaving Coffee and Beauboeuf in New Orleans, Ferrie made his way to Southeastern University in Hammond, Louisiana where he spent the night with Thomas Compton, whom he had met in the Civil Air Patrol. According to Compton, Ferrie was very upset about being suspected by the authorities of involvement in the Kennedy murder. After several conversations with Gill, Ferrie decided to return to New Orleans and face questioning.[21]

With Ferrie cleared by the FBI, Garrison now closed the book on the Kennedy case and returned to "the prosecution of burglaries, armed robberies, and other local crimes."[22] His ignorance would not last.

544 Camp Street

On August 9, 1963, a strange thing happened on Canal Street in New Orleans. A man was passing out leaflets for his new chapter of the Fair Play for Cuba Committee. Out of nowhere, he was attacked by three Cubans. They assaulted him and attempted to steal his pamphlets. His name was Lee Harvey Oswald.[23] The leader of the Cubans was Carlos Bringuier of the Cuban Student Directorate, or DRE.[24] Oswald had visited him a few days before, offering to lend his support to the DRE. Immediately afterward, the four were arrested and taken to station. After speaking to Agent John Quigley of the FBI, Oswald was released.

Through his arrest, and the subsequent confiscation of several of the August 9 leaflets, Oswald unwittingly set in motion the pattern of investigation may have unraveled the conspiracy that used Oswald as its *agent provocateur,* and placed him on that street corner with those pamphlets in the first place. The reason was that it was on August 9 and August 9 alone that the leaflets bore this address:

FPCC
544 Camp Street
New Orleans, LA

After returning from his trip with Rault and Senator Long, Garrison had his office order the Warren Report and the accompanying 26 volumes of hearings and exhibits. He would spend the next several months studying those volumes in their entirety, learning of Oswald's strange military career, with all the fingerprints of intelligence training, and his equally strange and provocative summer in New Orleans. The following is what Garrison found in those volumes.

Myth of a Marxist

There are many theories as to the methods of the Warren Commission. According to one hypothesis, the Warren Report was simply a construct of the Commission's worst witnesses—and the denial of their best evidence. This pattern can be seen in many areas. Despite the many witnesses to shots from locations other than the Texas School Book Depository, the attention and praise of the Report was heaped upon perjured testimony of Howard Leslie Brennan. Despite the reports from the Parkland doctors placing an "avulsive" wound at the rear of Kennedy's skull, all conclusions are drawn from the accounts of James Humes, J. Thornton Boswell and Pierre Finck, who, if Finck's cross-examination at the Shaw trial is any indication, would not have held up in a real court. This pattern can be extended to the Commission's myth of Oswald's political life.

The Commission's interpretation of Oswald's politics is stated plainly on page 23 of the Report, in their Summary and Conclusions. The Report reads that although the Commission could not determine a complete, specific motive for Oswald, they did find as a factor of that motive:

> *His avowed commitment to Marxism and communism, as he understood the terms and developed his own interpretation of them; this was expressed by his antagonism toward the United States, by his defection to the Soviet Union, by his failure to be reconciled with life in the United States even after his disenchantment with the Soviet Union, and by his efforts, though frustrated, to go to Cuba.*[25]

The specifics are addressed in Chapter 17, "Lee Harvey Oswald: Background and Possible Motives," under the section "Interest in Marxism." Oswald's background is, of course, one of the most substantial gray areas to be found in assassination research. Jim Garrison realized this back in the fall of 1966 when he read the Commission's 26 volumes, and like others before him, he thought the key lay in California.

> *I began with El Toro Marine Base in California, where Oswald was stationed from November 1958 to September 1959. I figured his fellow soldiers should have had a pretty good look at Oswald in the close quarters of military training.*[26]

The Commission cited the testimony of three of Oswald's fellow Marines specifically: Nelson Delgado, John E. Donovan and Kerry Thornley (who ironically had written a novel, The Idle Warriors, with a character based on Oswald before the assassination). From the Report:

Thornley, who thought Oswald had an "irrevocable conviction" that his Marxist beliefs were correct, testified:

*I think you could sit down and argue with him for a number of years * * * and I don't think you could have changed his mind on that unless you knew why he believed it in the first place. I certainly don't. I don't think with any kind of formal argument you could have shaken that conviction. And that is why I say irrevocable. It was just—never getting back to looking at things from any other way once he had become a Marxist, whenever that was.*

. . .

*Lieutenant Donovan testified that Oswald thought that "there were many grave injustices concerning the affairs in the international situation." He recalled that Oswald had a specific interest in Latin America, particularly Cuba, and expressed opposition to the Batista regime and sympathy for Castro, an attitude which, Donovan said, was "not * * * unpopular" at that time.*

. . .

*Thornley thought that Oswald not only wanted a place in history but also wanted to live comfortably in the present. He testified that if Oswald could not have that "degree of physical comfort that he expected or sought, I think he would then throw himself entirely on the other thing he also wanted, which was the image in history. * * * I think he wanted both if he could have them. If he didn't, he wanted to die with the knowledge that, or with the idea that he was somebody."*

Oswald's interest in Marxism led some people to avoid him, even though as his wife suggested, that interest may have been motivated by a desire to gain attention. He used his Marxist. and associated activities as excuses for his difficulties in getting along in the world, which were usually caused by entirely different factors. His use of those excuses to present himself to the world as a person who was being unfairly treated is shown most clearly by his employment relations after his return from the Soviet Union. Of course, he made his real problems worse to the extent that his use of those excuses prevented him from discovering the real reasons for and attempting to overcome his difficulties. Of greater importance, Oswald's commitment to Marxism contributed to the decisions which led him to defect to the Soviet Union in 1959, and later to engage in activities on behalf of the Fair Play for Cuba Committee in the summer of 1963, and to attempt to go to Cuba late in September of that year.[27]

Nelson Delgado is important. He lived closest to Oswald, and for longer than any of Oswald's other Marine associates.[28] On Oswald's political leanings, he said, "He was a complete believer that our way of government was not quite right, that—I don't know how to say it; it's been so long. He was for, not the Communist way of life, the Castro way of life, the way he was going to lead his people. He didn't think our Government had too much to offer."[29] So Oswald may have felt there was something wrong with the American system—not an uncommon or unpatriotic sentiment then or today—but he was certainly not a Communist. Did Oswald ever say anything particularly subversive about the government? According to Delgado, "He never said any subversive things...."[30] Delgado's feelings on Oswald's alleged Communism were noted in the Report, however. What was left out was his feelings on another important subject: Oswald's skill with a rifle. "We went to the range at one time, and he didn't show no particular aspects of being a sharpshooter at all,"[31] he said. Questioning by Wesley Liebeler continued:

Mr. LIEBELER. He didn't seem to be particularly proficient with the rifle; is that correct?

Mr. DELGADO. That's right.

...

Mr. LIEBELER. Do you remember whether or not Oswald kept his rifle in good shape, clean?

Mr. DELGADO. He kept it mediocre.. He always got gigged for his rifle.

...

Mr. LIEBELER. Did you fire with Oswald?

Mr. DELGADO. Right; I was in the same line. By that I mean we were on line together, the same time, but not firing at the same position, but at the same time, and I remember seeing his. It was a pretty big joke, because he got a lot of "Maggie's drawers," you know, a lot of misses, but he didn't give a darn.

Mr. LIEBELER. Missed the target completely?

Mr. DELGADO. He just qualified, that's it. He wasn't as enthusiastic as the rest of us. We all loved—liked, you know, going to the range.[32]

The section of the Warren Report in question is filled with obvious fallacies. In drawing conclusions regarding Oswald's "Communism," it accepts the word of Kerry Thornley, who lived on a different part of the base[33] and had only served with Oswald from "Easter of 1959"[34] to the following June, when Thornley was transferred to Japan, over that of Delgado, who knew Oswald the whole time Oswald was at El Toro. [35] The cited testimony of Donovan indicated merely that Oswald found something wrong with the system in the United States, a sentiment not uncommon or unpatriotic even today. Donovan's testimony also makes clear that anything Oswald may have said about Castro was innocuous at the time (Castro was, in fact, something of a media darling during that era). The Report also accepts the Mexico City story, which we will see was anything but innocuous.

Despite all these flaws, the smoking gun is to be found in Volume 8 of the Commission's hearings. Delgado, Donovan and Thornley were not the only Marines interviewed by far. The rest have many interesting things to say about whether or not Oswald was a Communist.

Chapter Two

Semper Fi, Lee Harvey Oswald!

"I knew then what I know now: Oswald was on assignment in Russia for American intelligence."

–James Bohtelho, USMC[1]

Oswald's first assignment since completing his training in 1957 was the Marine Air Control Squadron No. 1 (MACS-1), stationed on the air base at Atsugi, Japan. Atsugi was home of the CIA's primary operational base in the Far East, as well as one of two bases where the Agency's U-2 spy planes launched from.[2] One of the Marines who served with him there was Peter Francis Connor of Connecticut. "I never heard Oswald make any anti-American or pro-Communist statements," Connor said. "He claimed to be named after Robert E. Lee, whom he characterized as the greatest man in history."[3] John Rene Heindel of Louisiana was also there; "Although I generally regarded Oswald as an intelligent person, I did not observe him to be particularly interested in politics or international affairs," he said.[4]

Daniel Patrick Powers was born in Minneapolis, Mississippi. A married man and father of two, he joined the Marine Reserves in December, 1954 and went Active Duty from 1956 to 1958.[5] It was during a 1957 trip to a training school in Biloxi, Mississippi that then-PFC Powers met Lee Harvey Oswald. Powers would be transferred, with Oswald, to Atsugi Naval Air Station in Japan.[6] Did Powers think Oswald was a Communist?

> *Mr. JENNER. Did he ever express any sympathy toward the Communist Party?*
>
> *Mr. POWERS. None that I recall.*
>
> *Mr. JENNER. Toward Communist principles?*
>
> *Mr. POWERS. None that I recall.*
>
> *Mr. JENNER. Or Marxist doctrines?*
>
> *Mr. POWERS. None that I recall; no, sir.*
>
> *Mr. JENNER. Or did he ever discuss those subjects with you or in your presence?*
>
> *Mr. POWERS. I'm not sure. He didn't discuss them to any great length or to any issues that I would recall.*
>
> *Mr. JENNER. Nothing to excite you?*
>
> *Mr. POWERS. Nothing that I would attach any political significance to.*[7]

Donald Peter Camarata was another Marine who knew Oswald. While stationed at Keesler Air Force Base in Biloxi, Mississippi and the Marine Air Station at El Toro, Camarata never observed "any remarks on his [Oswald's] part concerning Communism, Russia, or Cuba."[8] While at El

Toro, Oswald's Platoon Sergeant was Allen D. Graf of Buffalo, New York. Graf recalled, "Oswald never gave to me any indication of favoring Communism or opposing capitalism."[9] Henry J. Roussel would recall "no serious political remarks on the part of Oswald."[10] Despite this, Oswald did seem to have the mystique of Russian culture around him. Roussel continued:

> *On occasion, however, Oswald, when addressing other Marines, would refer to them as "Comrade." It seemed to me and, as far as I know, to my fellow Marines—that Oswald used this term in fun. At times some of us responded by calling him "Comrade." Oswald also enjoyed listening to recordings of Russian songs.[11]*

California Judge James Bohtelho served at El Toro during his service in the Marine Corps. While there, he spent some time as Oswald's roommate, even introducing Oswald to his parents at one point. Bohtelho told Mark Lane:

> *I'm very conservative now and I was at least as conservative at that time. Oswald was not a Communist or a Marxist. If he was I would have taken violent action against him and so would many of the Marines in the unit.[12]*

A look at the testimony of Lt. Col. Allison G. Folsom, USMC reveals the following:

> *Mr. ELY. All right. Now, moving further down page 7, we have the record of a Russian examination taken by Oswald on February 25, 1959. Could you explain to us what sort of test this was, and what the scores achieved by Oswald mean?*
>
> *Colonel FOLSOM. The test form was Department of the Army, Adjutant General's Office, PRT-157. This is merely the test series designation. Now, under "understands" the scoring was minus 5, which means that he got five more wrong than right. The "P" in parentheses*

indicates "poor." Under reading he achieved a score of 4, which is low. This, again, is shown by the "P" in parentheses for "poor."

Mr. ELY. This 4 means he got four more questions right than wrong?

Colonel FOLSOM. This is correct. And under "writes" he achieved a score of 3, with "P" in parentheses, and this indicates he got three more right than he did wrong. His total score was 2, with a "P" in parentheses meaning that overall he got two more right than wrong, and his rating was poor throughout.[13]

This testimony clearly raises more questions than it answers. Why was Oswald being tested in the Russian language in the first place? Would this be evidence he was receiving intelligence training? And did he really do that bad? Jim Garrison writes in *On the Trail of the Assassins*, "I am reminded of the man who said his dog was not very intelligent because he could beat him three games out of five when they played chess."[14] Other evidence indicates Oswald spoke Russian rather fluently during that period. In his Warren Commission testimony, Henry Roussel mentioned, "On one occasion I arranged a date for Oswald with my aunt, Rosaleen Quinn, an airline stewardess who, because she was interested in working for the American Embassy in Russia, had taken a leave from her job in order to study Russian. I arranged the date because I knew of Oswald's study of the Russian language."[15] Not only had Quinn left her job to study Russian, she had in fact been working with a tutor for over a year preparing for the State Department's foreign language test when she met Oswald. Quinn told Edward Jay Epstein that Oswald "had a far more confident command of the language than she did."[16] But no matter how fluently Oswald spoke Russian, the important thing was the exam. Garrison notes:

In 1959, when Oswald was taking that exam, I was a staff officer in the National Guard in a battalion made up of hundreds of soldiers. None of them had been required to show how much Russian they

knew. Even on that night in 1966 when I read Colonel Folsom's testi-
mony I was still in the military service—by now a major—and I
could not recall a single soldier ever having been required to demon-
strate how much Russian he had learned.[17]

The testimony of the Marines Oswald served with at El Toro clearly
indicates that the Russian language training was for some purpose besides
an interest in Marxism. "I do not recall any remarks on his part concerning Communism, Russia, or Cuba," recalled Mack Osborne.[18] He continued, "Because the fact that he was studying Russian, fellow Marines
sometimes jokingly accused him of being a Russian spy. In my opinion he
took such accusations in fun."[19] Richard Dennis Call testified:

Although members of the unit often had discussions on foreign affairs,
Oswald seldom, if ever, participated. During this time, Oswald was
studying Russian. For this reason many members of the unit kidded
him about being a Russian spy; Oswald seemed to enjoy this sort of
remark.

. . .

In connection with this general joking about Oswald's interest in
Russian, he was nicknamed Oswaldskovich." However, I do not recall
Oswald's making serious remarks with regard to the Soviet Union or
Cuba.[20]

Oswald's stint in the Marines came to an end in 1959. That August, he
applied for a discharge on the grounds that his injured mother needed his
help. Oswald received a passport on September 10, and on September 11
was officially discharged from the Marines. Oswald then visited his
mother for a short time, withdrew $203 from the bank and went to New
Orleans where he bought a $220.75 ticket to France on the freighter
Marion Lykes. The Marine departed on September 20. France was merely
the first stop along the way—to the Soviet Union.[21]

Chapter Three

Spy Saga

"Now I don't know who killed cock robin, but we do know Oswald had intelligence connections. Everywhere you look with him, there're fingerprints of intelligence."

—Sen. Richard Schweiker, 1975

Oswald arrived in Le Havre, France on October 8, 1959, and made his way to Southampton, England the following day. The Warren Commission stated that Oswald then went to Helsinki, Finland that same day, checking into the Torni Hotel. British authorities, however, stamped Oswald's passport on October 10, not October 9. The sole direct flight to Helsinki that day did not arrive in time for Oswald to check in at the Torni Hotel at the time listed in the guest register.[1] It should also be noted that the Torni Hotel was one of the two most expensive hotels in Helsinki, the other being the Klaus Kurki Hotel-which Oswald moved into his second night in Finland. Oswald was getting far for a man of limited means.[2]

Oswald then visited the Soviet consulate where he received a visa after a mere two days. The Warren Commission later discovered that the shortest usual time for getting a visa was one week. Oswald went to Moscow by train where he told his Intourist (the Soviet state tourist agency) guide, Rima Shirokova, that he wanted to defect. Oswald's proclamations of his own "Communism" apparently did not catch the attention of the Soviet government, and he was informed on October 21 that his visa had expired and he had two hours to leave. Oswald responded by cutting his left wrist prior to a meeting with Shirokova, who took him to a hospital. He left the hospital on October 28 and checked into the Metropole Hotel. Two days later, October 31, he went to the U.S. Embassy in Moscow and stated his intention to "dissolve his American citizenship."[3]

Richard E. Snyder, the senior consular official, tried to persuade Oswald not to do what he was doing. Oswald gave him a handwritten note, reading:

> *I, Lee Harvey Oswald, do hereby request that my present citizenship in the United States of America, be revoked...I take these steps for political reasons. My request for the revoking of my American citizenship is made only after the longest and most serious considerations. I affirm that my allegiance is to the Union of Soviet Socialist Republics.*[4]

With Oswald and Snyder was John McVickar, who stated Oswald "was following a pattern of behavior in which he had been tutored by a person or persons unknown...[He] seemed to be using words he had learned but did not fully understand...."[5]

"In short," he McVickar said, "It seemed to me there was the possibility that he had been in contact with others before or during his Marine Corps tour who had guided him and encouraged him in his actions."[6] However, since it was Saturday, Oswald was not allowed to renounce his citizenship. A few days later he sent a letter to the embassy protesting what had happened, but he never returned to follow it up. Embassy personnel later contacted Oswald, but he refused to see them.[7] Several researchers have suggested that Oswald *intentionally* waited until a Saturday to renounce his citizenship in order to facilitate his later return to the United States.

During his stay in Russia, Oswald was given a spacious rent-free apartment in Minsk where he hosted members of Russia's high society. Oswald was a member of the Belorussian Society of Hunters and Fisherman, which allowed him to own a 16-gauge shotgun—a privilege not allowed to the average Soviet. And in March 1961, he met the woman he would marry, Marina Prusakova. As Oswald wrote in his historic diary, he was "living big."[8] Oswald later gave a description of this period that caused him and the government some embarrassment. During his debate with anti-Castro Carlos Bringuier in 1963, Oswald stated:

> *Er, well, as I er, well, I will answer that question directly then as you will not rest until you get your answer, er, I worked in Russia er,* **I was er under the protection er, of the er, that is to say I was not under protection of the American government** *but as I was at all times er, considered as American citizen. I did not lose any American citizenship.*[9] [Emphasis mine.]

In February 1961, Oswald wrote to the U.S. Embassy, saying, "I desire to return to the United States, that is if we could come to some agreement concerning the dropping of any legal proceedings against me," and pointing out that he had never officially renounced his citizenship.[10] Oswald did not have any trouble at all getting back into the United States. He even received a loan from the government with which to travel.

In addition to the government's suspicious permissiveness concerning Oswald's return, researchers have questioned why Oswald was not debriefed by the CIA upon his return? (Indeed, why would it be that alleged conspirator Clay Shaw's debriefs were considered routine, while Oswald was *not* debriefed upon returning from the Soviet Union?) Recent work by John Armstrong and John Newman seems to suggest that Oswald *was* in fact debriefed by the CIA's Domestic Contacts Service. A DCS officer named Donald Denesleya remembered the debrief, and that it was conducted by an officer named Anderson. The existence of the debrief was later confirmed to producers of a PBS *Frontline* documentary by several other DCS officers who would not go on the record.[11]

After Denesleya stated that Anderson had done the debrief, John Newman located a document containing the notation "OO Andy Anderson on Oswald." OO is the CIA's designation for the Domestic Contacts Service. This notation was the result of one document bleeding through onto another document during copying. The missing document would likely reveal much about what Oswald told the CIA after his return.[12] The House Select Committee was apparently aware of all this. A 1978 letter from the HSCA to a CIA attorney reads:

Dear Mr. Breckinridge:

In connection with its investigations into the circumstances surrounding the death of President Kennedy, the Select Committee on Assassinations has been informed that during the summer of 1962, a CIA contact report concerning the Minsk Radio Plant was routed to the Foreign Documents Division in the Soviet Branch of the Directorate of Intelligence. The source of this contact report is believed to have been a former Marine and defector to the Soviet Union who returned to the United States with his family during the summer of 1962. The source is believed to have stated that he had been employed at the Minsk Radio Plant.[13]

The report described in the letter seems eerily similar to Commission Exhibit 92, an "essay" known to be written by Oswald about the Minsk Radio Plant. This document (reprinted in Appendix A) features detailed descriptions of every aspect of the plant.[14] It is also significant to note that DCS officer J. Walton Moore encouraged Oswald's friend George deMohrenschildt to "unwittingly" debrief Oswald on his time in the

Soviet Union. As a result of this, Oswald gave deMohrenschildt a detailed memo on his Russian period.[15] Oddly enough, when Garrison was the subject of a laudatory news article in 1976 entitled "Was Jim Garrison Right After All?" it was Moore who authored a CIA memo stating, "We are somewhat more concerned about how we should respond to any direct questions concerning the Agency's relationship with Clay Shaw."[16] As the reader will see in Chapter Eight, Moore had much to be concerned about.

As Senator Richard Schweiker later stated, Oswald had the fingerprints of intelligence all over him. (More evidence of Oswald's relationship with the CIA can be found in Chapter Eight) Garrison's early study of the Warren Commission's evidence led him to conclude that Oswald was far more than the demented Marxist Kerry Thornley painted him to be. The case was *not* closed, and Garrison decided that Oswald's true background was worthy of a real investigation.

Chapter Four

The Garrison Probe

"The job done by the District Attorney of New Orleans was far more thorough than that of the Federal Government...and that fact alone [proves] the men of that office patriots of the highest order."

–Researcher Matt Allison[1]

After reading through the 26 volumes of the Warren Commission, Garrison was now thoroughly convinced that there had indeed been a conspiracy. He now went looking for it. Oswald's pamphlets had always been stamped with either his home address or post office box, but on the day of the altercation with Bringuier they were stamped with the address "**544 Camp Street.**" After noticing this peculiarity in the 26 volumes, Garrison decided to check the place out for himself.[2] What he discovered was that 544 Camp Street was the *side entrance* to Guy Banister's office at 531 Lafayette.[3]

This flew in the face of everything the Warren Commission had painted Oswald. Here he was, a dedicated Marxist and Castro-supporter working out of the office of New Orleans' most virulent anti-Communist. For Garrison a separate pattern was emerging, one where Oswald was not a Communist, but rather a man being used by people Garrison suspected—but could never prove—were working for the U.S. government. Garrison now sought out Carlos Bringuier, the DRE member involved in the leafleting altercation with Oswald. Bringuier told Garrison nothing of value, but did inform the New Orleans CIA station of Garrison's investigation.[4] Garrison also contacted Jack Martin, questioning him December 13, 1966. Martin now admitted to what he could not in 1963—that Oswald and Ferrie had associated together in Banister's office.[5] The difference was that Banister had suffered a fatal heart attack during the summer of 1964, which put him beyond Garrison's jurisdiction.[6]

On December 14th Assistant DA John Volz questioned Ferrie a second time. Again Ferrie denied having ever met Oswald and repeated his version of the Houston trip, which contradicted that of Coffee and Beauboeuf.[7] Garrison's men would later question Banister operatives Bill Nitschke and George Higginbotham. Nitschke remembered seeing pro-Castro placards in Banister's office that may have been Oswald's. Higginbotham was a Banister agent responsible for infiltrating left-wing groups suspected of being communist. When Higginbotham witnessed Oswald's fight with Bringuier, he (Higginbotham) informed Banister. Banister's reply: "Cool it. One of them is one of mine."[8] Additionally, Banister's wife, Mary, told Garrison's office in April of 1967 that she had come across an entire stack of "Fair Play for Cuba" and "Hands Off Cuba!" pamphlets—the same kind Oswald had distributed—while cleaning out Banister's office after his death.[9] Another witness that came forward at this point in Garrison's investigation was Banister investigator David F. Lewis, who was questioned by Louis Ivon on December 15th. Lewis told Ivon that he knew of five men in Banister's circle who were in the planning stages of an assassination conspiracy, which he described as a "quick, overkill-type of operation." The men were Oswald, Ferrie, Banister, Sergio Arcacha Smith and Carlos Quiroga.[10] Lewis proved to be a disappointment to Garrison when he (Lewis) faked a shooting attack against himself on Chartres Street. A polygraph examination revealed Lewis had lied to get attention.[11]

In Search of Clay Bertrand

In his research Garrison came upon the testimony of an old friend of his, New Orleans Attorney Dean Andrews. Andrews testified that in the summer of 1963, he had come into contact with Oswald and a group of "Gay Mexicanos." Oswald had come to Andrews seeking help in upgrading his Marine discharge from dishonorable (it had initially been an honorable discharge—until he defected to the Soviet Union). The relevant part of his testimony follows:

> *Mr. Liebeler.   Did there come a time after the assassination when you had some further involvement with Oswald, or at least an apparent involvement with Oswald; as I understand it?*
>
> *Mr. Andrews.   No; nothing at all with Oswald. I was in Hotel Dieu, and the phone rang and a voice I recognized as Clay Bertrand asked me if I would go to Dallas and Houston—I think— Dallas, I guess, wherever it was that this boy was being held—and defend him. I told him I was sick in the hospital. If I couldn't go, I would find somebody that could go.*
>
> *...*
>
> *Mr. Liebeler.   Now what can you tell us about this Clay Bertrand? You met him prior to that time?*
>
> *Mr. Andrews.   I had seen Clay Bertrand once some time ago, probably a couple of years. He's the one who calls in behalf of gay kids normally, either to obtain bond or parole for them. I would assume that he was the one that originally sent Oswald and the gay kids, these Mexicanos, to the office because I had never seen those people before at all. They were just walk-ins.*

Mr. Liebeler. You say that you think you saw Clay Bertrand some time about 2 years prior to the time you received this telephone call that you have just told us about?

Mr. Andrews. Yes; he is mostly a voice on the phone.

. . .

Mr. Liebeler Now [FBI Agent Kennedy] came and visited you at the hospital; is that correct?

Mr. Andrews Right.

Mr. Liebeler Now—

Mr. Andrews I remember that pretty good because I called the Feebees, and the guy says to put the phone, you know, and nothing happened.

Mr. Liebeler The Feebees?

Mr. Andrews That's what we call the Federal guys. All of a sudden, like a big hurricane, here they come.

Mr. Liebeler Do you remember telling them that Clay Bertrand had come into the office with Oswald when Oswald had been in the office earlier last spring?

Mr. Andrews No; I don't remember.

Mr. Liebeler Was Bertrand ever in the office with Oswald?

Mr. Andrews Not that I remember.

Mr. Liebeler Do you have a picture in your mind of Clay Bertrand?

Mr. Andrews Oh, I ran up on that rat about 6 weeks ago and he spooked, ran in the street. I would have beat him with a chain if I had caught him.

Mr. Liebeler   Let me ask you this: …in your continuing discussions with the FBI, you finally came to the conclusion that Clay Bertrand was a figment of your imagination?

Mr. Andrews   That's what the Feebees put on. I know that the two Feebees are going to put these people on the street looking, and I can't find the guy, and I am not going to tie up all the agents on something that isn't solid. I told them, "Write what you want, that I am nuts. I don't care." They were running on the time factor, and the hills were shook up plenty to get it, get it, get it. I couldn't give it to them. I have been playing cops and robbers with them. You can tell when the steam is on. They are on you like the plague. They never leave. They are like cancer. Eternal.

Mr. Liebeler   That was the description of the situation?

Mr. Andrews   It was my decision if they were to stay there. If I decide yes, they stay. If I decide no, they go. So I told them "Close your file and go some place else." That's the real reason why it was done. I don't know what they wrote in the report, but that's the real reason.

Mr. Liebeler   Now subsequent to that time, however, you actually ran into Clay Bertrand in the street?

Mr. Andrews   About 6 weeks ago. I am trying to think of the name of this bar. That's where this rascal bums out. I was trying to get past him so I could get a nickel in the phone and call the Feebees or [Secret Service agent] John Rice, but he saw me and spooked and ran. I haven't seen him since.[12]

Garrison now wanted to find out exactly who Bertrand was. Unbeknownst to him, the FBI had already investigated Bertrand in December of 1963 and learned he was actually Clay Shaw, Director of the

New Orleans International Trade Mart.[13] Several people had talked to the Bureau about Shaw, who was cleared of involvement in the assassination. Publicly, however, the Bureau wrote off Andrews' testimony when he changed his story and claimed Bertrand was a figment of his imagination that he had created while sedated in the hospital. This has been the standard anti-conspiracist response to the allegations against Shaw, but there are two problems with it. First, FBI Agent Regis Kennedy admitted under oath at the Shaw trial that he had been seeking Bertrand prior to Dean Andrews' contacting the FBI (see Chapter 6).[14] Second, Andrews received the call from Bertrand at least four hours prior to being sedated. Eva Springer, whom Andrews called and told about the call from Bertrand, fixed the time of Andrews' call at 4:00 PM. A review of Andrews' hospital records by FBI Special Agent Richard Bucaro revealed that Andrews did not receive any sedation until 8:00 PM.[15] Even Garrison critic Patricia Lambert has accepted the 4:00 PM time for Andrews' call to Springer.[16]

Oddly enough, the first person in the NODA to suspect that "Bertrand" was an alias for Shaw was Assistant DA Frank Klein, who would later run against Garrison for District Attorney. Scribbled in the margins of an NODA copy of the Warren Report, Klein asked himself who lived in the French Quarter who was named Clay, and answered with "Clay Shaw -?"[17]

While he was watching Ferrie and waiting, Garrison sent his Assistant DAs out to comb the French Quarter to find the true identity of Clay Bertrand. He had no other choice. When Garrison confronted Andrews about Bertrand over lunch, Andrews was evasive and indicated he was being threatened. "If I answer that question you keep asking me, if I give you that name you keep trying to get, then it's goodbye, Dean Andrews," he said. "I mean like permanent. I mean like a bullet in my head...Does that help you see my problem a little better?"[18] Unfortunately, Garrison's probe of the French Quarter came up dry. No one was talking. Garrison did, however, have other leads pointing to Shaw so he decided to call him in for questioning.

On December 23, 1966, two days before Christmas, Clay Shaw reported to the DA's office for questioning. Shaw was evasive and untruthful. When asked where he was when John Kennedy was killed, he said he was on a train, traveling to San Francisco for a speaking engagement. The truth was that Shaw was already IN San Francisco with J. Monroe Sullivan, Director of the San Francisco ITM. Later, he changed his story yet again and told the New Orleans Times-Picayune that he was actually at the St. Francis Hotel when JFK was shot down in Dallas. He also said he was invited to San Francisco by Sullivan. Sullivan denies this. He told journalist William Turner that Shaw contacted him two or three months before and asked to set up a luncheon for the purpose of wooing clients for the New Orleans ITM.[19]

Sullivan also raised some peculiar issues regarding Shaw's reaction to the assassination. After offering to pay for the luncheon and all the arrangements himself, Shaw showed up around mid-morning on the morning of November 22. When someone told them that JFK had been shot, Shaw showed no reaction. Though people who were shocked, even in tears over the news, surrounded him Shaw—who claimed to be fond of Kennedy—was unmoved. When Sullivan offered to call off the luncheon, Shaw told him not to.[20] Turner, recalling his interview of Sullivan, said, "Sullivan was struck by Shaw's seeming indifference to the president's death."[21]

Garrison had by now learned that Oswald had distributed his Fair Play for Cuba leaflets outside of Shaw's International Trade Mart. In February of 1967, Assistant DA Andrew Sciambra questioned Mrs. Carlos Marquez, the widow of the former Cuban consul in New Orleans who had worked out of an office in the ITM. Marquez remembered that a few days after the incident in which Oswald did his leafleting in front of the ITM, she saw him again—this time strolling through the ITM's lobby.[22] Two months later, Garrison's staff interviewed Ernesto Gonzales, who in addition to referring to Arcacha Smith as a "bad hombre," mentioned a rumor that Oswald had gone into the ITM after distributing his "Fair Play for Cuba" leaflets.[23]

During the December 23rd interview, Shaw denied knowing Oswald, Ferrie and Dean Andrews. In fact, Gordon Novel (who we will hear from again) had tried to open a concession in the ITM in 1964. The attorney who represented him: Dean Andrews.[24] Shaw also said he had never even heard of Clay Bertrand.[25] Garrison believed Shaw was lying, but had no evidence Shaw was involved in a conspiracy. Garrison thanked Shaw for his cooperation and told his staff to "forget Shaw." He would have to wait.[26] Garrison had no way of knowing he didn't have much time.

Gordon Novel and the Houma Raid

In late 1960, CIA asset Ed Butler was gearing up to launch the famed anti-Communist Information Council of the Americas (INCA). It was during this time that he met electronics expert Gordon Novel, whom he recommended to Sergio Arcacha Smith and Guy Banister. Novel then met Arcacha in a local coffee shop where they talked about their opinions on Marxism and Castro's new regime. Arcacha liked what Novel had to say, and invited him to a meeting in Banister's office later that week.[27] At that meeting, Novel met Banister and a man called Mr. Phillips for the first time. There is little doubt that Mr. Phillips was David Atlee Phillips, who would later go on to become the CIA's Chief of the Western Hemisphere Division. At this time the group discussed propaganda warfare against Cuba. Little came of this discussion, but it served to cement Novel's involvement in the New Orleans anti-Castro intelligence apparatus.[28]

Novel received a key in the mail from Banister a short time later, along with a message that a follow-up meeting would come soon. Novel would also receive, in time, half of a five hundred dollar bill and a key. He then met with David Ferrie, Arcacha, Banister, an ex-Marine named Jerome Blackmon and two Cubans. At this stage it was clear some kind of operation was being planned, and Novel was asked to procure a fleet of trucks in support of it. Arcacha found the trucks he needed without Novel's help and told Novel to meet him at Ferrie's home.[29]

Now, in February of 1961, Novel went to Ferrie's apartment dressed, as Arcacha had instructed, in entirely black. There he met Blackmon, Arcacha, Layton Martens (a mutual friend of both Shaw and Ferrie), Novel's friend Rancier Ehlinger and Marlene Mancuso, who would go on to become Novel's wife.[30] The group then left New Orleans and drove to Houma, Louisiana where they arrived at an old Navy blimp base owned by Schlumberger Wells Services Company.[31] According to a CIA report declassified in 1993, at least five of Schlumberger's executives and officers were approved for use as sources of intelligence during the 50s and 60s.[32] Inside a padlocked bunker, which the group unlocked with Novel's key, the group procured what author William Davy described only as "crate after crate" of war materiel, all of which was labeled "InterArmco, Alexandria, Virginia." InterArmco was a CIA dummy corporation. The group returned to New Orleans in Arcacha's truck, where they stored the weapons in Banister's office and at Ferrie's house. These weapons would later see use in the failed Bay of Pigs invasion in April of that year.[33]

Novel came under Garrison's suspicion early in the New Year of 1967 when he began probing into the Houma raid. Novel went on to do much for the CIA and it's anti-Castro operations after this raid. He once helped channel money to the Evergreen Advertising Agency, a CIA front that bought radio ads featuring cryptic messages designed to alert agents to the date of the Bay of Pigs invasion.[34] By 1967, Novel even had the ear of CIA Counterintelligence Chief James Jesus Angleton, whom we will return to at length.[35] Garrison began to suspect Novel's connection to the Agency, and it was this connection that led him to believe Ferrie, Shaw and others might have also been CIA assets (a suspicion that was later confirmed). After Garrison questioned Novel, Novel promptly reported the progress of Garrison's investigation to the local FBI office.[36]

Novel was summoned before the Orleans Parish Grand Jury on March 16, 1967, whereupon he testified about general matters.[37] Novel was scheduled to be questioned again in more detail on March 22. He fled New Orleans instead and began a nationwide flight from extradition. Though this prevented Garrison from potentially using Novel as a witness to prove Ferrie or Shaw's CIA connections, it confirmed Garrison's suspicions about Novel.[38] The two young girls from whom Novel had rented his New Orleans apartment found a letter left by Novel in the apartment. Written in January of 1967 and addressed to a "Mr. Weiss," portions of it read:

> *I took the liberty of writing you directly and apprising you of current situation expecting you to forward this through appropriate channels. Our connection and activity of that period involved individuals presently about to be indicted as conspirators in Mr. Garrison's investigation.*
>
> ...
>
> *My reply on five queries was negative. Bureau unaware of Double-Chek association in this matter.*[39]

Double-Chek was, of course, a rather notorious CIA front based out of Miami. Novel initially denied his CIA connection, but after Garrison began releasing evidence regarding the Houma Raid the *New Orleans States-Item* printed a story that publicly revealed Novel's association with the Agency.[40] After Novel went on the run, he began employing the services of New Orleans attorney Stephen Plotkin. Plotkin now did not deny Novel's CIA connection, but refused to comment on it.[41] Plotkin and Novel were birds of a feather. After Garrison's famed Playboy interview, Novel sued Garrison for defamation. During a deposition Novel stated that his legal fees to Plotkin were "clandestinely remunerated by a party of parties unknown to me." A former CIA employee named William Martin told Garrison in May of 1967 that Plotkin was being paid by the CIA to represent Novel via cutout Stephen Lemman.[42]

End of the Line

On January 23, 1967, crime reporter Jack Dempsey got a tip that the New Orleans DA's office was investigating the assassination. When he tried to include this in a column for the New Orleans States Item, his employers referred this story to a more appropriate reporter Rosemary James as Dempsey had a longrunning feud with Garrison. James pursued the story, checking it out by looking at the vouchers from the Fines & Fees account that Garrison used to fund the investigation (these were public property and could not be legally destroyed).[43]

On February 17, 1967, the States Item printed James' story. "DA HERE LAUNCHES FULL JFK DEATH PLOT PROBE," read the headline that soon drew national attention. The light was on Garrison. His hopes of a quiet investigation were shattered.[44] Inexcusably, Garrison responded by issuing highly inflammatory statements to the press:

> *My staff and I solved the case weeks ago. I wouldn't say this if I didn't have evidence beyond a shadow of a doubt. We know the key individuals, the cities involved and how it was done....*
>
> *There will be arrests, charges will be files, and on the basis of these charges, convictions will be obtained.*
>
> *We solved the assassination.... We're working out the details of evidence which will probably take months. We know that we are going to be able to arrest every person involved—at least every person who is still living.*[45]

At the time Garrison issued these statements, his only witnesses *specifically claiming knowledge of a conspiracy* were Jack Martin and David Lewis.

By the next day it was known that Garrison's prime suspect was David Ferrie. Ferrie told the *New Orleans States-Item* that the Garrison probe was nothing more than "a big joke."[46] On February 18, Assistant DA Andrew Sciambra and Chief Investigator Louis Ivon against questioned Ferrie, this time at his apartment. Ferrie was very weak, had trouble keeping his food down and took an inordinately large amount of time just to climb the stairs to the second floor of the apartment. Sciambra and Ivon wrote this off as "a phony act," something they would regret only days later.[47] Nervous and erratic, Ferrie first recalled the Houston trip as the "worst trip that he had ever made in his life," and only moments later said, "I have never been to Texas."[48] Sciambra now asked Ferrie, "Dave, who shot the President?" Ferrie replied, "Well, that's an interesting question and I've got my own thoughts on it." Ferrie then went on into a long lecture about the insanity of scientific improbability of the lone assassin theory, concluding by saying "the question would never be answered because the doctor that performed the tracheotomy had 10 thumbs and left unanswered the most important question of all time." According to the memorandum Sciambra wrote from the interview, "FERRIE then laughed and said that doctors are almost as stupid as lawyers, but that lawyers are worse because they are always in your pocket."[49] Sciambra continued:

> I then said, "In other words Dave, you don't buy the 'one-shot theory'?" FERRIE said he wasn't saying anything because he didn't want J. Edgar on his tail, that he had enough with Garrison to contend with. FERRIE said that in time he would work the whole thing out and then laughingly said he would contact our office.[50]

Mysteriously, Ferrie also said "he had been contacted by some big attorneys in Washington DC, and they wanted to help him."[51] The meeting concluded ominously:

> I then asked him if he would like to tell me some more about his trip to Hammond and he smiled and said "Go to hell." I then asked if he stayed with CLAY SHAW. He said, "Who's CLAY SHAW?" I said, "All right, if that doesn't ring a bell, how about CLAY BERTRAND?" He said, "Who's CLAY BERTRAND?" I said CLAY BERTRAND and CLAY SHAW are the same person. He asked, "Who said that?" I

said, "Dean Andrews told us." [Author note: Sciambra is bluffing. Andrews did not say Shaw was Bertrand until much later, talking to Harold Weisberg, who quickly wrote off the admission.] He said, "Dean Andrews might tell you guys anything. You know how Dean Andrews is."[52]

First Ferrie denies even knowing who one of the most prominent men in New Orleans is, then only moments later seems to be highly concerned that this man he has never heard of has been connected to an alias he also hasn't heard of.

Ferrie continued to deteriorate, and the following day called Ivon and asked for help. Ivon checked Ferrie into the Fontainebleau Hotel under a fake name, and, according to Ivon, Ferrie proceeded to recant parts of what he had told Ivon and Sciambra the previous day. Ferrie now admitted that he had known Oswald and had performed contract work for the CIA. In addition, Ferrie now said he did know Shaw, whom Ferrie said worked for the CIA and hated Kennedy. Ivon described Ferrie to author Bill Davy as "very scared—a wild man."[53] Ferrie did not, however, admit anything in regard to the assassination. The problem with Ivon's claim is that he did not make it until years after the end of the probe—it was in fact first told to Oliver Stone's people during the production of *JFK.* Ivon left around 2:00 AM and returned several hours later to find Ferrie missing. Ivon and several police officers unsuccessfully looked for Ferrie the next day on Decatur Street, home of a Cuban community where Ferric was known to have stayed.[54] Two days later, Ferrie granted his final interview to George Lardner.[55]

Lardner later said Ferrie had been in a good mood. Ferrie told Lardner he had been investigating the assassination on his own because he did not trust Garrison. Ferrie also told Lardner, in contradiction with his February 18th interview with Sciambra and Ivon, that he (Ferrie) believed the Warren Report and that he had recently resolved any doubts he had had about the autopsy. Lardner left Ferrie's apartment around 4:00 AM.[56] The next day, February 22nd, Ferrie was found dead in his apartment.[57] He was 48.[58]

Ferrie was found in the presence of two unsigned notes, which Garrison interpreted to be "suicide" notes. In fact, Ferrie had been sick for a long time and had probably realized he didn't have much time left. One of the notes was addressed to no one, and the other was addressed to Al Beauboeuf. Ferrie probably had decided to write his final messages to the world of the living well in advance of his death.[59] Garrison theorized that Ferrie could have been murdered if he had been force-fed an overdose of Proloid, a thyroid medication. Garrison thought, based on Ferrie's nervousness, that Ferrie had had hypertension (Proloid was for treating low-thyroid conditions). In fact, Ferrie had been prescribed the Proloid and it is unlikely Ferrie could have ingested enough of it to constitute a fatal dosage.[60] Garrison's theory was later supported by New Orleans Coroner Frank Minyard who revealed that there had been a contusion on the inside of Ferrie's lower lip, which Minyard concluded had been caused by "something traumatically inserted into his mouth."[61] An April 1, 1967 report from two NOPD cops who had talked to Gordon Novel for a short time indicates that Novel told them that Ferrie was killed.[62] These leads remain uncorroborated.

The Big Break

It was only a few days after Ferrie died that Garrison found his first witness to the actual planning of the assassination. On February 24th, a story broke that a Baton Rouge resident named Perry Russo had known Ferrie in 1963 and had knowledge of Ferrie's participation in a possible conspiracy. Russo told the Baton Rouge Morning Advocate and the Baton Rouge State-Times that he had heard Ferrie say about a month prior to the assassination, "We will get him and it won't be long."[63] Russo, a Republican and Goldwater supporter, had not taken Ferrie's statements seriously—in light of Ferrie's almost pathological hatred of Kennedy—until Russo saw Ferrie's picture in the paper and learned of his involvement in the

Garrison probe. After Ferrie died, Russo sent Garrison a letter (it was lost in the mail) and talked to the media.[64] The press on the 24th brought Russo to Garrison's attention, leading Garrison to order Assistant DA Andrew Sciambra to go to Baton Rouge the following day.[65] On that afternoon of the 24th, Garrison's office received an additional tip—this time from an FBI informant (the Bureau was also informed of what Garrison's office was told) who contacted Lou Ivon on the telephone and said that Clay Shaw and Clay Bertrand were one and the same.[66]

The next day, Sciambra arrived in Baton Rouge. After some general discussion about Ferrie's homosexuality, his involvement with the Civil Air Patrol, his interest in hypnotism and his involvement with Al Landry, Russo described Ferrie's gradual obsession with the murder of President Kennedy.[67] According to Russo, "During the summer of 1963 Ferrie became obsessed with the idea that an assassination could be carried out in the United States very easily if the proper amount of planning was made....Ferrie said that the whole key to a successful assassination would be the availability of exit and the use of the mass confusion that would result from such a plot."[68] Ferrie had said he "could jump into any plane under the sun and fly it...to a place that would not extradite...."[69]

Russo then described a meeting that occurred in the aftermath of a party at Ferrie's New Orleans apartment in early September of 1963.[70] After the party had wrapped up, only Ferrie, Ferrie's friend Leon Oswald (whom Russo identified as Lee Harvey Oswald after whiskers were drawn on the photo Sciambra had with him), some anti-Castro Cubans and a tall white-haired man who was introduced as Clem Bertrand (whom Russo identified to Sciambra as Clay Shaw) remained.[71] The group discussed Cuban politics, specifically their hatred of Castro and Kennedy and proposed that Castro should be assassinated.[72] The Cubans then left, and Ferrie again raised the potential assassination of President Kennedy. It was at this party that Ferrie had said, "We will get him and it won't be long."[73] According to Russo, Ferrie now proposed that Kennedy be assassinated in a "triangulation of crossfire," or a shooting from three locations. Bertrand pointed out that they would need to establish alibis both away from the scene of the crime and away from each other.[74] Ferrie would be at Southeastern University in Hammond, and Shaw would travel to the West Coast on business.[75] As the interview wrapped up, Sciambra informed Russo that he would "be in touch with him," and left.[76] That night, Sciambra briefed Garrison about Russo's story.[77] Garrison then instructed Sciambra to get Russo to New Orleans.[78]

Russo arrived February 27th, and Garrison, not entirely sure of Russo, requested that Russo be administered Sodium Pentothal®, commonly known as truth serum. Russo consented and repeated the same story he had told Sciambra in Baton Rouge. Garrison believed Russo's story, as did Orleans Parish Coroner Nicholas Chetta who administered the truth serum. Chetta told Oser, "There's not a chance at all that what this kid [Russo] said [under sodium Pentothal] is not true…it had to happen."[79] Russo's recollections would later be partially corroborated by his friend Niles "Lefty" Peterson, who was at the party but left before the discussion between Shaw, Ferrie and Oswald occurred. Peterson remembered the presence that night of a Leon Oswald.[80] On February 28, Sciambra took Russo by Shaw's apartment, where Russo again identified Shaw as Bertrand, first from inside a parked car as Shaw stepped outside to greet a friend and a second time having gone up and briefly spoken to Shaw, posing as an insurance salesman. Garrison now had a *prima facie* case of conspiracy against Clay Shaw.

The Command Decision

Two days later, Garrison subpoenaed Shaw to appear for questioning. Sciambra and Ivon questioned Shaw that afternoon, and again he said he knew neither Ferrie nor Oswald. Shaw subsequently denied visiting Ferrie's apartment on Louisiana Avenue Parkway, as well as his service station on Veterans Highway.[81] (Russo had also stated that he had seen Shaw talking to Ferrie at the service station. Four of Ferrie's friends later told Garrison's office that they had seen Shaw there as well. See Chapter

Seven.) Sciambra asked, "What would you say if we told you we have three witnesses who could positively identify you as having been in Ferrie's apartment and in Ferrie's gas station?" Shaw looked at Sciambra and told him that the witnesses "were either mistaken or they were lying."[82]

Shaw was then asked to take either a truth serum or a polygraph test. He refused, claiming that he needed time to go home and rest first. Garrison didn't buy it, and ordered Shaw's arrest on the charge of conspiracy to murder President Kennedy.[83] It was March 1, 1967. Garrison next did something unprecedented. In his own words:

> *Next, I took a step in the defendant's behalf. I made a motion for a preliminary hearing. Customarily in a major case it is the defense attorneys who request a preliminary hearing. The object is to force the district attorney to demonstrate that there is a sound basis for bringing the defendant to trial. This procedure was developed to prevent a prosecutor from holding a frivolous charge over a defendant's head for a long period before trying the case on the merits.*
>
> *In this case I made the motion out of fairness to Shaw because of the extraordinary seriousness of the charge.... This was the first time in the history of Louisiana that such a motion ever was filed by the prosecutor on behalf of the defendant.*[84]

The Preliminary Hearing

Shaw's preliminary hearing began on March 14, 1967. March is a hot month in the humid port city of New Orleans, and after thirteen days of silence, the media eagerly gathered in the Orleans Parish Criminal District Court building to see what Garrison had. The press had very little to go on, and Garrison had thus far refused to reveal his "confidential informant"—Perry Russo. The result was a stuffy courtroom filled with reporters sticky with perspiration. Presiding over the hearing was a three-judge panel of Judges Bernard J. Bagert, Matthews S. Braniff, and Malcolm V.

O'Hara. Russo, who had been virtually forgotten by the news writers a short time after his late-February interviews, now took the stand to the surprise of everyone.[85]

Garrison, in his third actual courtroom appearance as DA, questioned Russo personally. Russo identified photos of David Ferrie and described his (Ferrie's) gradual obsession with Kennedy—constantly carrying around news clippings and whatnot. "Around the middle of September, I had occasion to go to his house on Louisiana Avenue Parkway," Russo recalled. "I walked in and there seemed to be some sort of party in progress."[86] Russo repeated his story that after he was left alone with Ferrie, "Bertrand" and Leon Oswald, the trio discussed killing Kennedy. Garrison asked Russo if the man introduced to him as "Bertrand" was in the room, and Russo replied affirmatively. "Would you point out that man?" Garrison asked. Russo pointed squarely at Clay L. Shaw.[87]

Coroner Nicholas Chetta took the stand next, testifying that he had administered the Sodium Pentothal® to Russo and that it could help sharpen a witness' memory and recall. By the time of the preliminary hearing, Russo had also been placed under hypnosis three times by Dr. Esmond Fatter, to further aide his recall, and Dr. Fatter appeared to testify to that effect.[88]

While the preliminary hearing was going on, Dean Andrews testified before the Orleans Parish Grand Jury. Andrews continually equivocated about naming the true identity of "Bertrand." Nevertheless, a Grand Juror stubbornly asked, "Would you state positively that Clay Shaw and Clay Bertrand were not the same people?" "I could not do it...I can't connect the two. I can't say he is and I can't say he ain't...."[89] Later, Andrews stated, "I get the impression you all want me to identify Clay Shaw as Clay Bertrand. I'll be honest with you that is the impression I get...." "Well?" Assistant DA Richard Burnes intoned.[90]

"And I can't," Andrews said. "I can't say he is and I can't say he ain't...I cannot say positive, under oath, that he is Clay Bertrand or he is not."[91]

Based on his earlier conversation with Andrews, Garrison concluded that "Andrews was protecting Shaw," and had him indicted for perjury.

The next witness at the preliminary hearing proved to be a controversial one. On March 16, 1967, Garrison's office learned of a 29-year-old heroin addict in the Orleans Parish Prison that claimed to have information about Clay Shaw. Specifically, Bundy said he saw Shaw speak with Oswald at Lake Pontchartrain. He was deposed that night by William Gurvich, and repeated his story to Garrison himself the following day. Garrison then ordered Bundy to take a polygraph examination. Assistant DA Charles Ward escorted Bundy to polygraph examiner James Kruebbe around noon on March 17. Ward asked Kruebbe to ascertain whether or not Bundy was acting on anyone's instructions (fearing that perhaps Bundy might have been a defense team plant) and to see if he was telling the truth. After the examination, Kruebbe reported to Ward, Assistant DA James Alcock and Garrison that Bundy "wasn't telling the truth" and that "no one put him up to it...."[92] Alcock and Ward told Garrison that Bundy's testimony was not necessary to prove probable cause and recommended he not be called as a witness. With less than two hours until Bundy was due to testify, Garrison disagreed, saying, "We didn't tell him what to say...let the jury decide whether or not he's telling the truth."[93]

At 2:30 that afternoon, Bundy appeared and was sworn in. Bundy testified that in the summer of 1963 he had been preparing to shoot up at the Pontchartrain lakefront when a black sedan pulled up. Out walked a tall gray-haired man, who Bundy identified as Clay Shaw. Shaw greeted Bundy and walked on about twenty or twenty-five feet where he was met by a "young fellow" who Bundy identified as Lee Harvey Oswald. The pair began to talk and Shaw passed Oswald "a roll of money." Oswald stuck the money in his pocket, dislodging some papers that fell onto the ground. Oswald and Shaw left, and Bundy shot up his heroin. Later, he picked up one of the papers that dropped from Oswald's pocket, noting that there was "something about Cuba written on it."[94] Defense counsel F. Irvin Dymond cross-examined Bundy and got him to admit to breaking into and stealing from cigarette machines, on occasion, to support his narcotics habit. Bundy also indicated some uncertainty about the month and part of the day that he saw Shaw and Oswald, but held to his story.[95]

The state rested its case, and F. Irvin Dymond tried to introduce the Warren Report into evidence to prove Oswald had already left for Mexico City during part of the approximate timeframe Russo had given for the conspiratorial meeting. Judge Bagert's incredulous reaction: "You are not serious, are you?"[96] After an impassioned closing argument in which defense counsel William Wegmann pleaded with the court to "Let this gentleman walk out of here without this stigma," the three-judge panel ruled that probable cause had been established and Shaw should be held to trial.[97] The Grand Jury followed up later that month with an indictment against Clay Shaw. The stage was set for the trial of the century.

Chapter Five

Charging Cemetery Hill

"He says that whatever happens, the Shaw case will end without punishment for him because federal power will see to that."

–Harold Weisberg,
referring to Bannister agent Tommy Baumler

On May 6, 1967, the *Saturday Evening Post* printed an article on Garrison's case by journalist James Phelan. Phelan, who had earned Garrison's trust a few years earlier after writing a laudatory article about his campaign against French Quarter vice, was allowed access to certain documentation regarding Perry Russo's testimony. Using these memos, prepared by Assistant DA Andrew Sciambra, Phelan attempted to prove that Russo's story had been *planted* under Sodium Pentothal® and hypnosis rather than confirmed by it. The article was printed under the mean-spirited title of "Rush to Judgment in New Orleans."

Phelan's laughable argument is false on its face. Both Russo (Russo also independently confirmed this to Phelan when interviewed prior to the infamous *Saturday Evening Post* article of May 6) and Sciambra testified that Russo told of the assassination party in Baton Rouge. Sciambra then divided his notes into two memos, one covering the assassination party and the Sodium Pentothal® examination and one concerning the other details related in Baton Rouge. The assassination party memo was actually the *first* Sciambra memo, which the reader can clearly see by merely looking at the date in the signature block of the memo—February 28, 1967. The other memo was turned in sometime before March 6, about a week after Shaw's March 1 arrest.[2] If the D.A.'s Office was engaged in prosecuting innocent men based on false testimony, they sure had a lot of time in which to cover it up.

We need not even consider Phelan's misrepresentation of the intent of Sciambra's memos, however. The affidavit filed by Lou Ivon on March 2 (before Sciambra even finished writing the Baton Rouge memo) requesting a search warrant for Shaw's apartment makes clear that Russo told Sciambra about the assassination party during the Baton Rouge interview and only *repeated* it in New Orleans:

> *One of the sources of information of the affiant is a confidential informant who was present at the meetings and saw the conspirators and heard the plans. The confidential informant saw David W. Ferrie and Clay Shaw (alias Clay Bertrand) and Lee Harvey Oswald and others and this confidential informant heard these subjects agree to kill John F. Kennedy, and heard the subjects discuss the means and manner of carrying out this agreement.*

> *That the said confidential informant **after giving this statement to the affiant** voluntarily submitted to sodium pentothal commonly called truth serum, which was administered under the care and control and supervision of the coroner for the Parish of Orleans, a medical doctor. That the said confidential informant while under the sodium*

*pentothal **verified, corroborated and reaffirmed** his earlier state-ments.[3] [Emphasis mine.]*

So in essence, the defense team's entire strategy was based upon a two-word typo in an ordinary office memo—Sciambra writing "twice" instead of "two other times," as he had meant to. One can see this reasoning in the Sodium Pentothal® memo, where Sciambra writes that Russo recalled "he had seen BERTRAND on two other occasions." This was before any mention of the assassination party. Since Sciambra uses the phrase "two other occasions" without establishing the original occasion, we can reason that he already knew about the assassination party and had told Garrison about it. Also, the first mention of the party is when Sciambra writes, "I then asked him if he could remember any of the details about CLAY BERTRAND being up in FERRIE'S apartment...."[4] Again, this shows that Sciambra was already familiar with the assassination party. Phelan, a writer, apparently forgot how to parse sentences when he read this memo. Besides, why would Garrison tell Sciambra to get Russo to New Orleans if his testimony was not very important?

Phelan's supporters claim that he was merely an objective reporter doing his job. However, when one looks at him closely, this simply does not hold water. Phelan testified at the Shaw trial that Russo had admitted to him that the first mention of the conspiracy meeting was in New Orleans, after the Baton Rouge interview.[5] He also testified that he had taken photographer Matt Herron with him to the meeting with Russo, "As a witness."[6]

Shaw's defense team subpoenaed Mr. Herron, Phelan's "witness." As Alcock held up a piece of paper during closing arguments he explained, "This is the return on the subpoena, and on this side it reflects personal service, which means that this subpoena for this trial was physically put in the hands of Matt Herron."[7] Evidently, Shaw's lawyers did not like what Mr. Herron had to say because he was not called as a defense witness. Somehow, Garrison got wind of this and Herron was apparently interviewed by the NODA, who liked *very much* what he had to say. At this point, they decided to use Herron as a state witness to impeach Phelan.[8] For unknown reasons Herron never testified at the trial, but his absence from the Shaw camp did bring serious doubts as to Phelan's credibility toward the end of the trial.

Another problem with Phelan's story was the fact that he appeared on a WDSU radio program in April of 1967, during which he warned Sciambra to "watch out" because Phelan taped his interview with Russo. When confronted with this at the trial, Phelan first denied making that statement and then simply back-peddled, admitting that he had lied on the program.[9] That same month, Phelan wrote the *Saturday Evening Post* article. When confronted under cross-examination with the fact that he had left out Russo's "admission," Phelan claimed that he had been facing a tight deadline and some points had been lost.[10] One supposes this kind of omission must only be unforgivable in the case of Andrew Sciambra. In the words of Mark Lane, "It was a Rush to Judgment in New York."[11]

The media attack continued nine days later when *Newsweek* ran "The JFK Conspiracy" by Hugh Aynesworth, who said that Russo testified at the preliminary hearing under hypnosis (Russo's last hypnosis session actually occurred more than two days before the hearing began) and that Garrison investigators Lou Ivon and Lynn Loisel had attempted to bribe and threatened to kill Ferrie's traveling companion Alvin Beauboeuf.[12] Aynesworth also alleged that Beauboeuf's lawyer, Hugh Exnicios, recorded this bribe.

The tape did exist, however, the NOPD (not Garrison's best friends) conducted an internal investigation on the matter that cleared Loisel and Ivon (Garrison had nothing to do with it) of any wrongdoing in a 37-page report. The pair was not trying to suborn perjury; they were offering to pay Beauboeuf's witness fees should he provide favorable (and factual) testimony. Beauboeuf issued a retraction saying that his lawyer told him the "bribery" tape would be a good chance to make some quick money. His wife, who was supposedly there when Loisel and Ivon threatened to kill Beaubeouf if he would not testify, said she had never heard such a threat.[13]

Finally, after Beauboeuf and his new attorney, Burton Klein, read the transcript prepared by the Exnicios for the media, they discovered several parts of the conversation were edited out that negated the "bribery" allegation. When Exnicios was asked to produce the tape for the NOPD investigation, he refused.[14]

It was later revealed that Aynesworth had applied for a visa to Cuba in 1962, and offered to gather intelligence for the CIA if the visa were granted. A few years after that, Aynesworth even went as far as seeking out an Agency recruiter for possibly going to work permanently for the CIA. Available documentation does not reveal whether or not Aynesworth made contact with the recruiter. Before the publication of the *Newsweek* article, Aynesworth took the liberty of forwarding a copy to the White House, as well as informing the FBI on *Life* magazine's coverage of the Garrison probe.[15] Aynesworth became rather cozy with Shaw's defense team, even inviting them to stay at his home.[16]

Both Aynesworth and Phelan were later subject to criticism by the *Columbia Journalism Review* for their actions:

> *Jim Phelan and Hugh Aynesworth, both fiercely anti-Garrison, became in effect special advisers to the defense. They consulted frequently with Shaw's attorneys, passing along tips on aspects of the case they knew best from time spent covering it as reporters. The two of them, says chief defense attorney F. Irvin Dymond, were "extremely valuable" to the defense case.... Aynesworth could have chosen between his twin functions of reporter and participant. He could, for instance, have taken a leave of absence to join the defense team and let someone else cover the Shaw trial for his magazine. Failing that, Newsweek's editors should have made the choice for him, to protect their own interests and the interests of their readers.[17]*

On June 19th, NBC aired an hour long program entitled "The JFK Conspiracy: The Case of Jim Garrison." The "White Paper" was largely the work of reporter Walter Sheridan, whose tactics were markedly similar to those generally attributed to Garrison. As soon as Sheridan arrived in the Crescent City, he offered Perry Russo a job with an airline, legal support and a move to California if he would recant his testimony. Sheridan also offered Dean Andrews a recording studio, a small dream of Andrews', and paid Gordon Novel $500 a day before telling him to leave New Orleans, after which Novel was paid an additional $750 (this time trying to block Garrison's extradition request in Ohio).[18]

Documents released by the Assassination Records Review Board in the 1990s reveal that Sheridan had been granted a CIA security clearance in 1955. Sheridan then went to work for the National Security Agency (NSA), an organization so secret its very existence was once classified. Afterward, Sheridan again received security approval from the Agency so he could take a "Basic Orientation Course." Sheridan later spent his days in the Justice Department's investigation of Jimmy Hoffa, all the while remaining in touch with the Agency. In May of 1967, Sheridan himself informed Richard Lansdale, the CIA Associate General Counsel made famous for Operation MONGOOSE, about the NBC special. Lansdale was told, "NBC regards Garrison as a menace to the country and means to destroy him."[19] The FBI was also aware of the purpose of the "White Paper":

> *A local FBI agent reported that Richard Townley, WDSU-TV, New Orleans, remarked to a special agent of the New Orleans office last evening that he had received instruction from NBC, New York, to prepare a one hour TV special on Jim Garrison with the instruction "shoot him down."*[20]

When the special finally aired, Sheridan attempted to discredit the testimony of heroin addict Vernon Bundy using two of Bundy's associates from Angola. The first, John Cancler, convicted burglar and pimp, said that Bundy had confided to him that he intended to lie about Shaw to get out of prison. Miguel Torres was the other "witness" against Bundy. Torres had a record of burglary, assault, substance abuse, and even attempted murder. He claimed that Bundy had told him the same thing he had told Cancler.[21] In fact, Bundy did not need help getting out of prison. In an NODA interview from 1967, William Gurvich writes "Bundy claimed he was in Parish Prison at the time because he went there voluntarily when he felt himself reverting back to the use of narcotics and feared the consequences of his addiction. Official records corroborate this."[22] After the NBC program aired, Garrison called Cancler and Torres before the Orleans Parish Grand Jury to tell their stories under oath. Both pled their Fifth Amendment right against self-incrimination, and subsequently had time added to their prison sentences for being in contempt of court.[23]

Another "witness" on the NBC special was Fred Leemans, proprietor of a French Quarter Turkish bath house who had told Garrison's office that Clay Shaw had visited his business under the name Clay Bertrand. Leemans then appeared on the "White Paper" saying that Garrison's investigators had offered him $2500 for his testimony. However, after the show aired, Leemans made out a rather incriminating sworn affidavit:

> *...I would like to state the reasons for which I appeared on the NBC show and lied about my contacts with the District Attorney's office. First, I received numerous anonymous threatening phone calls relative to the information I had given Mr. Garrison. The gist of these calls was to the effect that if I did not change my statement and state that I had been bribed by Jim Garrison's office, I and my family would be in physical danger.*
>
> *In addition to the anonymous phone calls, I was visited by a man who exhibited a badge and stated that he was a government agent. This man informed me that the government was presently checking the bar owners in the Slidell area for possible income tax violations. This man then inquired whether I was the Mr. Leemans involved in the Clay*

Shaw case. When I informed him that I was, he said that it was not smart to be involved because a lot of people that had been got hurt and that people in powerful places would see to it that I was taken care of.

One of the anonymous callers suggested that I change my statement and state that I had been bribed by Garrison's office to give him the information about Clay Shaw. He suggested that I contact Mr. Irvin Dymond, Attorney for Clay L. Shaw, and tell him that I gave Mr. Garrison the statement about Shaw only after Mr. Lee offered me $2,500. After consulting with Mr. Dymond by telephone and in person, I was introduced to Walter Sheridan, investigative reporter for NBC, who was then in the process of preparing the NBC show. Mr. Dymond and Mr. Sheridan suggested that I appear on the show and state what I had originally told Mr. Dymond about the bribe offer by the District Attorney's office.

I was informed by Mr. Dymond that should the District Attorney's office charge me with giving false information as a result of my repudiating the statement I had originally given them, he would see to it that I had an attorney and that a bond would be posted for me. In this connection Mr. Dymond gave me his home and office telephone numbers and advised me that I should contact him at any time of day or night should I be charged by Garrison's office as a result of my appearing on the NBC show.

My actual appearance on the show was taped in the office of Aaron Kohn, Managing Director of the Metropolitan Crime Commission, in the presence of Walter Sheridan and Irvin Dymond.[24]

Garrison was later granted 30 minutes under the "Equal Time" law to rebut the NBC allegations after the FCC determined that the "White Paper" was slanted and biased towards Shaw.[25]

Dean Andrews on Trial

As we saw earlier, Dean Andrews had gone before the Orleans Parish Grand Jury on March 16, 1967 and stated under oath that he could not say whether Clay Bertrand was in fact Clay Shaw. Garrison, who knew from his strange lunch conversation that Andrews was afraid for his life, was forced to conclude, "Andrews was protecting Shaw." Andrews was swiftly indicted for perjury by the Grand Jury.[26]

By that summer, Andrews was now claiming that Bertrand was actually his friend Eugene Davis—a claim Davis hotly denied.[27] This was incredible as well, because while Andrews said he had only met Bertrand in person a few times, he had visited Davis at least once every few months since they met in law school in 1950.[28] The Grand Jury subpoenaed Andrews to appear June 28, where he said under oath that Davis was Bertrand. Andrews made a mockery of the probe, calling the Shaw case "a joke," and boasting to the Grand Jury, "Indict me if you want to." The following day, Garrison filed additional charges of perjury against Andrews.[29]

Andrews went to trial August 9, 1967. For the first time, Garrison would attempt to prove at least part of his case to a courtroom jury— beyond reasonable doubt. Assistant DAs James Alcock and Richard Burnes prosecuted the case. They focused on testimony establishing that Andrews had changed his story numerous times. Witnesses included policemen, bondsmen and Andrews' own assistants, whom each had heard conflicting versions of Andrews' claims. Alcock and Burnes introduced as evidence the claim Andrews' made to the New Orleans Press Club that he had "made up Bertrand," which didn't jive with his testimony that Bertrand was Eugene Davis, nor his FBI and hospital records (although these were out of Garrison's reach and unfortunately could not be introduced at the trial).[30]

Andrews based his defense on what author Patricia Lambert termed, his "uncontrollable loquaciousness." According to the defense, Oswald could not have visited Andrews because if he had, Andrews would have told everyone under the sun about it.[31] However, Andrews' employee R.M. Davis told Garrison that Oswald had been in Andrews' office that summer.[32] Defense attorney Harry Burglass also called disreputable journalist Hugh Aynesworth, who testified that Garrison had told him that Andrews "doesn't know anything" about the JFK murder and had been giving Garrison a bunch of "bull."[33] One wonders why this hearsay would be allowed in court anyway, but it doesn't make much sense factually either. Why would Garrison say such a thing after Andrews' personally told Garrison that he (Andrews) would be killed if he talked.[34] Andrews had previously told Mark Lane—the spring before the Garrison probe began—that he would not talk because he was being threatened.[35]

Radio Station WNAC broadcaster Bob Scott interviewed Andrews during the Garrison probe. He told Scott, "I just don't want to get involved in it. Besides that, I like to live. If a guy can put a hole in the President, he can just step on me like an ant. It's not my fight...." Scott asked if Andrews had received any additional attention from the Federal Government since the Garrison investigation went public. "Yeah, they watch me," Andrews said. "Got a tap on the phone you're talking on now...."[36] Andrews would later express that same fear to Anthony Summers, who wrote, "He [Andrews] said later that to reveal the truth about his caller would endanger his life, and my own brief contact with Andrews suggested that the fear stayed with him years afterwards."[37] Before his death in the early 80s, Andrews at last admitted to Harold Weisberg that Clay Bertrand *was* Clay Shaw, but by this time Weisberg had become disenchanted with Garrison's case and it was too late to do Garrison any good anyway. "You understand," Weisberg told researcher Dave Reitzes, "Andrews was the biggest liar that ever lived." Indeed he was.[38]

The jury was not convinced. Andrews was convicted on three counts of perjury on August 14, 1967.[39] Presiding Judge Frank Shea sentenced Andrews to eighteen months in prison, before issuing the solemn observation that perjury "must not be condoned. If not suppressed, it will make meaningless the truth and will encourage willful and irresponsible false-hoods among those who now fear the consequences of such a lie." Shea also took Andrews to task for violating the legal ethics he should have upheld as a lawyer. Perjury is "all the more reprehensible in the words of an attorney since it can only lead to contempt for the law and courts."[40]

Andrews subsequently appealed and lost. His defense attorneys, concerned that his heart problems would prevent him from living out his eighteen-month sentence, approached Garrison. "I knew this was true, and I advised them to file a motion for a new trial. When they responded that the Supreme Court would never grant such a motion, I told them to note on the papers that the motion was approved by the district attorney. It would then be granted pro forma, as it was. When the case was sent back to my office, I dismissed the charges. Andrews never served any time...."[41] The conviction against Andrews was reversed on June 9, 1972.

After the Garrison investigation concluded, Andrews slowly faded into personal oblivion. Working at jobs ranging from French Quarter restaurants to being a mere legal clerk, Andrews at one point was forced to sleep on a cot in the back of a law library. Andrews died in April 1982. His passing was barely noticed.[42]

Andrews made one final appearance, as a defense witness at the trial of Clay Shaw. There, he claimed again that Davis, not Shaw, was Bertrand. This testimony was admissible due to a technicality in Louisiana law that allowed it as long as his perjury conviction was on appeal.

Finding Thornley

All the while, Garrison continued to wonder about Kerry Thornley. But he just could not be found. Oddly enough, it was author David Lifton that put the DA in touch with Thornley. This is a story in itself, and given the amount of disinformation going around about it, deserves comment. In early 1967, Lifton, who had befriended Thornley, learned that Oswald had spoken Russian with his fellow Marine John Renee Heindel, who revealed in his Warren Commission affidavit that he had gone by the nickname Hidell, also Oswald's alleged alias.[43] Lifton was suspicious of this. After all, how common were Russian speaking Marines?

Lifton reported the information he had received from Thornley regarding Heindel to Garrison's office. Heindel, who lived in New Orleans, was questioned by Garrison's office that September. If you believe Lifton's version, offered up in a May 1968 article for *Open City Magazine*, the situation now gets downright bizarre.[44] According to Lifton, a Garrison aide (not Garrison himself, mind you) told Lifton that Garrison thought Heindel was "lying through his teeth" and that Garrison had developed evidence that Oswald had met Heindel at several New Orleans bars in the summer of 1963.[45] This is interesting, because Garrison's case against Thornley was originally built on testimony along the same lines, except that it dealt with Oswald meeting with Thornley. Lifton says that Garrison wanted Thornley to "confront" and "identify" Heindel, or at the very least send Garrison some sworn statements to the effect that he had personal knowledge that Heindel was lying when he denied knowing Oswald in the summer of 1963. This would be to suborn perjury, something Garrison was known for—wrongly of course.

Lifton's narrative gets stranger still. There is no evidence in the archives that Garrison actually had information placing Heindel with Oswald in the summer of 1963. Yet, Garrison must have at least been suspicious of Heindel in some way (besides, Oswald's alias was Heindel's nickname—a fairly suspicious thing) because, according to Lifton, Thornley promptly prepared those statements and mailed them off.[46]

Lifton then meets Garrison at the Century Plaza Hotel in Los Angeles, where Garrison was "utterly frightened and...convinced that he was constantly followed, bugged, etc."[47] Garrison is supposed to be paranoid. However, he was not the only one that shared those sentiments. In James Alcock's famous telephone interview with David Logan, the following piece of information was exchanged:

A.   *Oh. Well, let me just call you and maybe in, how about the middle of the week and perhaps you'll have that name?*

L.   *Oh. Okay. Well listen—Well, I'll tell you what. Well, let's see, you don't want to call me you because you don't want me because you want to call from another phone?*

A.   *Well, I'm at a pay station now, you see, and I want to move because I just don't trust our office phones.*

L.   *Okay. Why don't—okay.*[48]

Lifton then attacks Garrison for the use of his theory of propinquity to connect Oswald and Ruby through telephone calls to the KTVT TV station in Fort Worth, Texas. But this is really an attack against the eccentricities of one investigator, and besides, Garrison had valid reasons for his theory. As he explained in a letter to HSCA staffer Jonathan Blackmer, the usual investigative techniques were less effective due to the secret nature of the assassination. Therefore, Garrison sought out other techniques. Propinquity may be a frankly dumb idea, but Garrison apparently believed in it.[49] On this issue Garrison told Lifton "Law is not a science," and that "After the fact, there is no truth. There is only what the jury decides."[50] But this is not indicative of a disdain for due process, but rather his malaise with the legal system. As Tom Bethell recorded in his famous diary, Garrison was taught in law school that any case could be argued in any way depending on the precedents employed in making the arguments. When Garrison realized that the truth had little effect on the outcome, disenchantment set in.[51] This is one reason Garrison took his campaign to clean up the French Quarter and the JFK investigation so seriously.

After this conversation, an amazing thing happened. Lifton talked to another Marine who witnessed Heindel and Oswald speaking Russian together. However, this Marine's story made it obvious that Thornley's "identification" of Heindel was false.[52] Lifton informed Garrison of this, and Thornley again came under the DA's suspicion. This caused Thornley to tell Garrison, in Lifton's words, "to shove off."[53] Garrison would do no such thing, but strangely, Lifton was offended. To Lifton, Garrison was in the wrong for reading his friend Thornley's perjured statements about Heindel. That Thornley had made out the statements was of no consequence. From here on out, Lifton considered Garrison the enemy.

Evidence Surfaces

On October 26, 1967, Assistant DA Andrew Sciambra interviewed a French Quarter hanger-on named Peter Deageano. Deageano had spent much of his time in the summer of 1963 hanging out at the Bourbon House, and it was there that he was introduced by Kerry Thornley and Thornley's girlfriend, Jeanne Hack to Lee Harvey Oswald.[54] Earlier that summer Deageano had ran into Oswald passing out leaflets on Canal Street:

> *When he saw me he handed me one of his leaflets. I looked at it and when I saw that it said something about helping Cuba, I just threw it down and walked off. I then remembered that I also saw him a few days before this incident in the Bourbon House. It was between 2:00 and 4:00 o'clock in the afternoon either in August or September of 1963. I was sitting at a table in the Bourbon House eating a hamburger. There weren't too many people in the Bourbon House and as I looked around I noticed Kerry Thornley, Jeanne Hack and him sitting at a table close to me. I looked at them and said hello and either Kerry Thornley or Jeanne Hack introduced him to me. I cannot remember how he was introduced or any of the conversation that we may have had as it was a very casual meeting. However, I remember thinking to myself that he might be related to Kerry Thornley as he resembled him quite a bit.*

After the assassination of President Kennedy a picture of Lee Harvey Oswald appeared on television and I immediately recognized him as being identical to the person I had seen handing out leaflets on Canal Street, and identical to the person that I saw sitting in the Bourbon House with Kerry Thornley and Jeanne Hack.[55]

Deageano also told Sciambra that Hack's father had been a teacher at Tulane Medical School and that Deageano's friend, Clint Bolton, was with the anti-Communist group Friends of Democratic Cuba.[56] Deageano's recollection was soon confirmed by an acquaintance of his, Barbara Reid.

Reid recalled that in mid-September of 1963, she had been having a hamburger in the late afternoon with Deageano and Thornley. Then someone else showed up.

I recall associating a sense of familiarity with this individual as the same individual who had received some publicity as a Communist because of his earlier activity of distributing Fair Play for Cuba leaflets in front of the International Trade Mart in New Orleans.

Also, I associated him as the person who was interviewed by Bill Stuckey of WDSU.

We engaged in casual conversation for a short period of time and then approximately ten to fifteen minutes later, I left the Bourbon House.[57]

Other witnesses interviewed at that time remembered Thornley as a regular at the Bourbon House. Two, referred to in Garrison's files as "J.S." and "J.D." placed Thornley there the night of the assassination and said that Thornley was glad to learn of JFK's death.[58] In a memo from Sciambra to Garrison, concerning witness Bernard Goldsmith, Sciambra noted the following:

He repeated that THORNLEY was a right-winger and so set in his political beliefs that he, GOLDSMITH, and THORNLEY made an agreement not to talk politics.[59]

Goldsmith, a friend of Thornley's, also recalled that Thornley had said, "he had known Oswald," though he did not specify if he had meant in New Orleans or not. Thornley also told Goldsmith "that Oswald was not a communist."[60]

On November 6, 1967, Sciambra spoke to Mr. Jack Spencer, who had been Thornley's landlord in 1963. Apparently, at around 8:00 P.M. the night of the assassination the Secret Service came knocking on Spencer's door wanting to speak to Thornley. By this time Thornley was at the restaurant where he worked nights, so Spencer directed the Secret Service Agents there. Thornley was able to get off work, and he returned, with the agents, to his apartment where they talked for some two to three hours.[61] The next day, the FBI also interviewed Thornley.[62] But unbeknownst to both Spencer and Garrison, Thornley said some very interesting things to the FBI. Thornley had only been with Oswald in New Orleans for two weeks, between the time Thornley got there after a trip to Mexico City (according to him, he wished to exercise his knowledge of the Spanish language) and the time Oswald *left for* Mexico City.

As mentioned earlier, Mexico City is the nexus where the case for conspiracy converges—an issue to be explored in Chapter 8. Note the following, however. Thornley told the FBI "he made this trip by himself and emphatically denied that Oswald had accompanied him from New Orleans to California or from California to Mexico."[63] This is extremely interesting—after all, how many people knew the day after the assassination that Oswald *had* been in Mexico City? It gets even more intriguing. An FBI telex written that same day reports that the FBI was informed by Grand Prairie Police Detective J.C. Murdock that "Thornley is presently employed as a waiter in New Orleans and has recently been in Mexico and California with Oswald. Secret Service has been notified."[64]

At any rate, Mr. Spencer told Sciambra that Thornley disappeared about two or three days after the murder. Spencer found a note in his mailbox that read, "I must leave. I am going to Washington, D. C. area, probably Alexandria, Virginia. I will send you my address so that you can forward my mail."[65] Spencer had other interesting information to offer. As Sciambra put it in a memo:

> *SPENCER said it was quite unexpected as THORNLEY had at least 10 days left in the month before his rent would have been due; that from the way the note was written he got the impression that THORNLEY was under some pressure and for some reason had to leave.*
>
> . . .
>
> *He said that after the note he went to THORNLEY's apartment which was Apt. "C," and every bit of paper in the apartment was torn up in little bitty pieces resembling confetti. THORNLEY had even watered down the paper so that the ink was blurred preventing anyone from reading any part of it.[66]*

Spencer, did not, however, see Oswald at Thornley's apartment at any time during those two weeks. After Thornley got to Virginia, he worked at the famed Shirlington House apartment complex. Mrs. Doris Dowell, Thornley's assistant manager, also knew that Thornley had lied about Oswald's "communism."

> *Mrs. Dowell said that about one month before THORNLEY left for California he told her that he had been in the Marine Corps with LEE HARVEY OSWALD, and also that they were buddies in New Orleans. He said that he had met OSWALD again in New Orleans, and that they had met at a place in the French Quarter that she would probably not like.[67]*

On January 10, 1968, Assistant DA Richard V. Burnes received a telephone call from a Florida newsman by the name Cliff Hall. In 1963 Hall had been Program Director of WSHO Radio in New Orleans. During his time in New Orleans, Hall became familiar with several denizens of the French Quarter, among them Kerry Thornley.[68] Very shortly after the assassination Hall accompanied Thornley to the WDSU TV station where he was interviewed about Oswald. Thornley revealed essentially the same information he later gave to the Warren Commission, but later that evening Thornley and Hall had drinks at the Bourbon House where Thornley added something. "'I didn't tell this guy,' he said, 'But I have seen Oswald since then, since the Marine Corps.'"[69]

Hall probed further. "I said, 'Did you know him well,' and he said, 'Yes.'"[70] Burnes then questioned Hall further, attempting to clarify the answer (Burnes was not familiar with the Thornley case, having only read Thornley's Warren Commission testimony and nothing more).

> *H. You see. Now I didn't know whether this would have any bearing on your investigation or not, but it might.*
>
> *B. It's certainly good information. Now let me ask you something. He told you that he knew Oswald since the Marine Corps?*
>
> *H. Yes sir.*
>
> *B. Which could only mean in New Orleans.*
>
> *H. Yes sir. That's what he said. He said that he had seen him in New Orleans since his service in the Marine Corps and he said that to me in the presence of other people.*
>
> *...*
>
> *B. I'll pass this along to Mr. Garrison and if it becomes an issue of whether or not Kerry Thornley actually saw Lee Harvey Oswald here in New Orleans, we will know that he admitted it to you at that particular time.*[71]

On February 22, 1968 the picture of Thornley's association with Oswald in New Orleans became even clearer when the NODA received a letter from John Schwegmann, Jr. of Schwegmann Bros. Super Markets:

An employee of our store, Mrs. Myrtle LaSavia [LaSavia had been a neighbor of Oswald when he and Marina Oswald had lived on Magazine Street.]…says that she, her husband, and a number of people who live in that neighborhood saw Thornley at the Oswald residence a number of times—in fact they saw him there so much they did not know which was the husband, Oswald or Thornley.[72]

Garrison now had a basis for an opinion of Thornley. He had reams of evidence that Thornley had lied when he told the Warren Commission Oswald was a dedicated communist. Yet, what are the odds that the only one of Oswald's Marine buddies to call him a communist was also the only one that closely associated with him the summer before the president's murder? Garrison again reached out for Thornley.

Kerry the Liar

Going back to his early FBI and Secret Service interviews, Thornley denied he had associated with Oswald in New Orleans in the summer of 1963, or even known Oswald was there. Thornley said the same thing to the Warren Commission:

Mr. JENNER. During none of that period of time did you have any contact with or hear anything about Oswald?

Mr. THORNLEY. Definitely not.[73]

Thornley's New Orleans friendship with Oswald is then suspicious in that Thornley later buried Oswald as a communist and then denied knowing him after the Marines. Yet there is an indication that even the Warren Commission might have known that Thornley was lying. Deep in volume eleven of the Warren Commission's hearings is this intriguing nugget from the testimony of Dean Andrews:

Mr. LIEBELER. Is it an extraordinary thing for a bunch of gay kids to come into your office like that, or did they come from time to time?

Mr. ANDREWS. Well, let's see. Last week there were six of them in there. Depends on how bad the police are rousing them. They shoo them in. My best customers are the police. They shoo them into the office. God bless the police.

Mr. LIEBELER. Did you ever know a man by the name of Kerry Thornley as one of these gay kids?

Mr. ANDREWS. No.

Mr. LIEBELER. Have you ever beard of Thornley?

Mr. ANDREWS. No; I represent them and that's about all there is to it. When they owe me money, I know where to go grab them, and that's about as far as it goes. Is he supposed to be down here?

Mr. LIEBELER. Thornley?

Mr. ANDREWS. Yes; I can find out if he ever made the scene here real easy.

Mr. LIEBELER. No; he is not in New Orleans, I don't think, at the moment. When Oswald told you about his discharge, did he tell you what branch of the service he had been in?[74]

Note how quickly Liebeler changes the subject when Andrews offers to check around about Thornley. Other evidence raises doubt as to whether or not the Commission truly believed Thornley. In Thornley's November 26, 1963 FBI interview he stated that Oswald "was not a Communist while he was assigned to the El Toro Marine Base."[75] This document, which was classified until 1993, is a bombshell in itself but is even more intriguing when studied in context of other information. The Commission had no independent investigative staff, relied on the FBI and CIA for investigative materials and presumably had access to the interview in question. We know with certainty that the Commission saw a newspaper article from the New Orleans States Item entitled "Wrote Novel About

Oswald, Says Orleanian" because a copy of the article appeared in the Commission's volumes. This interview of Thornley was printed on November 27, the very day that the memo recording Thornley's FBI interview was dictated. In it, Thornley says:

> *I think Oswald became a Communist before he became a Marine, but I believe the Marines only made things worse with him.*[76]

Thornley later revealed in a non-fiction (if only on the level of *The Idle Warriors*) book that he had spoken with Warren Commission counsel Albert Jenner several times prior to his official testimony, we can only assume in preparation for it.[77] Thornley's disdain for the truth continued to the era of the Garrison probe, as recorded in a pair of memos authored by Andrew Sciambra in early February of 1968. During a February 7 visit to the offices of the NODA, Thornley denied knowing David Ferrie and said he "might have met" Guy Banister.[78]

Yet in a 1976 affidavit to the HSCA, Thornley finally admitted he "accidentally" met David Ferrie in 1962, though he cautions that he was "nearly sure that no significant conversation transpired."[79] Thornley also admits to "accidentally" meeting Guy Banister in New Orleans in 1961 and discussing *The Idle Warriors*, but even here, Thornley does not reveal the whole truth.[80] In a pair of interviews conducted in September of 1994 by author James DiEugenio, Banister agents Allen and Dan Campbell both place Thornley at 544 Camp Street, apparently working for Banister. In fact, on the very day Kennedy was shot, Allen Campbell was in the company of none other than Kerry Wendell Thornley.[81] Dan Campbell told DiEugenio that Thornley, who at the time of the interview was very ill, was deathly afraid of revealing what he knew "about New Orleans."[82]

Thornley was finally summoned before the Orleans Parish Grand Jury on February 8, 1968. Rather than reveal major elements of his case against Thornley during the testimony, Garrison focused on the visit with Oswald in the Bourbon House witnessed by Peter Deageano and Barbara Reid. This was wise, in that it prevented Thornley from savaging Garrison's key witnesses before a trial could be held, during which time Garrison would be unable to defend himself because of the rules concerning pre-trial publicity. By holding a public preliminary hearing for Shaw, Garrison unwittingly opened himself up to the media assault that followed. Therefore, in dealing with Thornley in front of the Grand Jury, Garrison focused entirely upon Barbara Reid.[83]

Thornley's answers under questioning were evasive and dishonest. Note the way Thornley avoid making any outright confirmations or denials of anything:

> *Q. Did she see you with Oswald?*
>
> *A. I don't think she did because the next day I started asking people....*
>
> *Q. You don't think so?*
>
> *A. I don't know whether it was Oswald, I can't remember who was sitting there with me, I don't think it was Oswald for two reasons, the first thing is if I could remember who it was then I could say definitely, in view of the fact that....*
>
> *Q. I understand those facts, but in view of the fact that you were writing a novel about him, I should think you would recognize him.*
>
> *A. Yes, this was Barbara's theory.*
>
> *Q. Was her theory right?*
>
> *A. I don't know. First of all, the next day I started saying to people Barbara is sure she saw me with Oswald in the Bourbon House. That is the first thing. I kept asking people.*
>
> ...
>
> *Q. Did you ask them if they saw you at the Bourbon House with Oswald?*

A. No, I did not ask them, how would they know. Barbara was there. I said Barbara is sure she saw me at the Bourbon house with Oswald, I don't know whether it is true of nor but she is sure she saw me there and she has convinced me that she saw me. And everybody said, "Oh, Barbara Reed gets involved with everything that happens."

Q. Is it possible that you were with Oswald at the Bourbon House?

A. I don't think it possible. For here is the other reason. I remembered this thing that happened after she turned away and after she went back to conversing with this person sitting with me that is Barbara Reed, she is a character around here, to somebody who did not know Barbara she is a witch or something like this, and I felt that there was a barrier to my explaining this to this person and this could only have been one of the Cuban waiters at the Sheraton-Charles, and the only barrier would have been a language barrier, why did I feel that this was a barrier, and on the basis of that—that is all I know. On the basis of that I am sure I was not with Oswald, but Barbara is sure I was.

. . .

Q....Are you sure that you never saw Lee Harvey Oswald in New Orleans in 1963, for a while you seemed to be on the fence.

A. No, the only time I ever thought I did was when Barbara Reed was so sure about it, and I became convinced, but I am sure I did not see Oswald and recognize him in New Orleans of 1963.

Q. You are telling me there was a point when she had convinced you that you were with Oswald?

A. Yes, she convinced me, certainly, there was the two hours or so she was talking to me and she said, Kerry, what must have happened was this, you must have walked into the Bourbon House and he must have

*walked in, you must have seen that his face was familiar, but not rec-
ognized him our of uniform and all this stuff, and he must have sat
down next to you...she was so certain, so positive ...*

Q. Did it seem to you that it was possible?

*A. It seemed to be possible, when she got all through, until the next day
and people began to say Barbara Reed connects herself with everything
that happens, then it seemed impossible ...*[84]

Thornley apparently took Garrison's bait and focused entirely upon
arguing that Reid's testimony was an exaggeration of a mistaken recollection and attacking her involvement with occult religions (was this really
that uncommon in the French Quarter?), never considering that Garrison
had other evidence. Thornley must have been very surprised when, two
weeks later, Garrison had Thornley arrested and indicted for perjury.[85]

The Reaction

Jim Garrison could have only been amused at the way the media, the
government and Kerry W. Thornley reacted to Thornley's February 22,
1968 indictment for perjury. Thornley ironically claimed to the press that
he was the victim of a *conspiracy* to frame him, or failing that the Grand
Jury was merely misled by "an overwhelming amount of circumstantial
coincidentals." The young perjurer then intoned that the witnesses against
him "deliberately lied," but lamented that he had "neither the resources
investigative-wise nor legal-wise to prove that these witnesses were
lying."[86] Garrison's staff, however, suspected that if there was one thing
Thornley did not lack it was "resources."

According to Mort Sahl, Thornley demanded at one point in 1968 that
Assistant DA Sciambra meet him at the National Aeronautics and Space
Administration (NASA) complex on the eastern side of New Orleans.[87]
Garrison investigator Jim Rose would later learn that Thornley had two
homes in Florida, one in Miami and one in Tampa, as well as two cars.

The Tampa residence, where Thornley lived, was large white frame house on a one-acre lot. Thornley was single and supposedly had only worked as a waiter and doorman at a few apartment houses.[88]

That summer, *Open City Magazine* published the aforementioned David Lifton article. Lifton predictably singles out the only witness he could have known of: Barbara Reid.

> *To understand where Garrison's witnesses come from is to understand that his "investigation" should more accurately be termed a "Witness Recruitment Program...."*
>
> *The witness recruiting program for Kerry Thornley is now on in full force. Barbara Reid and Harold Weisberg are now turning up "witnesses."*
>
> *Fringe benefits for such testimony include the dropping of charges, plus one fantastic ego trip on the witness stand, as you chip in your portion of Garrison's solution to the assassination.*[89]

Garrison had the last laugh—most of his witnesses either turned up before Barbara Reid, or as in the cases of Cliff Hall and Myrtle LaSavia were unsolicited entirely. Rather than respond to these incessant attacks, Garrison simply pointed out that it was "thought provoking that the only one of Oswald's former Marine comrades who testified that he was a 'Marxist'...is also the only one who was in personal association with Oswald in New Orleans in 1963 before he returned to Dallas before the assassination."[90] Then a strange thing happened—as soon as the attacks against him concerning Thornley died down, Garrison went right back to rebuilding his case against Clay Shaw. On June 13, 1968, Garrison had to respond to a complaint filed by Shaw's attorneys in the U.S. District Court for the Eastern District of Louisiana. Shaw's complaints included attacks against the Grand Jury, Russo's "drug induced" testimony, illegal search and seizure (Garrison had a warrant to search Shaw's home), plots to harass citizens who disagreed with Garrison, and the recycled claims of William Gurvich.

The remainder of that summer was spent keeping straight the many different tales of Reverend Raymond Broshears and investigating the leads concerning Loran Hall, Fred Lee Chrisman and Thomas Edward Beckham. Then came the complicated set of legal battles on the road to getting Clay Shaw to trial. On one occasion F. Irvin Dymond and Edward Wegmann, Shaw's defense counsel, went as far as Washington, D.C. to beg the Justice Department for help, warning that "The District Attorney is a dangerous, irresponsible man and must be stopped."[91] Garrison also had to contend with requests for a change of venue and numerous delays brought on by the defense.[92]

All this resulted in one of Garrison's biggest mistakes. Garrison focused on nailing Shaw almost obsessively (see Chapter 8 for the reason why). That August, a paid volunteer by the name of Tom Bethell secretly met with defense lawyer Salvatore Panzeca and turned over to him the prosecution's whole trial brief. It was only at this point that the defense stopped trying to delay the trial.[93] In January of 1969, rumors began to spread around the NODA about a leak, resulting in an internal investigation. When confronted by Louis Ivon, Bethell confessed.[94] The motivation of Tom Bethell, who has been lauded as a hero by Shaw's defenders, may be explained by one intriguing fact. During the summer of 1963, Bethell was good friends with Warwick Reynolds, none other than Kerry Thornley's roommate.[95] At this point, Garrison could have requested a mistrial, but he did not. *Why?*

For some reason that has never been adequately explained, Garrison pressed on to try Clay Shaw. Perhaps Garrison—like General Robert E. Lee at Gettysburg—thought one decisive victory would be enough to turn the tide of the case and win the war. After almost two years of negative publicity, Garrison may have believed prolonging the conflict would only reduce his chances of breaking the conspiracy wide open.[96] Indeed, he may have seen the Shaw trial as his last opportunity. In Garrison's own words, "I could hardly count on being the district attorney in 2039 when the federal government proposed to release its great mass of evidence."[97] With the media, the government and New Orleans high society all arrayed against him, Garrison now went to trial against Clay L. Shaw.

Kerry Wendell Thornley would have to wait.

But the wait would be longer than Garrison could have ever realized.

Chapter Six

The Trial of Clay Shaw

"I do concur with Mr. Dymond, this is certainly an important case. Thank God it got to a jury such as yourselves despite the efforts of the Jim Phelans, the Walter Sheridans, and the Friends of NBC, because this is where it belongs, and whatever your verdict is, you have got the right to make that verdict."

—Rebuttal Arguments of James Alcock at the trial of Clay Shaw

The strategy employed by District Attorney Jim Garrison at the trial of Clay Shaw was remarkably simple—simply present enough witnesses to make the case, with few surprises and no forays into the murky world of Shaw's personal life. Garrison intended to prove several specific allegations that he hoped would force the jury to convict Shaw.

1. That Shaw had conspired with David Ferrie and Lee Harvey Oswald to arrange the murder of President Kennedy.[1]

2. That Shaw had made at least one overt act in furtherance of the conspiracy, as required under the laws of Louisiana (as in most states) to prove criminal conspiracy.

Furthermore, since Shaw had denied knowing Ferrie and Oswald and denied using the Bertrand alias, Garrison sought also to prove essentially that Shaw was a liar. Garrison was going to have a problem getting more than a scant few credible witness on the stand to prove Shaw's use of the alias. Apparently, many in the Quarter were fearful of the consequences of testifying publicly against Shaw. To demonstrate the size of Garrison's problem, consider the following:

a. Journalist Lawrence Schiller, who supported the conclusions of the Warren Commission, found several witnesses. Schiller told the FBI in March 1967 that "three homosexual sources in New Orleans and two homosexual sources in San Francisco have indicated that Clay Shaw was known by other names including Clay Bertrand."[2]

b. Assassination researcher Edgar Tatro was a college student during the time of the Shaw trial, and came down to New Orleans to watch the trial. One night in a French Quarter bar, several people noticed Tatro's Boston accent and asked him what he was doing in New Orleans. When Tatro told them, they started giggling. Tatro asked what was so funny. Their response: "Look, everybody down here knows that Shaw uses the name Bertrand. But that poor devil Garrison can't prove it to save his soul."[3] Shaw's high-society stature combined with the secret nature of his sexuality and the French Quarter tipped the balance in Shaw's favor.

c. New Orleans homicide detective and later HSCA investigator L.J. Delsa said Shaw's use of the name Bertrand was an "open secret."[4]

d. Previous New Orleans police reports had mentioned a wealthy homosexual known as Clay Bertrand.[5]

Finally, since the defense team had set out to prove that not only was Shaw not involved in the conspiracy, but also that there was *no* conspiracy, Garrison would introduce the Dallas evidence to further corroborate his assertions and to back up Russo's recollections about the planned triangulation of crossfire.

As far as the state's first two allegations, Garrison intended to introduce evidence of six overt acts of conspiracy. The first was the meeting with

Shaw, Ferrie, Oswald and the Cubans ("the assassination party") at Ferrie's apartment in September 1963. The second was the discussion of triangulation of crossfire and the need for each plotter to establish alibis away from the others on the day of the assassination. The third was Shaw's trip to San Francisco; the fourth was Ferrie's trip to Houston. The fifth act was Oswald's taking a rifle into the Texas School Book Depository (TSBD), as allegedly witnessed by Buell Wesley Frazier (ironic since Frazier is widely used by Warren Critics to rebut the allegations against Oswald).[6] The sixth and final act was an alleged September meeting between Shaw, Oswald and Jack Ruby at a Baton Rouge hotel. Allegedly, Shaw gave Ruby money and killing someone "from Washington" was discussed.[7]

The witness to this meeting was an eccentric former third-party candidate for governor of Louisiana by the name of Clyde Johnson. Johnson's nickname was "Slidin' Clyde" due to his disreputable way of life (he was a "freelance" preacher who had had run-ins with the law), and he was every bit the shady character. During his 1963 campaign for governor, he said, Shaw had made $2,000 in contributions after learning of Johnson's vocal criticism of Kennedy.[8] According to Johnson, it was at the Capitol House Hotel in Baton Rouge that he had overheard the meeting between Shaw, Ruby and Oswald. When Ruby questioned Johnson's presence, Shaw replied, "That's alright. He's one of my boys."[9] Although Johnson had a questionable reputation, New Orleans journalist Ross Yockey interviewed him in June 1967 and believed that he (Johnson) was telling the truth but was very scared. Johnson for one did not relish the idea of being subpoenaed by Garrison's office and wanted to consult an attorney before talking to the NODA.[10]

Garrison's office was able to partially corroborate Johnson's testimony by questioning his running mate Edward McMillan. McMillan identified Shaw as one of the attendees of a party held at the Monteleone Hotel for Johnson's supporters in January 1964.[11] Believing his story, Garrison put Johnson on the witness list for the Shaw trial and mentioned the story during the jury selection phase of the trial.[12] A few days before the trial was to begin, Johnson told reporters plainly, "I'm the ace-in-the-hole in Garrison's case."[13] It was not to be. Johnson was subsequently beaten severely and did not testify against Shaw.[14] With this loss, the sixth overt act was dropped by the prosecution by the time opening arguments were made.

To prove the remaining acts and allegations, Garrison outlined in his opening statements the following incidents and witnesses:

1. Oswald's mysterious activity in the summer of 1963, as evidenced by the leafleting incidents.

2. Discussion by Shaw and Ferrie of killing the president during a June 1963 party. The witness was not named, but it turned out to be surprise witness Charles Spiesel.

3. A meeting of Shaw and Oswald on the lakefront where Shaw passed Oswald money, as witnessed to previously by Vernon Bundy.

4. A trip allegedly made by Shaw with Ferrie and Oswald to the small town of Clinton, Louisiana as witnessed by more than a dozen of Clinton's own citizens.

5. The "assassination party" at David Ferrie's apartment as witnessed by Russo.

6. Shaw's trip to San Francisco.

7. Ferrie's trip to Houston and mysterious behavior at the skating rink, as witnessed by owner Chuck Rolland.

8. Various witnesses and pieces of photographic evidence from Dallas.

9. "Clay Bertrand's" call to Dean Andrews.

10. Evidence that Shaw received mail addressed to a "Clem Bertrand."

11. Evidence that Shaw signed the VIP Book at the Moisant Airport using the name "Clay Bertrand."[15]

Day of Reckoning

The actual Shaw trial began on February 6, 1967 (jury selection had taken two weeks). Garrison began by reading an opening statement outlining the basic strategy described above. F. Irvin Dymond, lead defense attorney, then offered his opening statement, stating, "We are not here to defend the findings of the Warren Commission," though that is exactly what he did. Dymond also claimed that "not only did Clay Shaw not engage in a conspiracy with David Ferrie and Lee Harvey Oswald to assassinate President Kennedy, but that he never knew nor ever laid eyes on either of these two individuals," and that Perry Russo was a "liar, a notoriety seeking liar whose name does not deserve to be mentioned in the same sentence with honesty, justice, and propriety." Dymond then entered a not guilty plea on Shaw's behalf.[16]

The first prosecution witness was Edwin McGehee, a barber in Jackson, Louisiana. In late August or early September of 1963, McGehee recalled that a stranger entered his barbershop requesting a haircut and "information." McGehee identified the stranger as Lee Harvey Oswald. According to McGehee, Oswald asked him if he knew of any job openings in the Jackson area. McGehee told Oswald that there might be a job available at the East Louisiana State Hospital—a mental hospital—and that it would help if Oswald were a registered voter in East Feliciana Parish since a job at that hospital would be a Civil Service job. Oswald was referred to Louisiana Representative Reeves Morgan, who was that area's state representative. McGehee also mentioned Henry Earl Palmer, the local registrar of voters. After McGehee was finished with his (Oswald's) haircut, Oswald left.[17]

The next witness up was Reeves Morgan, who recalled that Oswald had come to his rural home one evening in early autumn of 1963 and introduced himself.

> *Q: Tell the Court what you told Lee Harvey Oswald that day that you talked to him in your home.*
>
> *A: I told him that I could not help him get a job at the hospital ahead of any of my constituents, at the East Louisiana State Hospital, but I was not going to try to prevent him from getting a job, and I told him all the procedure he would have to go to to get in position to get a job,*

about going and putting in his application and getting set up to take a Civil Service examination, and that you just didn't go over there and get a job and just go to work, you had to go through applications and take a Civil Service examination for a job in the electrical department or something like that. They did have some jobs over there maybe, but I didn't tell him all that, but to get into the electrical department or maintenance you had to have a Civil Service exam, and—he was from New Orleans—it wouldn't hurt if he was a registered voter up there, and I told him that I knew a fellow up there once trying to find out what he can from everybody around there, and I told him I knew a fellow up there whose first name was Oswald and I asked him was he any kin to him.[18]

After Morgan came John Manchester, town Marshall of nearby Clinton, Louisiana. Manchester testified that in late August or early September of 1963, Clinton was up in arms over a voting drive conducted by the Congress on Racial Equality (CORE). On one particular day, Manchester had been watching the area in front of the voter registration officer when Henry Earl Palmer drew his attention to a black Cadillac containing two men he had never seen before. Manchester checked out the automobile and talked to the driver, "a big man, gray-haired, ruddy complexion, a real easy-talking man" whom Manchester identified as Clay Shaw."[19]

Q: When you asked this individual where he was from, did he say anything?

A: He said he was a representative of the International Trade Mart in New Orleans.

Q: Did you ever talk to anyone from the International Trade Mart before this day?

A: No, sir, I hadn't.[20]

Henry Earl Palmer, the registrar of voters, took the stand next. He testified than while the registration drive was going on, he had noticed the
black Cadillac during his morning break and requested that Manchester
get a "1028," or license registration check, of the car in order to identify
the passengers and make sure they weren't there to cause trouble. Palmer
described the man on the passenger side of the car: "Well, the man on the
passenger side, all I can tell you about him, he appeared—his eyebrows
were heavy and his hair needed combing. He had messed-up hair, I
noticed that." The witness identified the man as looking generally like
David Ferrie, and positively identified the driver as Clay Shaw.[21]

Palmer saw Shaw and Ferrie still parked there during his lunch and a
mid-afternoon break. Finally, after a 3:30 coffee break a young white man
stepped into the registration office. Palmer identified the young man as
Lee Harvey Oswald.[22]

> *Q: Would you tell the Court what transpired when you talked to
> Oswald in your office.*
>
> *A: When Mr. Oswald came in there and gave me the identification,
> ID card, I looked at the name on it, had Lee H. Oswald with a New
> Orleans address—I don't remember what the address was. I asked him
> where he lived, and—can I state what he said, where he lived?*
>
> *. . .*
>
> *Q: In reference to what he was trying to do, tell us what you told him.*
>
> *A: He was trying to—wanted a job at the hospital in Jackson.*
>
> *. . .*
>
> *THE COURT: It is a difficult situation. Just tell us, if you will, Mr.
> Palmer, what you told him you had to find out from him if he told you
> that. Just tell us what you spoke to him about.*

A: His ID card didn't identify his living in the Parish of East Feliciana, so I told him, asked him if he knew the business manager at the hospital in Jackson or if he knew the Mayor of the Town of Jackson or if he knew the Representative of the Parish. He couldn't give me any proof that he was living in the Parish long enough, but I told him he did not have to be a registered voter to get a job at the Jackson Hospital. He thanked me and left.

Q: How long did you say you talked to Oswald at that—

A: Oswald was in the office approximately 15 or 20 minutes.

Q: How many times did you see Oswald in line before you talked to him in your office?

A: He was in line when I went down for coffee and when I come back and went for lunch and when I come back and when I went for coffee in the afternoon and when I came back, and then he came in my office.

...

Q: Was the black Cadillac still parked outside when you left your office that day?

A: No, sir, it had gone.

Q: About what time did you say Oswald left your office?

A: A little after 4:00.[23]

Civil Rights Worker Corrie Collins had been with the CORE Registration Drive that day. He testified that he had seen the Cadillac when it first drove up in front of the voter registration office. Collins saw three men in the car; two were in front and one, who left the vehicle shortly after it pulled up, was in the back seat. This man was identified as Lee Harvey Oswald. Collins also identified the driver as Clay Shaw and the man in the passenger seat as David Ferrie.[24] The next day, Collins' testimony was corroborated by his assistant, William E. Dunn.[25]

The next two witnesses provided testimony indicating that Oswald returned to Jackson and indeed applied for a job at the hospital. Receptionist Bobbie Dedon stated under oath that she had directed Oswald to the administration building, and Maxine Kemp, a personnel office employee, testified that about a year after the assassination she had gone through old files to check out rumors that Oswald had applied for a job at the hospital. Kemp said she did find a file called, "Oswald, Lee" containing an application of the form used in 1963, returned the file to its place and later, when questioned by Garrison's staff, could not find it again.[26] The jury found the recollections of the Clinton witnesses highly credible.

Garrison Stumbles

The next major witness on the stand was Vernon Bundy, the heroin addict who two years earlier had testified at the preliminary hearing that he had been seen Shaw give Oswald money on the Lakefront while preparing to get high. Bundy's trial testimony was essentially the same on direct examination, but changed dramatically when Dymond began cross-examination. Dymond asked Bundy if Bundy had ever stolen to support his heroin habit. Bundy denied it, in spite of the fact that he had freely *admitted* to breaking into a cigarette machine for drug money at the preliminary hearing. Dymond had the preliminary hearing testimony introduced into evidence and Bundy walked off the stand in disgrace.[27]

Up next was surprise witness Charles I. Spiesel. Spiesel was an accountant from New York who testified that he had attended a party in the French Quarter in June of 1963, where Clay Shaw and David Ferrie talked about assassinating President Kennedy using a high-powered rifle and Ferrie's flying the assassins out of the country.[28] Spiesel's testimony was compelling. In the words of James Kirkwood, "This was no dope addict, thief, pimp, or pusher of pornographic films—here was a professional man."[29] Spiesel's effectiveness was lessened dramatically on his cross-examination by F. Irvin Dymond. Spiesel admitted to fingerprinting his own daughter to make sure she had not been replaced with a double, and to being spied on and hypnotized over fifty times by the New York City Police.[30] Spiesel was obviously discredited, but the question is why did he testify at all, and how did the defense know what to ask? As to the latter point, Salvatore Panzeca claims he received a call from his neighbor, Bill Storm, in the middle of Spiesel's testimony. Storm was supposed to have told Panzeca that he had worked with Spiesel years before and he was "a nut." Panzeca then pressed Storm for the details, resulting in the brilliant cross-examination.[31] The problem with this story is that Hugh Aynesworth had stated that the defense team had tried to contact Spiesel prior to his testimony, which should have been impossible since Spiesel was a surprise witness (Louisiana had no discovery law at the time). Declassified documents released under the JFK Act reveal the Wackenhut Corporation (hired by Shaw's attorneys to do research and investigation) had located Spiesel's daughter and son-in-law two days before Spiesel's testimony, indicating that Storm was not Panzeca's only source of information, as Panzeca implies. This raises the question of why he lied and what the whole truth actually is.

In regard to the why Spiesel was called to testify in the first place, it appears Garrison may have actually believed Spiesel. Garrison was aware of Spiesel's problems, but perhaps believed him anyway on the basis of the corroborating evidence. Spiesel had identified a building in the French Quarter, 906 Esplanade, as the building where the June 1963 party occurred. This building was at one time owned by Shaw, and was in fact identical in appearance to the adjoining building 908 Esplanade. Shaw owned 908 Esplanade at the time the party was supposed to have taken place and abutted Shaw's 1313 Dauphine Street apartment.[32] Garrison felt he needed Spiesel since the attack on Clyde Johnson had left him short of an "overt act" of conspiracy (one wonders if using Vernon Bundy—with Shaw giving Oswald money—was a similar strategic decision, with

Garrison gambling that the heroin addict was more credible than the psycho as Garrison only used Spiesel after Bundy had been discredited).

During the trial, Judge Haggerty allowed the prosecution to bring Spiesel and the jury out to the French Quarter so Spiesel could identify the apartment. The jury apparently disregarded Spiesel's testimony, but Haggerty expressed in a 1992 interview that he believed Spiesel was "an important piece of evidence."[33] (The author does not believe Spiesel. Garrison did not find Spiesel, Spiesel called the NODA one day with his story.[34] At the trial, Spiesel admitted that he had tried to sell his story to CBS for two thousand dollars.[35] Finally, the author contacted Spiesel in 2000 seeking an interview and was rebuffed. In this author's opinion, Spiesel was out to make a buck.)

The jury did not see it that way. Journalist William Turner later observed, "The Spiesel testimony was to the Shaw trial what the gloves that didn't fit were to O.J. Simpson's."[36] For Shaw's lawyers it was much simpler. "Had we been unsuccessful in our efforts to secure information with regard to Charles I. Spiesel...the results could well have been a verdict of guilty," wrote defense counsel Edward Wegmann.[37]

Star witness Perry Russo went next. Again, the defense focused on the issues of the Sciambra memoranda and Russo's hypnosis. Russo denied those allegations, although the defense did gain some mileage off Russo's admission that for all he knew the discussion at Ferrie's apartment may have been just talk, not an actual conspiracy, and that Ferrie and only Ferrie had said that the group had decided to murder Kennedy.[38] Dymond also tried to get Russo to say that the man he identified as Clem Bertrand was not Clay Shaw, but rather Guy Banister or James Lewallen. Re-direct examination by James Alcock clarified matters:

> *BY MR. ALCOCK:*
> *Q: Perry, are you today identifying the Defendant Clay Shaw as the same man that you saw in Ferrie's apartment in mid-September, 1963, who was identified to you as Clem Bertrand?*

MR. DYMOND: Object as a leading question.

THE COURT: Overrule the objection.

MR. DYMOND: To which ruling Counsel reserves a bill of exception, making the State's question, the Defense objection, the Court's ruling, the reason for the objection, and the entire record up until this point part of the bill.

BY MR. ALCOCK:
Q: Answer the question.

A: The question is whether Clay Shaw and Clem Bertrand are one and the same? They are.

MR. ALCOCK: No further questions.[39]

Dymond also questioned the certainty of Russo's identification. Russo explained, "In a case as serious as this, you would have to be 1,000 per cent sure although it was impossible to be that, but I was 100 per cent sure [that Shaw was Bertrand]." The questioning continued:

Q: Well, 1,000 per cent in your way of putting it would be surer than 100 per cent?

A: Well, 100 per cent is completely sure.

Q: What do you mean by 1,000 per cent?

A: 1,000 per cent is something that you can never reach, if you really want to know....At this point I am absolutely sure 100 per cent that the Defendant is the man that was there.[40]

On other points, however, Russo was less than certain and it hurt the prosecution's case.

BY MR. DYMOND:
Q: In your presence, did David Ferrie ever agree to kill the President of the United States, John F. Kennedy?

A: He said, "We will kill him."

Q: He had said that many times before, had he not?

A: Right.

Q: As a matter of fact, he had made that direct statement to you alone, had he not?

A: Right.

Q: Did Leon Oswald ever, in your presence, agree to kill the President of the United States?

A: No.

Q: Did Clem Bertrand ever agree to kill the President of the United States?

A: No.

Q: Would I be correct in saying then that you never hear anyone actually agree to kill the President of the United States?

A: Well, when you say "agree," it is the problem, that is the word "agree," you know, I mean, all I do is hear people talking about it, I don't know if they agreed or not. It would seem to me they were in agreement as far as certain things were concerned, I don't know if they actually—I can't remember either any of the three ever saying yes, this is how we will do it, let's do it this way.

Q: Did you ever hear anybody say, "We will do it"?

A: Dave Ferrie, "We will get him."[41]

Damaging for Ferrie, but Ferrie was dead. Clay Shaw was the man on trial. Russo's two days on the stand ended with Dymond accusing him of psychological problems. Based on the challenge to Russo's mental state, the state pressed for and was allowed to read into the record the preliminary hearing of Dr. Nicholas Chetta, who had since died. Dr. Chetta's testimony was significant because it also helped Russo's credibility by explaining the scientific nature of the Sodium Pentothal® examination.[42]

Picking up the Pieces

Assistant D.A. Andrew Sciambra took the stand after Russo, to fully clarify the chronological order of his memoranda. Under cross-examination Sciambra got into it with Dymond over James Phelan's credibility:

> *Q: You told, you told Russo to lead Phelan on in May or June '67?*
>
> *A: That is right and can I give you my reason?*
>
> *Q: Can you say yes or no?*
>
> *A: At that particular time we didn't think an out-of-state Journalist, we considered at very best as a journalistic prostitute, should come into this State and try to hurt our case by trying to influence our case by showing him a picture of Guy Banister.*
>
> *Q: You've finished your explanation?*
>
> *A: By showing Perry a picture of Guy Banister, which he later did and telling him it was Banister and not Shaw and telling Perry he would be the patsy if Shaw were not convicted; that Perry would be on the edge of the limb and Garrison would go and get him; and also told Perry he should visit an attorney, a $200,000.00 a year attorney that they had and that he or Shaw would take care of the expenses.[43]*

At this point, Garrison's case was almost dead in the water. Even though some ground had been regained by the testimony of Dr. Chetta and Sciambra, Russo was still seen as questionable—especially in the face of a major community figure like Clay Shaw. The disastrous cross-examinations of Bundy and Spiesel had all but destroyed the credibility

Garrison had established early on with the Clinton witnesses. With the Russo situation out of the way, Garrison now focused on other areas.

Chuck Rolland, owner of the Winterland Skating Rink in Houston, Texas, took the stand next to testify to David Ferrie's strange behavior the weekend of the assassination. According to Rolland, Ferrie introduced himself to Rolland *six times,* spent most of his time waiting next to the pay phone and did not put on any skates.[44] Richard Jackson, a postal worker who in 1966 executed a change of address form for Clay Shaw, followed Rolland on the stand. Shaw had had his mail directed to the home of his friend Jeff Biddison at 1414 Chartres Street. Jackson could not locate the original change of address form or fix in his memory when the change of address had taken place, but he did have the cancellation form directing Shaw's mail *back* to 1313 Dauphine Street, dated September 21, 1966.[45]

Another postal worker, James Hardiman, then took the witness stand and stated that he had delivered the mail to Biddison's house in 1966, and remembered delivering letters addressed to Clay Shaw. *But* Hardiman also remembered delivering several letters addressed to a Clem Bertrand to that address. Hardiman's recollections were undermined under cross-examination by F. Irvin Dymond:

> Q: Have you ever delivered any mail to that address, that is 1414 Chartres Street, addressed to a Mr. Cliff Boudreaux?
>
> A: Yes.
>
> Q: Are you sure about that?
>
> A: I have seen that name before.
>
> . . .
>
> Q: Now, Mr. Hardiman, if I told you I just made that name up, would your testimony be the same?

A: Well, I wouldn't know. How would I know who made up a name and sent something there?

Q: But still you say you delivered Cliff Boudreaux mail to 1414 Chartres Street?

A: Maybe you have made it up, but I have delivered Boudreaux mail there, too. Now, maybe the "Cliff" might not be correct.[46]

Garrison's case against Shaw was hence dealt another blow. The state then regained some momentum by presenting the Dallas evidence, attempting to prove a conspiracy—specifically one with a triangulation of crossfire as recalled by Perry R. Russo. Witnesses included Abraham Zapruder, Robert West, Buell Wesley Frazier, Lyndal Shaneyfelt, Billy Joe Martin, Roger Craig, Elizabeth Carolyn Walton, James Simmons, Frances Gayle Newman, William Newman, Mary Moorman, and Herbert Orth. It was during the testimony of Abraham Zapruder that the Zapruder film, which Garrison had subpoenaed from Time-Life, was shown publicly for the first time. The night before Zapruder's testimony, Garrison treated Andrew Sciambra and journalist Art Kevin to a special screening of the film. Kevin vividly recalled Garrison's enthusiasm at being able to bring the film out for the American people: "'Tomorrow morning', said Garrison, 'I will show the American people for the first time how the President of the United States was murdered. They will see without a doubt that there had to have been more than one shooter. I will show the 'Z' film, the Zapruder film'. With that, he shoved a copy in my hand. 'That's for you Art. Now Andrew', he told Sciambra, 'turn off the lights and let's show Art the film that will prove once and for all in an open court of law that the Warren Commission lied to the people of the United States.'…Garrison had a wide ear to ear grin as he looked at me."[47]

Later, Assistant DA Alvin Oser went through the film for the jury with Dr. John Nichols, an expert in forensic pathology. It was the testimony of Dr. Nichols upon which Oliver Stone's famous "back and to the left" scene in *JFK* was based. After displaying the film for the jury once again, Dr. Nichols was asked if he could make a conclusion as to the source of the fatal headshot. Dr. Nichols answered, "Having viewed the Zapruder film, the individual 35 MM frames and the particular exhibits here, I would say that this is compatible with a gunshot having been delivered from the front."[48] Dr. Nichols came under some scrutiny from the CIA during his involvement in the Shaw case. After Dr. Nichols' testimony, CIA Counter-Intelligence Chief James Jesus Angleton had the FBI compile a dossier on Nichols.[49]

After going through the Dallas evidence, the state called retired FBI Agent Regis Kennedy. Kennedy could certainly be called a hostile witness. Earlier, he had testified before the Orleans Parish Grand Jury and spent almost the entire time issuing ringing denials or claiming "executive privilege." Kennedy had of course been the agent that interviewed Dean Andrews about Clay Bertrand in 1963. During Kennedy's testimony, Assistant DA James Alcock wanted two questions answered: First, whether or not Kennedy had been investigating the JFK assassination prior to interviewing Dean Andrews, and secondly, whether or not he had been looking for Clay Bertrand as part of that investigation. Kennedy refused to answer, again claiming "executive privilege" and asking to speak with U.S. Attorney Harry Connick, Sr. (Connick would run against Garrison for district attorney later that year. Connick was defeated, ran again in 1973 and won. After taking office, Connick ordered the Grand Jury transcripts from the JFK probe destroyed. It was only because a young policeman defied Connick's order that the transcripts exist today.) Connick told Kennedy he could answer Alcock's question.

> Q. Mr. Kennedy, prior to your interview with Dean Andrews, were you engaged in the investigation of the assassination of President Kennedy?
>
> A. Yes, I was.

Q. Mr. Kennedy, were you seeking Clay Bertrand in connection with your over all investigation into the assassination of President Kennedy.

A. I was.[50]

Kennedy *had* been looking for Clay Bertrand before talking to Dean Andrews—Clay Bertrand was not a figure of Andrews' imagination. The defense team then shot down this revelation in cross-examination.

CROSS EXMAMINATION BY MR. DYMOND:
Q. Mr. Kennedy, did you ever locate Clay Bertrand?

A. No, sir.[51]

Thanks to new evidence, we can now say Regis Kennedy was lying.

The 1963 Investigation of Clay Shaw

On March 2, 1967, Acting Attorney General Ramsey Clark stepped out from his confirmation hearing and was confronted by droves of reporters eager for any insight he could give into the case against Clay Shaw, who had been arrested in New Orleans the day before. What Clark said became the center of an Associated Press report that lent credence to many of Garrison's allegations.

> *Atty. Gen. designate Ramsey Clark said today the Federal Bureau of Investigation already has investigated and cleared Clay L. Shaw—a businessman arrested in New Orleans—of any part in the assassination of President John F. Kennedy.*
>
> ...
>
> *Clark said Shaw "was included in an investigation in November and December of 1963.*
>
> ...

> *"On the evidence that the FBI has, there was no connection found"*
> *between Shaw and the assassination of the President in Dallas on*
> *Nov. 22, 1963, Clark said.*[52]

Washington Post reporter George Lardner (the last man to interview David Ferrie) added one piece of information in his March 3 article:

> *The Attorney General's remarks consequently amounted to an accept-*
> *ance of Garrison's charge that Clay Shaw and "Clay Bertrand" are one*
> *and the same. "It's the same guy," said one source in the Justice*
> *Department.*[53]

The New York Times reported that "a Justice Department official said tonight that his agency was convinced that Mr. Bertrand and Mr. Shaw were the same man, and that this was the basis for Mr. Clark's assertions."[54] So the FBI had already investigated Clay Shaw and cleared him! The FBI, of course, had cleared David Ferrie as well, within three days of the assassination and after just one interview. But the FBI *had* connected Clay Shaw to the alias "Clay Bertrand." When the Justice Department figured out what Clark had done, they tried to straighten things out with an official statement:

> *Clay Shaw, New Orleans businessman, was not investigated by the*
> *Federal Bureau of Investigation during its inquiry into the assassina-*
> *tion of President Kennedy....A Justice Department spokesman said*
> *that Mr. Clark's statement last March 2, shortly after Mr. Shaw was*
> *arrested...was in error."*[55]

But in an interview given after the DOJ's official statement in June, Clark stuck to his original story. Clark said, "Yes. Clay Shaw was involved in an FBI investigation. So were other persons now being mentioned in connection with the Garrison investigation." Clark's interviewer reminded him of the DOJ's position that Shaw had not been investigated, and Clark responded, "I understand that the FBI information office did indicate that for part of one day recently. But they shortly received the correct information from their superiors in the FBI."[56] Clark's position is born out by an FBI document released many years after Shaw's trial. In a March 2, 1967 FBI memo, Cartha "Deke" DeLoach tells Clyde Tolson:

> *The AG then asked whether the FBI knew anything about Shaw. I told him Shaw's name had come up in our investigation in December, 1963 as a result of several parties furnishing information concerning Shaw.*[57]

Yet, as of 2001, no official documentation of that 1963 probe of Shaw has been found. This has led some to speculate that Shaw was not investigated at all, but the DeLoach memo and Clark's statements explicitly state otherwise. A closer look at Regis Kennedy may reveal exactly where those reports went.

In 1961, Guy Banister had been one of many New Orleans personalities involved in an organization called the Friends of Democratic Cuba (It was the FDC that "Oswald" supposedly represented in the famous Bolton Ford Incident. See William Davy's *Let Justice Be Done*, pages 15-16). The FDC was openly dedicated towards raising funds for the fight against Castro. Specifically, the money was supposed to go to the Frente Revolucionario Democratico (FRD), or Cuban Democratic Liberation Front, which an internal CIA memo describes as being "created by the Central Intelligence Agency in May of 1960."[58] The FDC was supposed to transfer the entire fund to the FRD through its New Orleans delegate, the ubiquitous Sergio Arcacha Smith, minus a twenty-percent discount to keep the FDC running. Investigation by Garrison's office revealed, however, that the FDC was a dummy organization for shipping and transporting people and supplies in and out of Cuba.[59] (Another FDC member was Martin McAuliffe, Jr., who apparently was the man who introduced Kerry Thornley to Guy Banister.)

According to a Garrison informant by the name of Betty Parrott, the lover of FDC member William Dalzell, the FBI had a liaison with the

Friends of Democratic Cuba—Regis Kennedy.[60] William Dalzell confirmed this information in his testimony before the Grand Jury on November 2, 1967. Dalzell said that Kennedy and another FBI agent, Warren deBrueys, had been the FBI delegates to the FDC for the purposes of insuring that the arms dealers with whom the FDC was doing business were not peddling stolen U.S. property.[61] Dalzell had previously done some P.I. work with Guy Banister Associates, had helped set up the anti-Castro "Free Voice of Latin America" and, according to a CIA memo declassified in 1983, had had three contacts with the New Orleans CIA office. An FBI memo describes Dalzell as being "a friend of Clay Shaw."[62]

With that information, one could reasonably postulate that Regis Kennedy knew more about the early '60s New Orleans anti-Castro scene than he let on. Indeed, perhaps Kennedy realized what had transpired when JFK was killed, and feared he would be held accountable for failing to stop a New Orleans based plot. Or maybe Kennedy actively supported those anti-Castro efforts enough to *want* to cover for the plotters of the assassination. Whatever the case may have been, the possibility exists that Kennedy hid or destroyed the documentary history of the 1963 probe of Shaw. It is already an established fact that Kennedy falsified his report on Shaw/Bertrand's call to Dean Andrews to indicate that Andrews was under sedation when the call was received. On December 5, 1963, Special Agent Richard Bucaro checked Andrews' hospital records, which stated that Andrews received no sedatives until 8:00 P.M. on November 23, the day of the call.[63] Kennedy interviewed Andrews' employee Eva Springer the following day, December 6, and learned that Andrews had called her on the 23rd to tell her he was going to Dallas to be counsel for Lee Harvey Oswald. The reason? "Bertrand" asked him to. Springer said she received the call at 4:00 P.M., a fact she could be certain of because she had just gotten back from her weekly trip to the grocery store.[64] As noted earlier, even Patricia Lambert has accepted 4:00 P.M. as the approximate time of the call (see Chapter 4). Later that day, Kennedy nevertheless wrote that the call had been a figment of Andrews' imagination—under sedation.[65]

To conclude that it is reasonable to believe Kennedy covered up the 1963 investigation of Clay Shaw requires one more piece of evidence: proof that Kennedy knew about that investigation. It can be found in Kennedy's testimony to the New Orleans Grand Jury on May 17, 1967. As a clue as to what was at stake, it is worth noting that A.G. Clark ordered Kennedy not to appear before the Grand Jury. It was only after Judge J. Bernard Bagert ruled that Kennedy had to testify that Kennedy answered Garrison's subpoena.[66] Garrison's first serious questions towards Kennedy were about his relationship to the Friends of Democratic Cuba; Kennedy's response set the tone for the rest of the session:

> Q. *Mr. Kennedy are you familiar with an organization known as the Friends of Democratic Cuba? Back in '61?*
>
> A. *Will you define what you mean by familiar with?*
>
> Q. *Did you ever hear of an organization known as the Friends of Democratic Cuba?*
>
> A. *I have heard of that organization.*
>
> Q. *Did you ever know any of the members of the organization?*
>
> A. *I don't think it would be proper to call it an organization. I think it was a corporation.*
>
> Q. *Well, a corporation?*
>
> A. *Do I know any of them? I have heard some of the names?*
>
> Q. *Will you tell me some of the names you remember?*
>
> A. *For the record I state that I regretfully decline to answer the question on the ground that the answer to the question will require me to disclose information and material which have been acquired by me in the performance of my official duties and official status as a special agent of the Federal Bureau of Investigation. I would like to further*

inform this Grand Jury that I have been directed by a telegram from the Attorney General of the United States as follows:

"The subpoena served on you to testify before the Grand Jury in New Orleans Parish Criminal District Court May 16, 1967 this confirms that pursuant to departmental order 32464 dated October 8, 1964 in Federal Register Vol. 29, No. 199, page 14027, dated October 10, 1964, you are directed to respectfully refuse to testify about or disclose information or material acquired in the performance of your official duties or because of your official status...."[67]

Kennedy then either answered inconsequential questions, or when faced with serious questioning, stonewalled at every turn.

Q. Do you know whether or not any Federal agents regularly attended the meetings of the Cuban Revolutionary Democratic Front in the summer of 1963?

A. I make reference to my previous comment.

Q. Is it not a fact that that agent was Warren DeBrueys? [Sic]

A. I would like to respectfully reserve...

Q. Were you yourself aware of the activities of Friends of Democratic Cuba in January of 1961?

A. I would like to exert the privilege again please.[68]

This is known to be a lie. Indeed, based on some of Garrison's next questions, one can assume Kennedy would be forced to answer in the affirmative or confirm Garrison's beliefs whenever he claims executive privilege:

Q....I have the distinct impression that you questioned him [David Ferrie] at the First District–you asked him questions in connection with his trip.

A. I did not question him at that time.

Q. Somebody else did?

A. I have to reserve the privilege on that.[69]

Kennedy was telling the truth—he did not question Ferrie the weekend of the assassination. But Garrison was right: someone else did, specifically Special Agents Ernest Wall and L. M. Shearer. Their interview of Ferrie can be found in Warren Commission Document 75, which was classified at the time of the Garrison probe. But what about Clay Shaw? Kennedy's answers are telling.

Q. . . . Did you know Clay Shaw?

A. No sir.

Q. Did you know anyone who knew Clay Shaw?

A. I will reserve the privilege on that.[70]

Later, Assistant D.A. James Alcock picked up where Garrison left off.

<u>*Q. BY MR. ALCOCK:*</u>

You said you did not know Clay Shaw, is that correct?

A. That is correct.

Q. Did you know Clay Bertrand?

A. No sir.

Q. Do you know whether or not the Federal Government ever made a check on Clay Shaw?

A. I have to reserve the exception to that.

Q. Do you know whether or not the Federal government, or particularly the Justice Department, determined as a matter of fact whether Clay Shaw and Clay Bertrand were the same person?

A. **I reserve the exception on that.** *[My emphasis.]*

. . .

Q. Do you know of any investigation conducted of Clay Shaw by the Justice Department after the assassination?

A. I have to reserve an exception to that.

Q. Then you do know as a matter of fact?

A. I am just asserting the privilege.

. . .

Q. Based on your reservations, might we assume then, without revealing any content thereof, that there is such a file on such an investigation having been conducted relative to Clay Shaw after the assassination?

A. I will just reserve the exception.[71]

Kennedy's silence speaks volumes. We have already seen that Kennedy was not above lying in his FBI reports, and that it appears he was aware and had personal knowledge of the FBI's probe of Shaw in November and December of 1963. All this puts one part of Dean Andrews' Warren Commission testimony in a very interesting context:

Mr. LIEBELER. Let me ask you this: When I was down here in April, before I talked to you about this thing, and I was going to take your deposition at that time, but we didn't make arrangements, in your continuing discussions with the FBI, you finally came to the conclusion that Clay Bertrand was a figment of your imagination?

Mr. ANDREWS. **That's what the Feebees put on.** *I know that the two Feebees are going to put these people on the street looking, and I can't find the guy, and I am not going to tie up all the agents on something that isn't that solid. I told them, "Write what you want, that I am nuts. I don't care." They were running on the time factor, and the hills were shook up plenty to get it, get it, get it. I couldn't give it to them. I have been playing cops and robbers with them. You can tell when the steam is on.* **They are on you like the plague. They never leave. They are like cancer. Eternal.**[72] *[My emphasis.]*

Of the two "Feebees" in question, Andrews said one was Regis L. Kennedy.[73]

The VIP Room Revisited

After Regis Kennedy left the stand, Garrison next called Jessie Parker. Here he would introduce the VIP Room evidence, which forms one of the most intriguing but often overlooked items of evidence against Clay Shaw. This was the allegation that Shaw, in the winter of 1966 (prior to questioning by the D.A.), signed the VIP book at Moisant Airport under his alleged alias—Clay Bertrand. To Garrison critics like Patricia Lambert and Dave Reitzes, the signature in that book is an obvious forgery and one of the more dubious areas of evidence delved into by Garrison and his staff.[74] The VIP room evidence was even largely written off by those in the Garrison camp until the work of William Davy in 1995 produced some interesting new twists on an old story.

To summarize, in 1967, NODA investigators learned that someone using the name "Clay Bertrand" had signed the guest book in the VIP room at Moisant Airport in New Orleans. In early September of that year, the signature was located and photographs were made of the book on the morning of September 2.[75] Ten days later, the hostess of the VIP room, an unassuming African American woman named Jessie Parker, made out a sworn affidavit stating the previous December two white men and four foreigners (from Caracas, Venezuela) had visited the VIP room and identified a picture of Clay Shaw as the one that signed the VIP book.[76]

In her book *False Witness,* Patricia Lambert makes the following argument against Parker:

> [Parker] claimed that on December 14, 1966, she saw Clay Shaw sign the name "Clay Bertrand" in the guest book. The prosecution offered no theory to explain why Shaw, if he had conspired to murder the president using this alias, would have continued to use it afterwards. The signature appeared on the last line of a page, where it could have been added at any time by anyone.[77]

Shaw's alleged alias did not necessarily revolve around the assassination. Even if it did, the new evidence renders Lambert's point moot. Besides, at that point Shaw hadn't even been questioned by the D.A.'s office nor did he have any idea Perry Russo would come forward with his story. Lambert's second argument is flawed as well. The signature wasn't added at the bottom of a page, it was on the last line. There is a difference. By Lambert's reasoning, any signatures on the last line of any page in the VIP book could have been added to support a wrongful prosecution against anyone. This argument also depends on the coincidence that Garrison's men were able to forge a signature immediately prior to that of four men from Caracas (who also recorded their visit as happening on the 14th) and after that of Arthur Q. Davis (who *also* recorded his as visit as happening on the 14th).

Lambert's other mention of the VIP room incident is her treatment of defense witness Charles Appel, a handwriting expert who determined that the signature was not Shaw's.[78] Lambert lauds Appel as being "nationally known for breaking the Lindbergh kidnapping case."[79] In defending Appel, Lambert, it seems, is one of the few in this country who still believe that Bruno Richard Hauptmann wasn't framed and was in fact guilty.[80] The reader is informed in passing that Appel "waived his fee when told the defendant couldn't afford it."[81] Why was the fee waived? In Appel's own words, because he wanted to prevent "an injustice occurring."[82]

To rebut the testimony of Appel, the prosecution called another handwriting analyst, Elizabeth McCarthy. Dave Reitzes argues against McCarthy's credibility in his article "Who Speaks for Clay Shaw?" noting that she had "no formal training" and that her presentation was less detailed than McCarthy's.[83] On the same note, Lambert writes, "None of her degrees had included handwriting analysis classes...."[84] Is this really an issue? Not according to Lambert's favorite analyst, Charles Appel.

> *Q. Now, what training have you had in this field, Mr. Appel?*
>
> *A. I just described it.* [Appel described researching the subject and studying under other experts, just as McCarthy had.] ***There are no courses in colleges concerning this.***[85] [Emphasis mine.]

In fact, McCarthy's training was remarkably similar to Appel's. The skill of McCarthy's presentation is, of course, highly subjective. Reitzes also attacks McCarthy because she only studied photographs of the signature (not the originals), she first worked on the case the previous evening and expected to be paid for her work. As far as the pay issue goes, McCarthy is way ahead of Appel.

Appel does no better on the other issues either. He too only studied photographs and did not see the original until his trial testimony.[86] This was not a real issue with the analysis of the handwriting "if the evidence in this case you are dealing with concerns the design of the letters, the quality of the lines, because these show very well even in Xeroxed copies." Such was the case at the Shaw trial.[87] Under cross-examination, Appel admitted that he was not present when Shaw made the samples he compared to the VIP signature. He was given other samples from letters Shaw wrote in 1966, but curiously the only one blown-up for his presentation was one that Shaw made specifically for his analysis.[88] It was only at the request of the prosecution that the other signatures were made available for the jury to view.[89] If McCarthy is to be criticized for only beginning her work the previous evening, it should be noted that she took four hours to analyze the signatures in question.[90] Appel testified it took him two hours.[91]

Additionally, Reitzes tells us that the state also contacted Gilbert Fortier about analyzing the signature, noting that he was the expert most frequently called upon by the prosecution in such matters.[92] Fortier, of course, never testified at the Shaw trial. If this is a sin on Garrison's part, Dymond and co. are no worse. The Shaw trial transcript reveals that on February 7, 1969, Dymond asked Judge Haggerty "for permission to withdraw…from evidence…the document referred to by the State in its opening statement as the "VIP Book of Eastern Airlines" for the purpose of having Mr. Gilbert Fortier, a duly qualified handwriting expert, make an examination of the purported signature in that book." Fortier never testified for the defense either.[93]

When James DiEugenio asked Dymond about the switch from Fortier to Appel, Dymond stated that the defense changed their mind when they were contacted by Appel offering to work for free. However, it was Appel that was first contacted by Shaw's partner Lloyd Cobb. Cobb, interestingly enough, was cleared for access to a CIA "cleared attorneys panel."[94] As far as why the state never used Fortier, no one really knows. Garrison passed away in 1992, so it is impossible to ask him.[95]

Witness Parker is criticized because she did not identify Shaw as the man who signed the book until offered the chance to take a polygraph test. Though critics have said she was threatened, Parker herself said, "They didn't threaten me, they asked me."[96] The prosecution apparently felt comfortable about her polygraph results; they mentioned it in closing arguments.

The only witness offered to dispute Parker's *recollection* was Arthur Q. Davis, the gentleman who signed the VIP book immediately prior to the "Bertrand" signature. Davis, who knew Shaw for more than 10 years and was friendly with him, testified that he didn't see Shaw in the VIP room that day.[97] It is possible the defense called him thinking he might be the second white man Parker saw with Shaw and the Venezuelans. Under cross-examination, Davis admitted that he was only in the VIP room for 20-30 minutes, that during that time no one other than him signed the VIP book and that the "Bertrand" signature had not been there when he left, rendering his testimony essentially moot.[98] Nevertheless, Reitzes used Davis in his arguments against Parker, though Lambert left him out of her book.

Although it was irrelevant, Davis' story seems quite damning at first glance. A friend of Shaw's was there and said he didn't see Shaw. It is then ironic that the exact opposite should prove true when, in 1995, William Davy discovered buried in CIA documents what may amount to the smoking gun on the identity of Clay Bertrand.

In November 1967, the NODA questioned a man named Alfred Moran. He was also in the VIP room that day, and told Alcock that Shaw, whom he knew (like Davis), was definitely not there.[99] A recently declassified CIA memo reveals that the next evening Moran hosted a cocktail party at his home. One of those there was Hunter Leake of the New Orleans CIA office who was a friend of Moran's. That evening Moran told Leake about his experience the previous day with the NODA, and, in addition, told him that Clay Shaw *was* in the VIP room contrary to his statement to Garrison's staff. He also told Leake that "Garrison had 'an ironclad' case against Shaw."[100]

Since this came to light, only one author, Dave Reitzes, had attempted to rebut Moran. His argument is based on two facts. The first, that the CIA memo on the subject says Moran told Leake that he did identify Shaw's presence to Alcock, is obviously flawed. Reitzes says, of course, that one of the memos (Alcock's or Lloyd Ray's) was mistaken. If Alcock was mistaken, then he let one of Garrison's best potential witnesses just slip away, after hearing his very damning testimony. If Ray was mistaken, he inadvertently misrepresented Leake's recollection of the evening or Leake simply misheard Moran.

Reitzes' second argument is that both the Ray memo and a later one from CIA Attorney Lawrence Houston both indicate that the authors are not aware that Shaw and Bertrand are supposed to the same man (it is probable Moran just didn't see it when Shaw signed the book). For instance:

> *It makes no sense for Clay Shaw to use the name Clem Bertrand at such a meeting so we assume they were two different people, but if Moran could confirm this it might be a very important point.*[101]

This, Reitzes argues, indicates the possibility that Shaw might not have been the Bertrand that signed the VIP book. This doesn't make much sense as Gene Davis, Clem Sert nor anyone else was seen signing the book as "Bertrand." It is clear that the CIA people writing these memos are actually merely ignorant of the details of Garrison's theories. Both use the 'Clem' variation on the alias that Alcock apparently miscommunicated to Moran (the signature clearly reads 'Clay'). Besides, these memos were never followed up so no evidence ever developed to indicate that the Clay Bertrand in the VIP room was anyone but Shaw.

The possibility exists that Houston's speculation was accurate (as noted, Moran did not witness the actual signing of the book), though this possibility lacks credence. The important thing is that Reitzes' arguments against Moran are intended to disprove the notion that Shaw perjured himself in denying using the "Bertrand" alias. Therefore, an alternative is that the Shaw and Bertrand of the VIP room were different people. Does this mean Clay Shaw did not lie under oath? From the Shaw trial transcript:

> *Q. Now, Mr. Shaw, I take it you are familiar with Moisant Airport here in New Orleans, are you not, sir?*
>
> *A. Yes, I am familiar with it.*

Q. Are you familiar with a room known as the VIP Room in Moisant Airport?

A. No, I didn't know that room existed until this trial.[102]

The previous facts considered, it is the conclusion of this author that the VIP room evidence is the *best* evidence of Clay Shaw's use of the "Bertrand" alias. It is highly interesting that researchers studying the Garrison investigation so often neglect the VIP room incident.

The Booking Card

To close the state's case, Garrison decided to call a policeman named Aloysius Habighorst. Habighorst had been the officer who booked Shaw after his arrest in March of 1967, and when Habighorst heard a new commentator the following day mention Garrison's allegation that Shaw had used the alias "Clay Bertrand," Habighorst recalled that Shaw had *admitted* to using the alias. Habighorst was taking fingerprinting classes at the time and had taken cards home on occasion to practice identification techniques. Habighorst realized he had made three copies of Shaw's booking card, which included the "Bertrand" alias and was signed by Shaw. The alias later showed up in Shaw's arrest record as well.[103]

With all the problems Garrison had been having with his witnesses, he elected to keep Habighorst under protective surveillance. It was during this period, immediately prior to Habighorst's testimony, that some strange things happened. Two days before he was to testify, spouse Elsie Habighorst received a phone call asking if "Al" was home. Mrs. Habighorst thought this was strange since Habighorst's friends called him "Hotsie," his boyhood nickname. The man on the phone asked her when Officer Habighorst would be getting off work. Elsie replied in the negative and asked if the caller would like to leave a message, upon which he said, "No," and hung up.[104] The following day was Mardi Gras, and since Habighorst was with his fellow officers guarding the parade, Garrison decided to take the protective surveillance off the officer. What followed was like something out of a suspense thriller. Habighorst was suspiciously relieved early, and while driving home was surprised by a yellow truck that pulled out of an alley in an attempt to ram him. While trying to avoid the truck, Habighorst suffered facial lacerations.[105]

Assistant D.A. James Alcock knew the defense team was sure to object to Habighorst's testimony when it was introduced, since it amounted in some respects to hearsay. Therefore, Alcock suggested that the jury be removed while Haggerty heard oral arguments about the booking card. NODA Investigator Louis Ivon was sworn in, and under questioning by F. Irvin Dymond, seemed to forget certain facts pertaining to Shaw's arrest.

> Q. Did you examine the original Arrest Register Sheet on Clay Shaw at any time?
>
> A. I don't know if I did.[106]

Dymond then showed Ivon the arrest record that Ivon had filled out on March 1, 1967, and asked where Ivon had filled it out. Ivon could not recall whether or not he had signed the arrest record or the search affidavit for Shaw's home and only remembered when Dymond showed him (Ivon) his own signature on the form. Ivon could not remember when or where he had signed the forms.[107]

Aloysius Habighorst then took the stand and testified that he had booked Shaw, that the information on the booking card had come from Shaw himself (not the arrest register), including the "Bertrand" alias, and that he had not threatened, bribed or abused the arrestee.[108] William Wegmann then cross-examined Officer Habighorst:

> Q. While you were taking the fingerprints of Mr. Shaw, was any attorney present with him?…Was anyone with him or not?
>
> A. The attorney was at the door.
>
> …

Q. At the time that you got the information that is contained on the back of the exhibit, the fingerprint exhibit that Mr. Alcock just showed you, was the attorney present during that period of time?

A. No, sir.

Q. And was he present when Mr. Shaw signed that card?

A. Yes, sir.

Q. Now you are positive about that?

A. I recall him being at the doorway and Mr. Shaw was standing directly in front of me by the fingerprinting —

Q. Was he inside the door or outside the door?

A. He was just right inside the door proper.

Q. Physically in the room, physically inside the B of I?

A. There is a little hallway that is there. I would say that he was more in the confines of the B of I than he was outside in the booking area.

Q. Was the door open or closed during this procedure?

A. The door is always open.

Q. Never closed?

A. No, sir.[109]

Wegmann continued his questioning, and got Habighorst to admit that he wasn't sure whether or not Shaw's attorney had been present when he got the alias.[110] After Habighorst left the stand, Dymond called Captain Louis Curole who had been at Central Lockup the night of Shaw's arrest. Curole testified that attorneys were not allowed in the B of I room with their clients as a general rule of the NOPD, that Edward Wegmann had not been allowed in the B of I room (in direct opposition to Habighorst's statement that Wegmann had somehow gotten in) and that a copy of the defendant's arrest register (including aliases linked to the defendant) is always sent to the B of I room.[111]

Sergeant Jonas Butzman followed Curole, and testified that he had been within ten feet of Clay Shaw during the booking procedure and that he had not heard anyone utter the name "Clay Bertrand." Officer John Perkins came next, stating for the record that he had never fingerprinted a suspect without an arrest register and that generally the defendant is fingerprinted and information added to a booking card *after* the defendant signs the card.[112] Habighorst's recollections had been thoroughly shattered.

Shaw's attorneys, Edward Wegmann and Sal Panzeca, were sworn in next and testified that they were not allowed in the B of I room, and finally Shaw took the stand in his own defense (the first time, but not the last) to testify that he had signed a blank booking card.[113]

Alcock then moved to enter the booking card into evidence and admit Habighorst's testimony. The reader can imagine Judge Haggerty's decision. Specifically, the evidence was not to be admitted on the basis of the *Miranda* and *Escobedo* decisions, which required a suspect to be informed of his legal rights and to have the opportunity to consult counsel. Haggerty maintained that Shaw's constitutional rights were violated, and that Habighorst had no right to ask Shaw an alias without an attorney presence. Haggerty said, "If Officer Habighorst is telling the truth—and I seriously doubt it…" Alcock jumped up, and emotionally asked, "Your Honor. Are you ruling on the credibility of Officer Habighorst?"[114]

Haggerty replied, "No jurors are present." Alcock was insistent: "But you are passing on the credibility of a witness before the press and the entire world."[115]

Haggerty was unapologetic. "I don't care. The whole world can hear that I do not believe Officer Habighorst," he said. Haggerty repeated, "I do not believe Officer Habighorst." Alcock demanded a mistrial, which Haggerty refused. Garrison tried to get a 24-hour stay of Haggerty's ruling from the Louisiana Supreme Court, which was also denied. The following day, Haggerty refused to reconsider. Thus ended the prosecution's case at the trial of Clay Shaw—with a whimper, rather than a bang.[116]

Objectively, Haggerty's decision does not hold legal ground on the *Miranda* ruling. Shaw had been read his rights before he was taken to the booking room.[117] In the case of Rhode Island v. Innis (1980), the Supreme Court ruled that the word "interrogation" in *Miranda* excludes police questioning, words and actions *normally attendant to arrest and custody*. According to a 7th U.S. Circuit Court ruling in 1977, United States v. Prewitt, an alias counts as "identifying characteristics" exempt from *Miranda* and Fifth Amendment considerations.[118] Of course, these decisions came after the Shaw trial so Garrison couldn't argue them. In the opinion of this author, Haggerty was likely correct in his *Escobedo* ruling. On the other hand, Garrison biographer Joan Mellen informs the author that respected New Orleans attorney Ralph Whalen wrote a long article arguing that Haggerty was incorrect in refusing to admit Habighorst's testimony on the basis of the *Escobedo* decision.[119]

Two additional items must be held in consideration in judging Habighorst's testimony. First, Habighorst's reputation was beyond reproach. On one occasion the officer jumped into a river to save a drowning man, and Habighorst was even used in police training films.[120] Habighorst's daughter, Karla Kemp, remembered her father as a man who brought home stray pets and lost children and would make phone calls until the animals' owners and the children's parents had been found.[121] Habighorst felt great pain at having his word questioned at the Shaw trial, and retired from the police very shortly thereafter. After working as a P.I., Habighorst's vision began to fail, and he became a steamship dispatcher. Habighorst died of a heart attack in 1980, a broken man at the age of 47.[122] In all likelihood, Habighorst honestly believed Shaw had admitted to the alias while being booked and was simply suffering from a mistaken recollection.

The second consideration that must be afforded Habighorst is the incident before his testimony when he was almost killed by the driver of the
yellow truck. The fact that Habighorst had been relieved from Mardi Gras
duty early suggests the possibility of police involvement. If someone inside
the NOPD was trying to sabotage Garrison's investigation, it reflects neg-
atively on the credibility of Capt. Curole, Sgt. Butzman and Officer
Perkins. There is, however, no direct evidence of such a plot by policemen
to undermine the JFK probe. The conclusion of this author is that, all
things considered, the credibility of Habighorst's testimony and the booking card should have been a matter for the jury to decide. Given what
their conclusion likely would have been, however, perhaps Garrison was
fortunate they did not see that evidence—it may have well had a similar
effect to Charles Spiesel.

The Defense Makes Its Case

First up for the defense was Marina Oswald Porter, who Dymond got
to say that Lee Harvey Oswald was always clean-shaven and always wore
clean clothes (Perry Russo described Oswald as unshaven and disheveled)
and only spent one night away from their Magazine Street apartment the
whole time she was in New Orleans. On cross-examination, Alcock
exposed the fact that Oswald had lied to her about when he was fired from
his job at Reilly Coffee Company, had not even told her about his previous job at Jaggars-Chiles-Stovall, a Dallas photographic firm, and had
kept her in the dark about numerous other things.[123] Mrs. Oswald's testimony was easily impeachable, despite her closeness to the alleged assassin,
as is evident from Alcock's closing argument:

> *Mrs. Garner, again a Defense witness, a woman that they vouch for,
> said that Lee Harvey Oswald's apartment was filthy, that the sink was
> torn up and the toilet was torn up and it was generally filthy, and that
> the mattress was filthy, and yet they want you to believe that this man
> literally carried a Norelco shaving outfit along with him, never had a*

beard, despite the fact that Marina Oswald herself testified that there were days that Lee Harvey Oswald did not shave. Marina Oswald, frankly, gentlemen, could not recount to you the movements of Lee Harvey Oswald—and for good reason. How much did Lee Harvey Oswald confide in his wife? Before coming here to the City of New Orleans she didn't even know where he was employed, had no telephone number to contact him. Coming to the City of New Orleans, gentlemen, she knew one language, and that was Russian; she was pregnant, expecting a baby. Lee Oswald had told her never to go into his belongings, and she abided by that. Gentlemen, she attempted one day pathetically to find her husband by going to the coffee company where she thought he might have worked, and it was the wrong one. And you know why it was the wrong one, because Lee Oswald never told her where he worked, he never gave her a phone number, he never talked about anybody he met at work, he never told her about the post office box, he never told her where it was located. She did not have a key to the post office box. Frankly, gentlemen, she didn't know what Lee Harvey Oswald was doing. And there is one other point I would like to bring out in connection with her testimony. She on the witness stand said the farthest back she would put the firing of Lee Harvey Oswald would have been approximately one month before they left the City of New Orleans, and they left the City of New Orleans on September 23. That would have made it August 23, 1963. Lee Harvey Oswald was fired from the Reiley Coffee Company July 19, 1963. This is how much Marina Oswald knew about the activities of Lee Harvey Oswald.[124]

Lloyd Cobb, Clay Shaw's boss at the International Trade Mart, and Goldie Moore, his secretary, both appeared to testify that Shaw had been very busy during the period in 1963 of the alleged visit to Clinton, Louisiana. Supposedly, Shaw had only left for one day, to visit his parents. Both testified that they never saw David Ferrie with Shaw at any time.

Neither was shaken by cross-examination, but Moore did reveal that Shaw had allowed certain Cuban exile groups space in the ITM, free of charge.[125] Harold Weisberg later ascertained, however, that the leasing arrangements for the new ITM building—the ones that supposedly kept Shaw too busy to go anywhere—where actually handled by a man named James Lawrence during the period in question.[126] Dymond then called Rex Kommer, a meteorologist with the United States Weather Bureau, to impeach the Clinton witnesses, who had generally described cool weather. Kommer testified that the average high temperature during the last half of August was 92.1 degrees, and that the average high for the first half of September was 93.1. On cross-examination, Alcock made sure Kommer spelled out for the jury that of the evening low temperatures, there were nine days in August that the temperature was in the 60s and some as low as 60 degrees. The Clinton witnesses, of course, had described the *nights* as being very cool.[127]

The next defense witness was FBI ballistics expert Robert Frazier. Frazier gave the official version of the events in Dealey Plaza in an attempt to refute the testimony of the Dallas witnesses. For this, he suffered a blistering cross-examination by Assistant DA Alvin Oser that shattered the conclusions of the Warren Commission.

> *Q: Mr. Frazier, you said that the shot from the sixth floor was a relatively easy shot to hit President Kennedy while he proceeded on Elm Street. Can you name anybody in the Federal Bureau of Investigation or any expert rifleman under the Bureau's direction who could accomplish the same feat that is alleged to have been accomplished, by the Warren Commission, namely, that the rifleman was in the sixth floor some 60 feet off of ground level at a distance of 265 feet away at frame 313, and with a moving target?*
>
> *MR. DYMOND: If the Court please, we object to this on the grounds, number one, that it is argumentative, number two, it is not proper re-*

cross-examination. Nothing was brought out on re-direct which permits such a question as this.

THE COURT: You needn't argue, Mr. Oser, it is within my discretion to permit it, and I will overrule your objection.

*THE WITNESS: **I know of no such tests or individuals.***

MR. OSER: That is all.[128] *[My emphasis.]*

Forensic pathologist Dr. Pierre Finck, one of JFK's autopsy doctors, showed up ready to defend conventional wisdom and was likewise shot down. Much of Oser's cross-examination of Finck is worth quoting verbatim:

Q: Well, at that particular time, Doctor, why didn't you call the doctors at Parkland or attempt to ascertain what the doctors at Parkland may have done or may have seen while the President's body was still exposed to view on the autopsy table?

A: I will remind you that I was not in charge of this autopsy, that I was called—

Q: You were a co-author of the report though, weren't you, Doctor?

A: Wait. I was called as a consultant to look at these wounds; that doesn't mean I am running the show.

Q: Was Dr. Humes running the show?

A: Well, I heard Dr. Humes stating that—he said, "Who is in charge here?" and I heard an Army General, I don't remember his name, stating, I am." You must understand that in those circumstances, there were law enforcement officers, military people with various ranks, and you have to co-ordinate the operation according to directions.

Q: But you were one of the three qualified pathologists standing at that autopsy table, were you not, Doctor?

A: Yes, I am.

Q: Was this Army General a qualified pathologist?

A: No.

Q: Was he a doctor?

A: No, not to my knowledge.

Q: Can you give me his name, Colonel?

A: No, I can't. I don't remember.

…

Q: Did you have an occasion to dissect the track of that particular bullet in the victim as it lay on the autopsy table?

A: I did not dissect the track in the neck.

Q: Why?

A: This leads us into the disclosure of medical records.

MR. OSER: Your Honor, I would like an answer from the Colonel and I would as the Court so to direct.

THE COURT: That is correct, you should answer, Doctor.

THE WITNESS: We didn't remove the organs of the neck.

BY MR. OSER:
Q: Why not, Doctor?

A: For the reason that we were told to examine the head wounds and that the—

Q: Are you saying someone told you not to dissect the track?

THE COURT: Let him finish his answer.

THE WITNESS: *I was told that the family wanted an examination of the head, as I recall, the head and chest, but the prosectors in this autopsy didn't remove the organs of the neck, to my recollection.*

BY MR. OSER:
Q: *You have said they did not, I want to know why didn't you as an autopsy pathologist attempt to ascertain the track through the body which you had on the autopsy table in trying to ascertain the cause or causes of death? Why?*

A: *I had the cause of death.*

Q: *Why did you not trace the track of the wound?*

A: *As I recall I didn't remove these organs from the neck.*

Q: *I didn't hear you.*

A: *I examined the wounds but I didn't remove the organs of the neck.*

Q: *You said you didn't do this; I am asking you why didn't do this as a pathologist?*

A: *From what I recall I looked at the trachea, there was a tracheotomy wound the best I can remember, but I didn't dissect or remove these organs.*

MR. OSER: *Your Honor, I would ask Your Honor to direct the witness to answer my question.*
BY MR. OSER:
Q: *I will ask you the question one more time: Why did you not dissect the track of the bullet wound that you have described today and you saw at the time of the autopsy at the time you examined the body? Why? I ask you to answer that question.*

A: *As I recall I was told not to, but I don't remember by whom.*

Q: You were told not to but you don't remember by whom?

A: Right.[129]

Oser also exposed the fact that in his Warren Commission testimony, Finck had stated that CE 399 could not have caused the wound to Governor Connally's right wrist:

> *Mr. SPECTER. And could it [CE 399] have been the bullet which inflicted the wound on Governor Connally's right wrist?*
>
> *Colonel FINCK. No; for the reason that there are too many fragments described in that wrist.*[130]

The Magic Bullet did not shatter Governor Connally's wrist, ergo, the Magic Bullet Theory is untenable.

The Trial Winds Down

As the trial wound down, the defense called James Phelan. Much of Phelan's testimony was discussed in Chapter 5. The reader will recall that Phelan was caught in several lies under cross-examination, and had claimed Perry Russo admitted to him—in front of photographer Matt Herron—that Russo had not told Sciambra about the conspiracy meeting until after the February 25, 1967 interview in Baton Rouge. Herron remembered things differently. Also, Alcock got Phelan to admit that he had tried to convince Russo that the man Russo had seen at Ferrie's was Guy Banister.

> *Q. So why did you suggest Guy Banister?*
>
> *A. Because of his similarity to Mr. Shaw.*
>
> *Q. You think there is a similarity? Have you ever seen Guy Banister?*
>
> *A. No, sir.*[131]

Phelan admitted Walter Sheridan had suggested the idea of the "similarity" to him.

The defense ended their presentation with none other than Clay Shaw, testifying in his own defense. Shaw denied all of Garrison's charges. No party at Ferrie's apartment—he didn't even know Ferrie. No knowing Oswald either. Shaw never used any alias, nor did he have any connection with the Central Intelligence Agency. Never made it out to Clinton either.[132] Shaw's responses would earn him a perjury indictment after the trial was over, but until then, Garrison had his mind on other things.

The following day, February 28, 1969, Garrison called two rebuttal witnesses. Nicholas and Matilda Tadin were a married couple whose 21 year-old son had taken flying lessons from David Ferrie in 1964. One day, they had gone to drop off their son at the Lakefront Airport when they saw Ferrie walk out of a hangar with none other than Clay Shaw. Mr. Tadin recognized Shaw, who was well known locally, and asked Ferrie if Shaw was a student of his. "No," Ferrie said, "He's a friend of mine, Clay Shaw. He's in charge of the International Trade Mart." Mrs. Tadin confirmed her husband's story in every respect. When Mrs. Tadin stepped down from the witness stand, the trial came to an end.[133]

Assistant DA James Alcock gave the first closing argument, emphasizing the degree to which the plan made at Ferrie's apartment had been carried out, with Shaw in San Francisco, Ferrie traveling to Texas possibly as a getaway pilot and later going to Hammond, and Oswald in Dealey Plaza. Alcock reminded the jury of Dymond's promise to prove that Shaw never laid eyes on Ferrie or Oswald. "Gentlemen, I submit to you that within four hours of the beginning of this trial that promise was broken. That promise, gentlemen, lay shattered, broken, and forever irretrievable in the dust of Clinton, Louisiana," he said.[134] Assistant DA Alvin Oser went through the Dallas evidence once again. Oser tried to convince the jury that the Single Bullet Theory was an impossibility, and that there had to be three assassins in the Plaza: "It seems strange, doesn't it, gentlemen, that a triangulation of fire was talked about, and I submit to you we have proven a triangulation of fire resulted from the conspiracy and the agreement that was hatched with the defendant Clay Shaw present."[135]

Defense counsel F. Irvin Dymond accused the state of using Clay Shaw to put the Warren Report on trial. Shaw was, Dymond argued, a "patsy…picked" to question the government's conclusion of a lone assassin. "It will be clear," he said, "that this Defendant, Clay Shaw, while he is sitting here, a defendant charged with a crime, has been brought here for no other purpose than to create a forum for the presentation of this attack upon the Warren Commission, for such an attack as would downgrade the respect of the American public for the very Government of that public. Again I say, gentlemen, if they are accusing our Government of being a completely fraudulent institution, let them come before you and say so. And another good appropriate statement might be either 'Love it or leave it.'"[136] In rebuttal arguments, Oser responded to Dymond's attack thusly: "We are un-American. You know what he said, I guess insinuating about whether or not—if you don't like the country, you can leave it. Well, in answer to that statement, gentlemen, let me tell you what came from this witness stand about triangulation of fire, and if Mr. Dymond doesn't like it, then he can lump it, because what came from that witness stand is proof beyond a reasonable doubt that there was a triangulation of fire in Dealey Plaza on November 22, 1963."[137]

After Oser and Alcock responded to Dymond's closing arguments on points like the Sciambra memo and the Dallas evidence, Garrison made the final closing argument of the trial. Garrison's words resonated across the courtroom as he personally made his final move at the trial.

> So let me talk to you about whether there is government fraud in this case. Now, a government is a great deal like a human being: It is not necessarily all good, and it is not necessarily all bad. We live in a good country, and I love it and you do, too, but we have nevertheless a government which is not perfect, and there have been indications since November 22 of 1963—and that was not the last indication—that

there is excessive power in some areas of our government—and that the people have not received all of the truth about some of the things that have happened, some of the assassinations that have occurred, and particularly with regard to the assassination of John Kennedy. Going back to when we were children, I think most of us, probably all of us here in this courtroom, felt that justice came into being automatically, that virtue was its own reward and good would triumph over evil, that it occurred automatically. And later when we found that it was-n't quite so, most of us felt that, hopefully, that at least justice occurred frequently of its own accord, but now I think that almost all of us world have to agree that there is really no automatic machinery, not on this earth at least, which causes justice to happen automatically. Men have to make it occur, individual human beings have to make it occur, otherwise it doesn't come into existence, and this is not always easy. As a matter of fact, it is always hard, because justice presents a threat to power, and in order to make justice come into being you often have to fight power.

...

Now, you men in recent weeks have heard witnesses that no one else in the world has heard, and you have seen what happened to your President, and I suggest to you that most of you know right now that in that area at least a fraud has been perpetrated. That does not mean that our Government is entirely black, and I want to emphasize that. It doesn't mean that the President is bad, it doesn't mean that the Supreme Court is bad. It does mean that in recent years, through the development of excessive power, because of the cold war, forces have developed in our Government over which there is no control, and these forces have an authoritarian approach to justice, meaning they will let you know what justice is.

Well, my reply to them is, we already know what it is. It is the jury system.

...

I am telling you that I think we can do something about it. I think that there are still enough Americans left in this country to make it continue to be America. I think that we can still fight authoritarianism: the government's insistence on secrecy, the government force used in counter-attacks against an honest inquiry; and when we do that we are not being un-American, we are being American, because it isn't easy, and you are sticking your neck out in a rather prominent way, but it has to be done, because truth does not come into being automatically. Justice does not happen automatically. Individual men, like the members of my staff here, have to work and fight to make it happen, and individual men like you have to make justice come into being, because otherwise it doesn't happen. And what I am trying to tell you is that there are forces in America today, unfortunately, which are not in favor of the truth coming out about John Kennedy's assassination. As long as our government continues to be like that, as long as such forces can get away with these kind of actions, then this is no longer the country in which we were born.

The murder of John Kennedy was probably the most terrible moment in the history of our country. Yet circumstances have placed you in the position where not only have you seen the hidden evidence, but you are actually going to have the opportunity to bring justice into the picture for the first time.

Now, you are here sitting in judgment on Clay Shaw, but you as men represent more than jurors in an ordinary case, because of the victim in this case. You represent, in a sense, the hope of humanity against government power. You represent humanity which yet may triumph over excessive government power, if you will cause it to be so in the course of doing your duty in this case.

I suggest that you "ask not what your country can do for you but what you can do for your country." What can you do for your country? You can cause justice to happen for the first time in this matter. You can help make our country better by showing that this is still a government of the people; and if you do that, as long as you live nothing will every be more important than that.

Thank you.[138]

Garrison sat down. The trial of the century was over.

The Verdict

It was almost midnight on February 28, 1969 when the jury neverthe-less elected to enter deliberations. The two alternate jurors were excused by Judge Haggerty, but asked to record their votes anyway. They voted to convict. During deliberations, the general consensus had been that Garrison simply did not have enough evidence connecting Shaw to the assassination conspiracy. Perry Russo's admission that he never actually heard Shaw or Oswald agree to the conspiracy was the key part in this.

Many jurors were convinced, based on the Dallas evidence that Garrison had proven a conspiracy, but several were not. One actually indi-cated he believed in the Warren Report more after the trial. Juror Larry Morgan felt Garrison's witnesses were weak relative to the "seriousness" of the charge. On the other hand, several jurors later told the press they felt Shaw had lied when he denied knowing Ferrie or Oswald.[139] They were not alone; Judge Haggerty himself said he thought Shaw "lied through his teeth" and conned the jury.[140] In the initial vote, eleven jurors voted to acquit, with one voting to convict. After further deliberations the jury voted again—this time it was unanimous.[141]

At 1:04 A.M. on the morning of March 1, 1969, two years to the day after Shaw's arrest, the jury returned to the courtroom. Shaw was found not guilty.[142] Garrison had returned to his office after closing arguments. When an aide brought word of Shaw's acquittal, the DA reportedly went into a non-characteristic angry rage. Two and a half years of hard work, Garrison must have felt, went down the drain with the jury's verdict.[143] Shaw was all smiles, and after thanking the jury, was driven away in a sheriff's car a free man. That night the defense team and several journalists who had covered the case celebrated the verdict in a bar called The Spotlight. According to Patricia Lambert, one member of the defense team awoke the next day unable to remember where he had left his car.[144]

Chapter Seven

The Lie Takes Hold

"Does any sane human being believe that President Johnson, the Warren Commission members, law enforcement officers, CIA, FBI, assorted thugs, weirdoes, Frisbee throwers, all conspired together as plotters in Garrison's wacky sightings? And that for 29 years nothing leaked?"

–Jack Valenti

Literally days before the end of his trial, Clay Shaw—much to the surprise of the prosecution—took the stand in his own defense. While testifying, he denied having worked for the CIA. He denied using the alias "Clay Bertrand." He denied knowing David Ferrie. And he denied knowing Lee Harvey Oswald. All these points of testimony can now be shown to be false. On March 3, 1969, the first business day after his acquittal on conspiracy charges, Shaw was charged with a new crime—perjury.[1]

The Bill of Information, signed personally by Garrison, charged that Shaw perjured himself specifically when he denied knowing Ferrie and Oswald.[2] If convicted, Shaw would have faced ten years in prison (each count was worth five).[3] Garrison had a very good reason for not going after Shaw for his alias and intelligence work. That Shaw had used another name and worked for the government was—at the time—very hard to prove. Beyond the witnesses at the conspiracy trial, Garrison had *only* Edward Whalen willing to testify under oath that Shaw had gone by the name Bertrand.[4] However, Whalen's story would have been at odds with Shaw's self-cultivated image of a *genteel* southern gentleman. Whalen's claims did not make much logical sense and Whalen told many obvious lies and exaggerations. It was very unlikely that the jury would have found him credible. With the booking card evidence already ruled on by Judge Haggerty, Garrison likely would have been unable to call Aloysius Habighorst. On the other hand, Garrison had stronger witnesses as far as Ferrie and Oswald. Thanks to the efforts of the ARRB and others, we now know that the FBI received several reports concerning Shaw's alias, and that the CIA knew about it in some form or fashion.[5]

Once again, the media turned a blind eye. Early press reports from Rosemary James and others characterized the charges as an act of spite from a vengeful Garrison.[6] Shaw's lawyers immediately appealed the charge, going before Criminal District Court Judge Malcolm O'Hara to request that the charges be dropped. O'Hara refused, and set the trial date for January 18, 1970.[7] It is important to note that at this juncture, neither Shaw nor his lawyers denied that Shaw had committed perjury. Their argument against the charges was that Perry Russo's initial characterization of the conspiracy meeting as a "bull session" reduced the importance of the Shaw-Ferrie and Shaw-Oswald relationships beyond the scope of the laws regarding perjury.[8]

Shaw's defense team continued to appeal the charges through every avenue, resulting in delays that set the trial back a full year.[9] On the eve of the trial, Shaw's attorneys applied for a temporary restraining order against Garrison in order to buy more time. It was denied. The trial began in earnest on January 18, 1971. It didn't get far. After a few preliminary motions and before a jury had been selected, the U.S. Court of Appeals for the Fifth Circuit heard a new motion from the defense, one for emergency relief.[10] This was possibly Shaw's last chance to get off. Sadly, it worked. Following a brief conference with the defense and prosecution, it was ordered that the U.S. District Court for the Eastern District of Louisiana (New Orleans Division) hold a hearing on Shaw's motion for injunctive relief. The trial was suspended and the hearing was convened five days later on January 25th.[11]

To Shaw's surprise (hopefully), the judge assigned to preside over the case was none other than Judge Herbert Christenberry. Shortly after his acquittal on the conspiracy charges, Shaw received a letter from Christenberry's wife, Caroline. Part of it read, "Our most sincere congratulations! We shared your anxieties over the past two outrageous years. Should your case have eventually found its way to Federal Court and been allotted to my husband you most certainly would have had a <u>fair</u> trial."[12]

One of the witnesses called by Shaw's defense team was none other than William Gurvich. Gurvich got up on the stand and claimed that Garrison had hired him to help with the assassination probe, that he had been Garrison's "chief investigator" and that he had finally resigned the following June out of a moral quandary that resulted when he realized the Shaw prosecution was a "fraudulent, criminal act."[13] The record shows that the truth is quite different. Gurvich begged Garrison for a job, even suspiciously "donating" him a color television. Garrison's actual chief investigator was always Lou Ivon. Gurvich appears in all NODA documentation as an "aide." Gurvich didn't so much resign as simply drift off after stealing a copy of Garrison's master file on the probe. He then blasted Garrison and his staff on every media outlet he could get access to. The CIA saw this and recommended to Shaw's lawyers that they contact Gurvich, if they had not already done so. He, along with "reporter" Hugh Aynesworth, later went to Clinton to try to strong-arm the witnesses there into changing their stories.[14] What is interesting is that Gurvich told journalist Ross Yockey "he would not be working on it [the Garrison probe] if he felt there was no substance to it." Yockey told the Orleans Parish Grand Jury,

"He was the person who convinced me, and I remain convinced to this day, that this is an investigation worth conducting. He alone. He introduced me to Mr. Garrison after he convinced me there was substance to the investigation."[15]

Garrison took the stand in his own defense, to explain the change in his thinking that led to his reinvestigation of the Kennedy case after his 1966 flight with Senator Russell Long and Joseph M. Rualt, Jr. He admitted that Russo had been his only witness against Shaw, prior to his arrest. He didn't deny that he had been aware of the attempted polygraph exam. Garrison was, much like at the conspiracy trial, using a limited strategy and was counting on Perry Russo to testify at the hearing in order to explain his behavior during the polygraph exam and to recount his memories of the conspiratorial meeting at David Ferrie's apartment in the September of 1963. This strategy was based on the lessons learned at Shaw's preliminary hearing. In that instance, he had been as forthright as possible, revealing the state's star witness and putting him up for attack a full two years before the trial. In his attempt to demonstrate good faith, he opened up the can of worms that would allow Dymond and Wegmann to come at him later on claiming he had planted Russo's story through drugs and post-hypnotic suggestion. Rather than reveal the witnesses he had against Shaw this time around, Garrison preferred to assume Shaw could not sustain the burden of proof he carried as the plaintiff. He assumed that Christenberry would be as open-minded as the other judges who had heard Shaw's appeals and give the state as much room as necessary to try the case. Garrison couldn't have known how biased Christenberry was, or what Russo would do when he took the stand.

Sadly, the collective pressure of the last five years had taken their toll on Russo. In a final effort to find release from the burden that had earlier led to his breakdown in front of Lt. O'Donnell, Russo pled the Fifth Amendment against self-incrimination rather than testify. Many of Garrison's critics like to claim that Russo was recanting his story in doing this. However, in 1991 he told James DiEugenio that the media circus surrounding the Shaw case had ruined his life and that he had informed the Shaw defense team that he simply refused to testify for either side.[16]

The night before his testimony, Russo met with Shaw's lawyers and, in the words of critics like Patricia Lambert, "recanted" his story. Lambert and company do not tell us that Russo's recanting actually amounted only to saying, "Not really," when asked if he was positive that Shaw was the Clay Bertrand he saw at Ferrie's party.[17] At no time did Russo ever say that the party did not happen, and all other points he testified to in the session with Shaw's lawyers are about ancillary issues irrelevant to the conspiracy charge. We are also not informed that Russo only gave Shaw's lawyers this testimony because they threatened to make an issue of his sexual habits on the stand the following day if he did not recant.[18] Garrison could have tried this with Shaw to expose Shaw's double-life, lending credence to Shaw's use of an alias, but Garrison did not. Russo's story had already been partially corroborated by Niles "Lefty" Peterson anyway—Peterson remembered the party at Ferrie's and recalled a Leon Oswald being present.[19]

Since 1971, Russo has held to the version of events that he recounted at Shaw's trial. In interviews with Bill Davy, Jim DiEugenio, William Matson Law, Steven Tyler (this interview can be seen in Tyler's documentary, "He Must Have Something"), Will Robinson and Marilyn Coleman, he always placed Shaw, Ferrie and Oswald with several Cubans at a party in the summer of '63, plotting a triangulation of crossfire.

Nevertheless, Russo's withdrawal took the bite out of Garrison's defense. On January 28th, the proceeding ended—leaving the fate of the Shaw case in the hands of Herbert Christenberry. The bias in Christenberry's decision is evident. Christenberry accuses Garrison violating Shaw's rights countless times, knocks Garrison for speaking to the media about the assassination (despite the fact that Garrison *always* refused to discuss the specifics of the Shaw case) and accepts every bit of the official story. Nevertheless, Christenberry was now left with a problem—how to paint the perjury charge as "bad faith." His answer was to lie about it. Christenberry writes, "Subsequent to his acquittal, the defendant Garrison immediately, and without any witnesses other than those he used at the trial, charged Shaw with perjury," citing the testimony of Judge Alcock. However, what Alcock actually said was that the D.A.'s Office had only the witnesses *available* at the time of the conspiracy trial. As the reader will recall, Garrison used relatively few of the witnesses he had available (this was one of his major strategic blunders).[20] For instance, to bolster his charge that Shaw did indeed know David Ferrie, Garrison had the testimony of David Logan.

On April 13, 1968, then-Assistant D.A. Alcock conducted a phone interview with Logan that was recorded and subsequently transcribed. The contents of this interview are particularly damning towards Shaw's denial of his relationship with Ferrie, as well as his attempts to lie about his double-life.

> A.   ...Listen, but what I wanted to ask you about was you say you met Shaw at a party I think, as I understand it.
>
> L.   Right.
>
> A.   Who—and Ferrie was at the party?
>
> L.   Yes.[21]

Logan goes on to describe seeing Ferrie at the party with Shaw around the time of Mardi Gras in 1961. Shaw had invited Logan to the party (which took place on Governor Nichols Street, where Shaw had an apartment) after they met at a French Quarter bar called Dixie's. Logan went on to describe a brief sexual encounter with Shaw, and his statements contradict Shaw's claims about the items investigators removed from his apartment following his arrest.[22]

Another previously unheard witness was one of the Clinton witnesses that didn't make it to the Shaw trial. His name was Henry Burnell Clark. In the course of the CORE Voter Registration drive, he was walking down the sidewalk in front of the Stewart and Carroll General Store where he worked and saw a tall man in a business suit with a shock of gray hair, whom he identified as Clay Shaw. He then noticed a man using a pay phone, who he remembered "because of his unusual hair." In his affidavit, Clark said, "It was bushy and stood up all directions o n [sic] his head like he had been out on a drunk all night." Burnell identified this man as David Ferrie.[23] Ferrie associates Herbert Wagner, Jim Louviere, James Laurent and Tommy Clark had all told the District Attorney's Office that they had seen Shaw visit with Ferrie, just as Perry Russo had described, at his gas station on Veterans Highway.[24]

It should be noted that Alcock's statement was incorrect. Garrison's office went on to locate several witnesses after the trial, among them Mrs. June Rolfe, who in 1960 or 1961 saw Shaw driving a "light-colored Thunderbird with the top down in the French Quarter in New Orleans."[25] Rolfe said, "In the rear I recognized DAVID FERRIE whom I had seen at the old airport (New Orleans Lakefront Airport) and who occasions had been pointed out to me as being an instructor for the Civil Air Patrol."[26] The date on which Rolfe's statement was taken: 29 May 1969—almost three months *after* the Shaw trial. So much for Christenberry's contention that the investigation ended with Shaw's acquittal.

With this flimsy base for a conclusion, Christenberry issued his decision on May 27, 1971. Garrison was officially enjoined from "further prosecution of the pending criminal action entitled 'State of Louisiana v. Clay L. Shaw,' No. 208-260." Once again, Clay Shaw was home free.

Aftermath

Despite the acquittal of Clay Shaw and newspaper editorials calling for his resignation, Garrison easily defeated Harry Connick, Sr. and won a third term as district attorney.[27] While preparing for Shaw's perjury trial, and its illegitimate child, the Christenberry hearing, Garrison wrote a book on the assassination entitled *A Heritage of Stone*. The book did well, although Garrison could not go into the case against Shaw since the perjury case was still pending. Kerry Thornley was placed on the backburner while all this was going on. It was at this time that the strongest so-called "Garrison case" became the forgotten one. Later in 1971, after the Christenberry hearing, Garrison was arrested for accepting kickbacks from pinball machine operators. A federal case, the trial was given to none other than Judge Herbert Christenberry. The trial did not take place until 1973. In the mean time, journalist Rosemary James had interviewed former Garrison investigator Pershing Gervais, the government's star witness, who confessed that his testimony was false.[28]

> *James: You were forced to work for the government?*
>
> *Gervais: But more than that, I was forced to lie for them, that's a better description.*
>
> *James: What were you forced to do?*
>
> *Gervais: Well, it became clear in the beginning…that they were really interested in but one man, Jim Garrison, and in their minds, they knew that I was the guy who could get him.*
>
> …
>
> *James: What do you mean when you say they wanted Jim Garrison?*
>
> *Gervais: They wanted to silence Jim Garrison.*
>
> …
>
> *James: Well, now are, are you saying that you participated in a deliberate frameup?*
>
> *Gervais: A total, complete political frameup, absolutely.*[29]

Garrison, who defended himself in the trial, had the James interview introduced as evidence and called experts who proved that the tapes purporting to be of Garrison accepting the bribes were doctored.[30] Garrison was acquitted of all charges, but the trial ended mere weeks before the 1973 election. Garrison had no time to run a real campaign and was defeated by Harry Connick, Sr. by a mere 2,000 votes.[31] Shortly before Garrison left office in 1974 he was re-arrested by the federal government on charges that he did not pay income taxes on the money he had supposedly taken as kickbacks. Garrison defended himself once again and was acquitted a second time.[32]

Harry Connick, Sr. took over as DA on April 1, 1974. Within five months he had dropped all charges against Kerry W. Thornley. Garrison's last defendant was now a free man. Connick dropped the ball in other areas as well. Since Garrison left office, New Orleans has become the city with the highest murder rate per capita in the country. After he took over, Connick ordered an investigator named Gary Raymond to destroy the Grand Jury records from the Shaw case. When Raymond questioned the DA's decision, Connick said, "Burn this sonofabitch and burn it today!" Raymond instead kept the records in his garage before turning them over to the Assassination Records Review Board in 1995. Before Raymond gave the files to the ARRB, Connick had actually claimed that Garrison and his staff had stolen many of the records. Upon hearing Connick's claim the aforementioned attorney Ralph Whalen, who had worked on Connick's staff, spoke up and said he remembered Connick "destroying a bunch of Garrison stuff...some things that related directly to the Shaw case."[33]

It was not the first time Raymond had gone up against Connick. When Raymond left the police force in the mid 1980s, he had risen to become Connick's chief investigator. Later, as a PI, Raymond looked at a pedophile case for Connick as a favor and recommended Connick prosecute. Connick refused. Raymond would later run into one of the children he had seen in a pornographic video shot by the Catholic priest he had investigated. The boy refused to talk saying the priest had threatened his life. Raymond wrote a three-page memo on the subject, which infuriated

Connick because it left a paper trail. Raymond asked Connick when the priest would be charged, and Connick replied, "He won't. Not as long as I am the DA. And you can't do a thing about it." Raymond told his story to a reporter, who exposed Connick's negligence. The case became the famous Father Dino Cinel child abuse scandal.[34]

Clay Shaw died August 15, 1974 of a brain tumor.[35] Garrison was widely held as discredited until the disclosures of the Rockefeller Commission and the Church Committee about CIA abuses, domestically and internationally. In 1976, Garrison was the subject of a *New Orleans Magazine* article entitled, "Was Jim Garrison Right After All?" At last, Garrison was beginning to get some of the credit he deserved.[36] The growing trend towards public understanding of the Kennedy assassination and the intelligence agencies culminated in two things. The first was Garrison's 1978 election to a ten-year term as judge of the Louisiana Fourth Circuit Court of Appeals.[37] The second was a new investigation of the assassination. Everything seemed to be coming to a head in the mid-70s. Author James DiEugenio writes:

> *This was a qualitative leap up from Garrison. The New Orleans DA could only howl in the wind about what he knew to be the malfeasance, or worse, of those two agencies [the FBI and the CIA] in the Kennedy case. Now, with access to the actual documentary record, Frank Church and the U. S. Senate were certifying that much of what Garrison said was true and warranted. Further, Church was also saying that the CIA secretly plotted the deaths of political leaders and was tracing those plots in detail. At this time, New Orleans magazine ran a cover story on Garrison basically saying that he had said all this before and no one had listened to him. Researcher Mary Ferrell wrote him a letter apologizing for not standing by him more staunchly. She didn't suspect in 1967 that the CIA could do such awful things.[38]*

On March 6, 1975 researcher Robert Groden and comedian Dick Gregory appeared on Geraldo Rivera's ABC talk show to show the

Zapruder film publicly (outside of the Shaw trial, of course) for the first time. The response was huge. The son of U.S. Rep. Tom Downing of Virginia saw the film, and forced his father to watch it. Congressman Downing then drew up a bill creating a select committee of Congress to investigate the assassination.[39] The legendary Henry Gonzalez of Texas already had a bill on the house floor to investigate not only the JFK assassination, but also the murders of RFK, Martin Luther King, Jr. and the attempted assassination of George Wallace. Gonzales agreed to work with Downing, and the pair dropped all but the JFK and Martin Luther King cases from their bill. Finally, on September 17, 1976 the bill creating the House Select Committee on Assassinations passed by 280-65.[40]

Downing became chairman of the new HSCA, with Gonzalez in line to replace Downing when Downing retired at the end of the 94th Congress. As chief counsel for the committee, they hired Richard A. Sprague, a heavyweight prosecutor famous for prosecuting Tony Boyle's mob conspiracy to murder labor leader Jock Yablonski.[41] With the appointment of Sprague came a general feeling that a reckoning in the JFK case was at hand. Cyril Wecht recalled:

> *Dick Sprague was the ideal man for that job with the HSCA. Richard Sprague had probably prosecuted more murder cases than any DA in the United States....He knew how the police worked. He wasn't just the kind of guy who tried the case. He worked with the police. He knew thoroughly how homicide cases were conducted. He's tough, he's tenacious, he's aggressive. He has a strong streak of independence. He was the man for the job.[42]*

In the words of Gaeton Fonzi:

> *After talking with Sprague I was now certain he planned to conduct a strong investigation and I was never more optimistic in my life. I remember excitingly envisioning the scope and character of the investigation. It would include a major effort in Miami, with teams of*

investigators digging into all those unexplored corners the Warren Commission had ignored or shied away from. They would be working with squads of attorneys to put legal pressure on, to squeeze the truth from recalcitrant witnesses. There would be reams of sworn depositions, the ample use of warrants and no fear of bringing prosecutions for perjury. We would have all sorts of sophisticated investigative resources and, more important, the authority to use them. The Kennedy assassination would finally get the investigation it deserved and an honest democracy needed. There would be no more bullshit.[43]

Sprague chose Robert Tanenbaum to run the JFK side of the investigation. Tanenbaum came from the New York DA's Office and had never lost a murder case.[44] Both Tanenbaum, and his counterpart on the MLK case Bob Lehner, picked their investigative staff from experienced homicide detectives around the country, such as Al Gonzalez, Cliff Fenton, Bob Buras and L.J. Delsa.[45] The only non-detective was Gaeton Fonzi, a journalist who L.J. Delsa said "could have been a cop."[46] With a fine staff assembled, and plans for a thorough homicide investigation underway, Rep. Downing had every reason to be optimistic when he retired from Congress on December 31, 1976. Unfortunately, he would be let down.

Almost immediately, after it became clear that Sprague and Tanenbaum were going to investigate a murder, not just write a report, Sprague came under heavy attack by the Los Angeles Times, the New York Times and the Washington Post.[47] As HSCA investigator L.J. Delsa told the author, Sprague and Tanenbaum were not "Hill People," meaning Washington people.[48] This was why Congressional leaders joined the media in their attacks. Allegations that Sprague was tied to the Mob were read into the Congressional Record.[49] Sprague was accused of taking mob-paid vacations to Los Vegas and visiting the mob-connected Fontainebleau Hotel in Miami Beach.[50] In fact, the only time Sprague had visited Los Vegas was when he spoke before the National Trial Lawyers Association. He had never stayed at the Fontainebleau.[51]

When Sprague learned that early polling indicated that the Committee would not be reconstituted with him as chief counsel, he resigned.[52] Tanenbaum refused to take Sprague's job, but agreed to stay on long enough to find a new chief counsel.[53] Candidates included former Watergate Special Prosecutor Archibald Cox and former Supreme Court Justice Arthur Goldberg.[54] Finally, on June 20, 1977, Cornell Law Professor G. Robert Blakey was appointed chief counsel of the HSCA. Tanenbaum then resigned. "At that time I had a three year old daughter…and I didn't want her to read about American history that I knew to be absolutely false, that her father may have participated in," he said.[55]

Under Blakey and Tanenbaum's successor, Gary Cornwell, the HSCA became another cover-up. Medical and photographic evidence was ignored or classified, leads relating to the intelligence agencies were written off and experts bent over backwards to prove that Oswald was the lone assassin. It was only with the late introduction of the acoustical evidence of a shot from the Grassy Knoll by Gary Mack and Mary Ferrell, then seen as incontrovertible, that the Committee concluded that there had been a conspiracy. Blakey thought his job was to write a report, on time and on budget, and he did so. The HSCA's 1979 Final Report admitted the conspiracy existed, but blamed it on a new patsy—the mob. The media trashed the Committee's conclusion and a 1983 National Research Council (NRC) report refuted the acoustical evidence to the satisfaction of most researchers. The last investigation was over.

Stone's JFK Changes Everything

Garrison was re-elected to the Louisiana Fourth Circuit Court of Appeal in 1988. That same year he wrote his second book on the assassination, *On the Trail of the Assassins,* a slightly fictionalized account of the New Orleans investigation and the prosecution of Clay Shaw. Oliver Stone, director of *Platoon* and *Born on the Fourth of July,* optioned Garrison's book.[56] The film that resulted, *JFK,* opened in December of 1991 to severe criticism from the media for questioning the official story and for its positive portrayal of Jim Garrison and his investigation. (Garrison even had a cameo in the film, ironically, as Earl Warren. Perry Russo and Layton Martens can be found in *JFK* as well.) Stone's movie caused public support for a new investigation and a release of classified files to grow to a level unseen since right before the HSCA was created. As a result, President George Bush signed into law the President John F. Kennedy Assassination Records Collection Act on October 26, 1992, directing the National Archives to create a JFK Collection and ordering the creation of an Assassination Records Review Board to facilitate the release of those records.[57]

Garrison had passed away on October 21, only five days earlier, of natural causes.[58] When Shaw was acquitted, Garrison went into a tirade. He thought he had failed. Jim Garrison *didn't* fail. Thanks to his work, we are closer to an answer in the Kennedy case than we ever have been. Without Garrison's investigation, there would have never been an Assassination Records Review Board. While he could not convict Clay Shaw in 1969, or Kerry Thornley after, Jim Garrison left us a living, breathing record of the most turbulent period of American history.

Of all his achievements—soldier, prosecutor, investigator, author— surely that is what he should be remembered for.

Chapter Eight

The New Files

"To honestly study this new record is to see that Jim Garrison was anything but the caricature the media made him back in 1967."

–James DiEugenio

The ARRB finished their work and closed up shop in October 1998, having spent the better part of four years declassifying the records of everyone from the obvious CIA, the obscure President's Foreign Intelligence Advisory Board (PFIAB) and of course, Garrison's NODA. What can we learn from these new files on the assassination?

Ask, for example, what can we learn about Kerry W. Thornley? Well, this book couldn't have been written without those files. Except for those documents in the possession of James Lesar's Assassination Archives and Research Center in Washington, D.C., most had no idea exactly what kind of evidence Garrison had dug up. The Thornley case was forgotten in the media after a couple of days. Garrison devotes a couple of pages to him in his book. That's about it. While everyone in the research community was arguing about the case against Clay Shaw, the case against Kerry Thornley lay in boxes in a room somewhere. About everyone except Bernard Fensterwald treated Thornley as Garrison's victim. Looking in the HSCA's published 12 volumes of hearings and exhibits, one finds the following written about Thornley:

> *Thornley firmly denied contact with Oswald at 544 Camp Street in New Orleans or at any time since his Marine Corps days. His statements have been corroborated and no evidence has been found to contradict him.*[1]

But looking at the new files, we find that after interviewing Thornley in 1976, a House Select Committee staffer wrote this note on a memo:

"JG got only bullshit before"[2]

Jim Garrison wasn't the only one.

Mexico City

As noted in Chapter 5, Thornley protested way too much and knew way too much too soon about Oswald's visit to Mexico City two months prior to the assassination. We know Thornley had been in Mexico City before Oswald, but what he did there is still unclear. What is clear is this: something was going on in Mexico City, and it was the cause of the cover-up.

The key to these events was a phone call to the Soviet Embassy in Mexico City from a caller identifying himself as "Lee Oswald." This call was allegedly picked up by CIA surveillance, and in it, the man purporting to be Oswald speaks of his contact with KGB Agent Valeriy Kostikov.[3] The CIA station in Mexico City wrote a report on the subject describing a man "apparent age 35, athletic build circa 6 feet, receding hairline, balding top."[4] Clearly not the real Lee Harvey Oswald. This report was transmitted to CIA Headquarters, who responded by sending two messages, both referring to Oswald as "Lee Henry Oswald." The first message was sent back to Mexico City with a description of the actual 24-year-old Lee

Harvey Oswald. The other was sent to the FBI and contained the description of the 35-year-old.[5] These two cables were drafted by at least three people, including Charlotte Bustos, Mexico City HQ Desk Officer, Ann Egerter of CI/SIG, and Stephan Roll, CI liaison to the Soviet Russia division,[6] and the first of the pair of cables was signed off on by the Assistant Deputy Director for Plans.[7] The Mexico City cable "caused a lot of excitement" in Langley, so, as noted by Peter Dale Scott in *Deep Politics II,* "The misinformation in the cables is unlikely to have been accidental...."[8] Indeed, the CIA has a long history of keeping false information on Oswald, dating all the way back to 1960 when his 201 file was opened under the name of "Lee Henry Oswald."[9] This false information about Oswald came from two sources. One was the Counterintelligence Special Investigation Group, or CI/SIG, which was part of the CIA's Counterintelligence (CI) staff under James Jesus Angleton. The second source was a group of CIA officers in Mexico City.[10]

The purpose of CI/SIG was essentially similar to that of Internal Affairs in a police force. Angleton created the unit in 1954 to keep the rest of the Agency in line and to search for KGB penetration agents, called "moles." Angleton intentionally staffed his unit with former FBI personnel to insure that it would be very watchful of the rest of the CIA.[11] Evidence now seems to indicate that Oswald may have been used in just such a mole hunt. First, let us examine the importance of Oswald's alleged contact with Valeriy Kostikov. Warren Commission Document 347, a January 31, 1964 memo from Richard Helms to Warren Commission Counsel J. Lee Rankin, says:

> *17. KOSTIKOV is believed to work for Department Thirteen of the First Chief Directorate of the KGB. It is the Department responsible for executive action, including sabotage and assassination. These functions of the KGB are known within the Service itself as "Wet Affairs". The Thirteenth Department headquarters, according to very reliable information, conducts interviews, or as appropriate, file reviews on*

*every foreign military defector to the USSR to study and to determine
the possibility of utilizing the defector in his country of origin.*[12]

This is highly significant! Former defector Lee Harvey Oswald speaking with a KGB official who works in a department responsible for assassinations, two months before Oswald himself is arrested for assassinating the president of the United States. How likely would this be were there not a Soviet plot to kill Kennedy?

However, the Lee Harvey Oswald who made the call in Mexico City was likely not the Lee Harvey Oswald arrested in Dallas. The individual in Mexico City spoke in broken Russian.[13] This could hardly be the Oswald who spoke Russian so well his wife thought he was from the USSR when she first met him. This wasn't the Lee Harvey Oswald who greatly impressed Rosaleen Quinn, who had worked with a Berlitz tutor for over a year, with his use of Russian during his time in the Marine Corps (see Chapter Two).

If we look at the testimony of Eusebio Azcue and Silvia Duran of the Cuban Consulate in Mexico City, who were also visited by "Lee Oswald," we find that they describe a blonde man over 30-years-old.[14] HSCA Staffer Edwin Lopez interviewed two CIA employees who were used as double agents within the Cuban Consulate at the time of the "Oswald" visit. They told Lopez "that the consensus among employees within the Cuban Consulate after the Kennedy assassination was that it wasn't Oswald who had been there."[15]

Going back to the call to the Soviet Embassy, we are left with a question. The Mexico City CIA Station cable to headquarters describing the call says the man "spoke with Consul whom he believed to be Valeriy Vladimirovich Kostikov." But in the summary of the phone transcript quoted in the Lopez Report, "Oswald...said that he did not remember the name of the Consul with whom he had spoken. Obyedkov asked if it had been Kostikov.... The man outside replied affirmatively and repeated that his name was Oswald."[16] If the cable is correct, then the man pretending to be Oswald is the one who introduced the idea of the Kostikov visit. If the transcript is correct, the KGB connection was implied in the CIA cable. If the second case is correct, it is unlikely that implication was accidental. With all the false information already in the CIA files about Oswald, the misleading nature of the cable was probably intentional.[17] Of course, parts of the Oswald misinformation share the same author—Ann Egerter (one of the authors the two separate replies to the Mexico City cable about "Lee Henry Oswald") had earlier opened the 201 file for "Lee Henry Oswald."[18]

This brings us back to Oswald's time in the Soviet Union. As noted earlier (see Chapter Three), Oswald received a visa to enter the Soviet Union from Finland in just two days. For years researchers have seen this as evidence that Oswald was doing intelligence work, but they were not alone. Otto Otepka of the State Department was paying attention to Oswald's actions in Russia and feared Oswald may have defected to the KGB. The quick receipt of Oswald's visa, combined with Oswald's acquisition of an exit visa a month and a half early, led Otepka to be very suspicious of Oswald. Strangely, however, Otepka's attempts at learning more were thwarted by his superiors in the State Department. This led Otepka to suspect a subversive conspiracy ("moles" in the government) with Oswald as some kind of KGB agent.[19]

Angleton, another deeply paranoid individual with an intense fear of the Soviets, may well have shared these suspicions. Author Peter Dale Scott has pointed out the likenesses of the "Lee Henry Oswald" cables to what Angleton called a "marked card" operation, wherein false information, "like a bent card," is sent out "to see where it ends up."[20] If Angleton was unsure about Lee Harvey Oswald, he could have put the falsified cables in the file on "Lee Henry Oswald." If references to a "Lee Henry Oswald" showed up in KGB material the "mole" would have been found.[21]

With the newly released files there is more proof than ever of Oswald's impersonation in Mexico City. Though the CIA claimed they destroyed the recorded intercept of the "Oswald" phone call as a matter of routine, the weight of the evidence firmly indicates otherwise. Several FBI memos from 1963 show that agents in Dallas reviewed tapes of the call. From an FBI HQ memo to the FBI's Mexico City station:

> *If tapes covering any contacts subject (Oswald) with Soviet or Cuban embassies available, forward to bureau for laboratory examination and analysis together with transcript. Include tapes previously reviewed Dallas if they were returned to you.*[22]

A transcript of a telephone call from J. Edgar Hoover to President Johnson shows Hoover said:

> *We have up here the tape and the photograph of the man who was at the Soviet embassy using Oswald's name. That picture and the tape do not correspond to this man's voice, nor to his appearance. In other words, it appears that there is a second person who was at the Soviet embassy down there.*[23]

On top of all this, two Warren Commission counsels, William T. Coleman Jr. and W. David Slawson, both said they listened to a recording of the telephone call during their trip to Mexico City in the spring of 1964.[24]

It was the early falsehoods about the Mexico City trip that caused speculation about a Communist plot. The CIA's lies and obfuscations on the subject seem to have given birth to the line of thought that the assassination had to be covered up for the good of the American people. In the words of Deputy Attorney General Nicholas Katzenbach in a now famous memo, "Speculation about Oswald's motivation ought to be cut off, and we should have some basis for rebutting thought that this was a Communist conspiracy or (as the Iron Curtain press is saying) a right-wing conspiracy to blame it on the Communists. Unfortunately the facts on Oswald seem about too pat—too obvious (Marxist, Cuba, Russian wife, etc.). The Dallas police have put out statements on the Communist conspiracy theory, and it was they who were in charge when he was shot and thus silenced."[25] President Johnson himself used the threat of nuclear war to build and staff his Warren Commission.[26]

Kerry Thornley, who apparently frequented Guy Banister's anti-Castro apparatus at 544 Camp Street and was a frequent companion of Oswald during that turbulent summer in New Orleans, lied to the Warren Commission, the Orleans Parish Grand Jury and the American people about Oswald to draw attention away from the intelligence connection to Oswald's Soviet defection and to paint him as a communist loner. The Mexico City cover-up seemed aimed at disguising Oswald's involvement in some kind of Counterintelligence operation and painting him as a KGB assassin to kill the objective investigation of the assassination. Clearly, Thornley was sensitive about his own trip to Mexico City. Why? If Thornley had something to do with the CIA's Mexico City deception, it would appear he had far more to do with the assassination than anyone could have realized.

Clay Shaw's CIA Connection

Clay Shaw denied until the day he died that he had any connections at all to the Central Intelligence Agency. It took no more than one year for the late, lamented New Orleans socialite to be proven a liar. Victor Marchetti, a former CIA officer who had served as an assistant to the Director of Central Intelligence, gave an interview to *True* magazine in 1975. Marchetti revealed that during the period of the Shaw trial, DCI Richard Helms would ask on several occasions during staff meetings questions like, "Are we giving them all the help they need?"[27] Though Marchetti did not know who "they" were, he guessed, based on the general tone towards Garrison, that "they" was Clay Shaw's defense team. Helms would then direct all discussion on the matter to "later in my office" so nothing was on the record. Marchetti began to ask around about who Clay Shaw was. One of his fellow CIA officers told him, "Well...Shaw, a long time ago, had been a contact of the Agency.... He was in the export-import business...he knew people coming and going from certain areas—the Domestic Contact Service—he used to deal with them...and it's been cut off a long time ago...." Marchetti was then cautioned, "[W]ell of course the Agency doesn't want this to come out now because Garrison will distort it, the public would misconstrue it."[28]

Marchetti cautioned the interviewer that Shaw's links to the CIA might not have been so innocuous. Marchetti said, "I accepted these explanations on face value, never thought more about them until I...looked back. One of the reasons I accepted that at face value is usually when you were being put off you were told 'look, it's sensitive and you have no need to know.' Sometimes when it was really sensitive they would give you a phony excuse.... His association and contacts could have been extensive and I was just being put off."[29] Four years later, Richard Helms himself would confirm Shaw's Domestic Contact Service (DCS) utilization under oath. "The only recollection I have of Clay Shaw and the Agency is that I believe that at one time...he was one of the part-time contacts of the Domestic Contact Division..." he said.[30]

Shaw's defenders argued that Shaw was just one of thousands of businessmen and academics every year who were debriefed by the Agency upon returning from foreign travel. Shaw's actual DCS reports were released, however, in 1994 and they seem to indicate that Shaw did more than just report in about his time overseas. Shaw's first DCS contact was in 1948 and was a routine report about a Czechoslovakian trade exhibit in the ITM.[31] In 1949, however, Shaw was actually briefed by the CIA *before* leaving on a three-month tour of Latin American countries such as Cuba, Haiti, the Dominican Republic, Puerto Rico, Peru, Ecuador, Colombia, Venezuela, Panama, Costa Rica, El Salvador, Guatemala, Nicaragua and Honduras. When he returned, Shaw reported on the political and economic climate of Peru, criticism of Nicaragua's dictator Somoza and even the private lives of Juan and Evita Peron.[32]

A few years later when Shaw got his hands on a directory of German companies engaging in international trade, he made sure to pass it along to the CIA's Foreign Documents Division. In August of 1955, Shaw offered to attend the Czechoslovak Engineering Exhibition in Erno the following month as a CIA observer under the pretense of being an ITM representative provided the CIA agreed to pay his expenses. William Burke, Chief of the New Orleans DCS Office, wrote in a memo on this mission that Shaw was a "valued source" of the office, and further that, "[W]e deem it sufficiently important to compromise a 'Y' number to refer you to the reports submitted by Clay Shaw as Y 145.1 and particularly OO-B-54754, Subject: 'Observations on International Fairs at Milan, Brussels, Basel, Paris and London/Comments on Western European Economics and Desire to Trade with the Soviet Bloc.'"[33] This reads almost like a letter of recommendation. In 1956, Shaw offered to write letters of inquiry to producers of mercury in Spain and Italy, again under the pretense of representing the ITM, to gather intelligence on Spanish and Italian mercury producers.[34]

After 1956, all the official records indicate Shaw ceased to be a source of the DCS office. Why would Shaw, described as a "valued source" in 1955, no longer be of value in 1956? Not all of Shaw's CIA files have been released yet, and there are indications in the records that some may have been destroyed.[35] Nevertheless, there is room to speculate on what, if anything, Shaw might have done for the Agency after 1956. That year, a project called PERMINDEX ("permanent industrial exhibition") opened in Basel, Switzerland.[36] PERMINDEX featured a 13 floor office building, an exhibition building, and a 15 floor hotel, all modeled after the New Orleans International Trade Mart.[37] In charge of the project were Ferenc Nagy (the right-wing former prime minister of Hungary), Hans Seligmann (a fascist collaborator during World War II), George Mandel (Hungarian exploiter of the WW2 Jewish refugee racket), Hjalmar Schact (convicted war criminal) and Gutierrez di Spadaforo (a former member of

Mussolini's cabinet).[38] This strange grouping of the European far right caught the attention of the U.S. State Department, who, through the American Consulate in Switzerland, kept track of PERMINDEX as it developed. It was in the spring of 1958 that the consulate reported that Clay Shaw of New Orleans had had "from the outset great interest in the PERMINDEX project."[39]

When public suspicion and criticism of Nagy's project began to heat up in 1958, Nagy appealed to the Italian government to allow PERMINDEX to move to Rome. PERMINDEX made the transition that October, opening up an affiliate called the Rome World Trade Center or Centro Mondiale Commerciale deRoma.[40] When PERMINDEX came to Rome, an addition was made to the Board of Directors—Clay L. Shaw. Shaw remained with CMC/PERMINDEX until 1963 when suspicion and controversy forced the project to relocate again to South Africa.[41] After Shaw's arrest in 1967, the left-wing Italian newspapers *De La Sera* and *Paesa Sera* ran stories alleging that CMC was "a creature of the CIA" for the purposes of transferring money for illegal espionage activities in Italy. A mainstream Canadian newspaper called *Le Devoir* (*Le Devoir* is still in operation—it is one of the primary media organizations in the province of Quebec) repeated these allegations shortly thereafter.[42] However, the allegations in these articles were never confirmed, and, as author Patricia Lambert points out in her book *False Witness*, *Paesa Sera* was known for its pro-Soviet bloc articles, and recent research has revealed that leftist Italian dailies were often used for KGB propaganda purposes.[43] The CIA's Office of Security, in response to the *Paesa Sera* allegations, did an internal review and found no connection between the CIA and CMC/PERMINDEX.[44] It should be noted that CIA internal reviews have also concluded that the Agency never tried to kill Castro and, as we shall see, that known Agency employees did not work for the Agency.

In late March of 1967, aforementioned Garrison informant Betty Parrot told Assistant DA Andrew Sciambra that FBI Agent Regis Kennedy had stated privately that "Shaw was a CIA agent who had done work, of an unspecified nature, over a five year span in Italy."[45] Shaw's time on the board of CMC/PERMINDEX coincided with CMC's time in Italy, which lasted *five years*. However, in his Grand Jury testimony, Kennedy flatly denied making the statement. It was apparently Kennedy's practice to claim executive privilege if the Grand Jury was getting into territory he did have knowledge of but had to keep secret, and since Kennedy plainly said "no," we have no reason to doubt him.[46] In the end, all the PER-MINDEX story contributes to the understanding of the assassination are accusations that cannot be confirmed. However, other evidence strongly indicates that Shaw's relationship with the CIA did not end in 1956.

A CIA document released in 1992 contains the following:

> *A memorandum marked only for file, 16 March 1967, signed Marguerite D. Stevens, says that J. Monroe SULLIVAN, #280207, was granted a covert security approval on 10 December 1962 so that he could be used in Project QKENCHANT. SHAW has #402897-A.*[47]

The exact origin and purpose of Project QKENCHANT has still not been satisfactorily resolved. In 1998 the CIA tried to minimize its importance in response to an ARRB inquiry. According to the Agency, "QKEN-CHANT was the name of an Agency project used to provide security approvals on non-Agency personnel and facilities."[48] The CIA's confusing language does little more than to establish that Shaw was likely more to the Agency than a mere DCS contact. The CIA's memo also says that "Monroe Sullivan, Clay Shaw's boss, was granted a security approval in December 1962."[49] But Sullivan was Clay Shaw's counterpart at the San Francisco ITM, not his boss. This raises reasonable doubts as to the Agency's sincerity.

It is a known fact that Watergate burglar E. Howard Hunt also received a security approval for QKENCHANT in 1970 when he "retired" from the Agency and, the next day, took at job with the Robert R. Mullen Company, a CIA front corporation based in the same building as the CIA's Domestic Operations Division (DOD).[50] In addition to actual public relations work, the Mullen Co. provided cover overseas for CIA espionage activities and did PR for other Agency fronts. The offer of employment from the Mullen Co. was the result of a personal request from DCI Richard Helms, and Hunt continued to "work" for the firm after taking a job in G. Gordon Liddy's Special Investigative Unit at the White House. The CIA continued to provide Hunt with assistance including disguises and false identities during this period. It should be noted that Hunt had twice before "retired" from the Agency.[51]

When researcher William Davy brought up Shaw's QKENCHANT clearance with Victor Marchetti, Marchetti said, "If you're working with DCS, there's no need for a covert security clearance like that. This was something else. This would imply that he was doing some kind of work for the Clandestine Services."[52] Davy asked what division of Clandestine Services would be involved with QKENCHANT. Marchetti replied that it would be the DOD, the same division the Mullen Co. was fronting for. While Shaw was probably not working specifically in a front like the Mullen Co., it is clear that his CIA connections were more than that of a simple DCS contact. In the words of William Davy, "One could logically conclude that, at the time this memo was issued (early 1967), Shaw was an active covert operative of the CIA."[53]

What was Shaw doing for DOD? There is a possibility that the International Trade Mart itself was being utilized by the Agency for intelligence gathering. Let us look at the individuals working for the New Orleans ITM. For three years in the 1950s, a man called David Baldwin served as public relations director of the Trade Mart. Baldwin was a CIA operative who served in India using the North American Newspaper Alliance as a front.[54] After Shaw's arrest in 1967, Baldwin wrote him

[Shaw] a letter stating, "With my own CIA connections, I may be seeing you sooner than you think. I would be delighted to tell Garrison what an idiot I think he is."[55] Shaw's boss at the ITM, Lloyd Cobb, was given access to a Cleared Attorney's Panel for the CIA's Office of General Counsel in 1967, and had earlier had a Covert Security Clearance for utilization on an OGC Private Attorney's Panel. In March of 1969, CIA propaganda-guru David Atlee Phillips sought to use both Cobb and Paul Fabry, Managing Director of the ITM's sister organization, the International House, for some kind of propaganda broadcasts.[56] Another International House figure with CIA connections was attorney William Martin, who became Director of International Relations and World Trade at the IH in the early 60s. Martin had begun providing information to the CIA the year before, and during his time at the IH in 1964-65, Martin became a formal source. Martin was granted a "security status of ad hoc through Secret, dated 9 November 1964, and an NI (a)–Approved, 7 January 1965, Office of Security file no. 388412." The files also indicate that the CIA "always held him in high regard," and that Martin's CIA contact ended when he left the International House.[57] Shaw associate Dr. Alton Ochsner was president of the International House and, CIA records reveal, "was a cleared source (Approved Caution) since 13 May 1955," although Dr. Ochsner ceased to be a CIA source during the 1962-63 timeframe.[58] Ochsner did, however, fund a pet project of CIA agent William Gaudet called the Latin American Reports, ostensibly "a survey of political and economic conditions in Latin American countries." Gaudet's newsletter was co-funded by the Agency as published out of a nearly rent-free office in Clay Shaw's International Trade Mart.[59] Finally, we should note that the New Orleans States-Item quoted CIA asset Gordon Novel as speculating that Shaw may have used the ITM to gather intelligence on foreign trade for the Agency.[60] Indeed, it seems we should be surprised if Shaw had worked in the ITM and not performed some kind of intelligence work.

Shaw's intelligence credentials were even more extensive. It has already been shown that Shaw provided free space in the ITM for certain anti-Castro groups (see Chapter 6). One of Shaw's close associates was Bay of Pigs -vet Alberto Fowler who later became Director of International Relations for the City of New Orleans and worked out of an office in the Trade Mart. Fowler reported to the New Orleans DCS office in April 1967 that "Shaw, who is reported to have been in intelligence work in World War II in the Army, is now quite calm and assured because he, Shaw, feels that high-ranking Government officials are involved and will see that no harm comes to him."[61] This turned out to be the case, as we saw in earlier chapters.

Another incident sheds light on Shaw's possible CIA work and why the CIA records showing no connection after 1956 might be lying. Leslie Norman Bradley was a soldier-of-fortune who, along with Loran Hall (who we will return to shortly), John Wilson Hudson and others, attempted to stage an incident in Nicaragua to falsely implicate Castro in international aggression. The Cuban G-2 Intelligence outfit foiled the plan and Bradley and Hall were both' arrested and imprisoned before being released after Castro confidante Camillo Cienfuegos interceded on their behalf.[62] A May 1967 CIA memo states that Bradley "was briefly considered for employment as a co-pilot in Project ZR/CLIFF and filled out a personal information form, but the offer of employment was cancelled."[63] But then Bradley went to work as a pilot for a CIA proprietary airline called Southern Air Transport, according to two CIA memos from January 1968, one of which was written by David Atlee Phillips.[64] The ZR/CLIFF project remained classified until 2000, when it was revealed that ZR/CLIFF *was* Southern Air Transport.[65] So internal CIA memos cannot always be trusted.

While working on ZR/CLIFF at a Houston airport, Bradley resumed contact with an acquaintance named Sam Kauffroth.[66] Kauffroth reported Bradley's activities to the Houston FBI office in 1966 and said:

I asked him [Bradley] how he had been making a living since being released from the Cuban prison and he replied that it was pretty rough but that Clay Shaw of the International House was "helping us." He never did clarify who "us" were, but I assumed that he meant the released prisoners. I distinctly recall that I was impressed with the philanthropic activities of this prominent citizen who took the time and trouble to assist these victims of Castro. There was no further discussion on the manner in which Mr. Shaw was helping.[67]

The FBI's information indicates the possibility that, either wittingly or unwittingly, Shaw was providing some kind of assistance to ZR/CLIFF. (It is interesting to note that while flying a Douglas 553 for South Central Airlines, David Ferrie would periodically keep his plane at the ZR/CLIFF facilities in Houston.)

In addition to the ZR/CLIFF allegations, there is other evidence that CIA personnel files may be deceptive. A CIA Counterintelligence Officer, John Whitten, was interviewed by the HSCA about the Mexico City incident and revealed several facts relevant to the Garrison case. HSCA counsel Michael Goldsmith asked Whitten, "An agent is not somebody who you would consider to be a CIA employee?" "That is right," Whitten replied. "He is in a contractual relationship of some kind. This is a myth, of course, because there is not any contract, really, but there is an agreement."[68]

Goldsmith then acknowledged an intriguing fact while beginning a question to Mr. Whitten:

Goldsmith: We recently introduced an employee who, as I mentioned earlier today, indicated that looking at his records, every indication on that record would be that he had retired from the Agency in the mid-50's when actually he had been with the Agency throughout and had continued one way or the other, whether it was to be paid by the Agency or by the State Department, he was still working for the Agency. There was no record of his Agency connection at Langley.[69]

Whitten indicated that another branch of the Agency might have a file on Goldsmith's agent, but Goldsmith asked another question.

> *Goldsmith: So that it is possible that the personnel file would be purged in some manner, or would be written up in a manner to indicate that he was no longer with the Agency?*
>
> *Whitten: Sure. Very probably yes.*[70]

In the words of William Davy, "Those expecting to see a paper trail back to Langley for the likes of Banister, Ferrie and possibly Oswald are deluding themselves."[71]

Clay Shaw had quite the vested interest in seeing Castro out of power. Apparently, Shaw had a business connection to a company based in New York called Freeport Sulphur. This company planned to mine nickel and cobalt in Cuba and ship the minerals to a refinery near New Orleans. Production on this refinery, due to employ an estimated 600 men, stopped before it could start when Castro stepped into Havana in 1959.[72] Freeport Sulphur had already invested $44 million in the refinery project. During the Garrison probe, however, the NODA would develop evidence that showed Shaw and Freeport Executive Charles A. Wight attempted to salvage the operation by routing the ore through Canada, which had no trade restrictions with Cuba.[73]

First, a Texan named James Plaine told Assistant DA Andrew Sciambra "he had been contacted by a MR. WHITE of Freeport Sulphur in regards to a possible assassination plan for Fidel Castro." Plaine also recalled overhearing either Shaw or David Ferrie discussing nickel mines in Cuba.[74] This connection was corroborated by Jules Ricco Kimble, a witness stereotypically deemed unreliable, who told the NODA that "White" had flown with Shaw and Ferrie to Cuba for some kind of nickel deal.[75] In 1967, New Orleans police detective Sal Scalia had interviewed former newscaster Ken Elliot, who said "that Shaw and two other persons either purchased or attempted to purchase a nickel ore plant in Braithwaite,

Louisiana after the company had closed because of the broken trade relations with Cuba. At this time, David Ferrie flew Shaw and his two part-
ners to Canada in an attempt to receive ore from Cuba through
Canada."[76] Oddly, both Dean Andrews and newsman Richard Townley
told investigators for Shaw's defense team that Clay Shaw was alleged to
have an investment in a firm owned by David Ferrie. This likely erroneous
description may possibly refer to the Freeport Sulphur project.[77] Based on
this information, Garrison's office concluded that Freeport Sulphur, Shaw
and Charles A. Wight, the man mistakenly called "White" by Garrison's
sources, were trying to buy the Braithwaite plant to refine ore shipped to
Louisiana via a Canadian dummy corporation.[78]

Shaw's connections to the anti-Castro cause go further. Banister agent
Joe Newbrough told William Davy in 1995 that Shaw was familiar to
Banister's operation at 544 Camp Street. Secondhand information from
New Orleans States-Item reporter Jack Dempsey seems to confirm
Newbrough's recollection.[79] Another Banister operative, Tommy Baumler,
told Bernard Fensterwald and J. Gary Shaw in 1981 that Banister and
Shaw were "close."[80] And a recently released CIA memo reveals Clay Shaw
and his ITM associate Mario Bermudez may have traveled to Cuba
together in 1959 on a gunrunning operation.[81]

Garrison's contention that Shaw lied about not knowing David Ferrie
seems stronger than ever. New Orleans journalist David Chandler had
been a longtime Garrison supporter prior to the assassination probe.
Chandler was the best man at Garrison's wedding, and described Garrison
in a November 1966 *New Orleans* magazine article as "an incorruptible
crusader for justice. Which (blush) he is. He really is."[82] Chandler's
friendship with Clay Shaw, however, drove a wedge between him and
Garrison and caused him to assist Richard Billings in a *Life* article critical
of the investigation.[83] By 1992, however, Chandler was willing to admit
that he had "always found Garrison to be honest, a man of integrity with
a deep concern for individual rights."[84] In 1999, the late Chandler's son
revealed to researchers William Davy and James DiEugenio a secret his

father had kept for over thirty years. According to Chandler, Shaw admitted that he *had* known Ferrie and that he was lying about it to avoid "tossing Garrison too big a bone."[85] In recent years a similar bombshell was laid on the research community by former HSCA Deputy Chief Counsel Robert Tanenbaum, who disclosed to the ARRB that his investigators had located photographs depicting Shaw with Ferrie and Oswald.[86] Tanenbaum's recollection was confirmed to the author by HSCA photographic consultant Robert Groden.[87]

Tanenbaum had other intriguing information to offer about New Orleans. Garrison stated in *A Heritage of Stone* that David Ferrie had reportedly frequented the CIA-funded Cuban exile training camp on land owned by Bill McLaney near Lake Pontchartrain. According to an interview Tanenbaum gave to *Probe* magazine, the HSCA located a film of activities at this training camp. In the film were Guy Banister, David Atlee Phillips and Lee Harvey Oswald.[88] Both Groden[89] and HSCA investigator L.J. Delsa confirm that the film existed.[90] The footage was shocking to Tanenbaum:

> *The movie was shocking to me because it demonstrated the notion that the CIA was training, in America, a separate army. It was shocking to me because I'm a true believer in the system and yet there are notorious characters in the system, who are being funded by the system, who are absolutely un-American! And who knows what they would do, eventually. What if we send people to Washington who they can't deal with? Out comes their secret army? So, I find that to be as contrary to the constitution as you can get.*[91]

Considering all the evidence, it is no wonder the HSCA's New Orleans investigative team concluded, "We have reason to believe that Shaw was heavily involved in the anti-Castro efforts in New Orleans in the 1960's and possibly one of the high level planners or "cut out" to the planners of the assassination."[92]

The Federal Effort to Stop Garrison

Testifying before the Assassination Records Review Board in 1996, JFK autopsy pathologist Dr. J.T. Boswell opened up a can of worms and began to expose the full extent of the Clark Justice Department's efforts to stop the Garrison probe.

Q. Very early on in your deposition today, you made reference to Mr. Eardley from the Justice Department asking you to go to New Orleans; is that correct?

A. Mm-hmmm.

Q. What did he say to you about the reason he wanted you to go to New Orleans?

A. He was really upset. He says, "J, we got to get somebody in New Orleans quick. Pierre is testifying and he's really lousing everything up." And I called Jim to see if he didn't want to go, and he was having—his mother-in-law was ill, and he couldn't go. So they put me on a plane that day and took me to New Orleans, and that was one of the most interesting adventures in my life. I met—do you want to hear all of this?

Q. Yes, please.

A. Carl Eardley sent me to a hotel, and I went into the hotel and registered. I was already registered. I got up to my room, and there was a note on my bedside telling me to meet somebody at a certain place at a certain time. And this was a scary place. This was down around the wharfs, and the federal attorney's office was in a big warehouse down there. And that's—I met somebody on the street. He took me in there, and they told me what was going on. They showed me the transcript of Pierre's testimony for the past couple of days, and I spent all night reviewing that testimony....I spent two days down there and then came home, never appeared in court. And the government won their case.

Q. Actually, the government was the district attorney. So, my next question for you actually was: What was the United States Department of Justice doing in relationship to a case between the district attorney of New Orleans and a resident of New Orleans?

A. Well, they—I went over and met somebody, some lawyer in another firm that night, and I don't know who he was representing. But, obviously, the federal attorney was on the side of Clay Shaw against the district attorney....

Q. What did the government attorney say to you? Did he help prepare potential testimony for you?

A. They were getting ready to. I guess it all depended on what Pierre did that next day or something.[93]

The defense team was looking for something to undo Assistant DA Alvin Oser's devastating cross-examination of Dr. Finck, and the DOJ turned to Dr. Boswell. But for one reason or another—likely because a clinical pathologist like Dr. Boswell questioning the testimony of a forensic pathologist like Dr. Finck in a murder case would be absurd—Boswell never testified.

In 2001, Dr. Gary Aguilar discovered a 1969 memo by Dr. Finck proving that Finck's own testimony had itself been arranged by the Justice Department. Dr. Finck had been contacted on February 16, 1969 by defense counsel Edward Wegmann who wanted Finck to testify. Dr. Finck was then taken to the office of Deputy Assistant Attorney General Carl Eardley to review documents concerning the autopsy. Eardley gave Finck a check for his expenses and a Washington D.C. court order for Finck to testify in New Orleans. Prior to testifying, Dr. Finck met with Shaw's defense counsel and received a call from the Assistant U.S. Attorney in

New Orleans to who offered his help.[94] Finck's testimony, of course, turned out to be a disaster.

We saw in Chapter Four how attorney Stephen Plotkin was being paid to represent Gordon Novel via a CIA cutout, and in Chapter Seven how the CIA had passed along information to the Shaw defense team recommending they contact William Gurvich, if they had not already done so. It is worth noting that on three occasions the CIA's Richard Lansdale received packages of documents from Herbert Miller, the CIA lawyer representing journalist Walter Sheridan.[95]

As William Davy showed in his landmark book, *Let Justice Be Done*, James Jesus Angleton's Counterintelligence Office compiled a dossier on the Shaw trial jury and gave it to the Agency's Security Division.[96] (Angleton also spied on expert witness Dr. John Nichols.) It has long been suspected but never proven that the concerted campaign by the CIA and the media to undermine Garrison's investigation may have been aimed at prejudicing the jury pool.

Earlier this year, the author discovered at the National Archives a 1968 memo from Harold Weisberg to Jim Garrison describing a meeting at the home of informant Barbara Reid. Present was Tommy Baumler, a former agent of Guy Banister. Weisberg recalled, "He [Baumler] says that whatever happens, the Shaw case will end without punishment for him because federal power will see to that. This, he says, will also be the destinies of Andrews, Thornley, if he is convicted, and any others, and he is unconcerned about the import, entirely without indignation about injustice and the failure of justice."[97]

Weisberg said Baumler continued, "describing the activities of a man he said had to be CIA and engaged in what he wanted me to understand was a major propaganda campaign, designed to influence public opinion here, *including that of jurors* and about you [Garrison] personally."[98] [My emphasis.] Baumler indicated that if the Agency could put 500 similar men on the street throughout the country, it would destroy the investigation.[99]

Loran Eugene Hall

One major problem for the Warren Commission was the testimony of Silvia Odio, the Cuban woman in Dallas visited by a man she identified as Lee Harvey Oswald, along with two Cubans going by the war names "Leopoldo" and "Angelo" or "Angel." But the timeframe of the visit was troubling—it put Oswald in Dallas when he should have been just about to leave New Orleans or already on the way to Mexico City.[100] FBI Director J. Edgar Hoover laid the matter to rest for the Commission by offering up Loran Eugene Hall, who said he had visited Odio in Dallas along with two associates, including one who looked like Oswald. Thus the Warren Report explained the incident as a mere case of mistaken identity.[101] But when Hall's friends told the FBI they had never met Odio, Hall took back his claim. The FBI belatedly informed the Commission, who neglected to publish the retraction in their volumes of evidence.[102]

Though Hall later claimed he had never told the FBI he had visited Odio, the HSCA nevertheless called his story "an admitted fabrication."[103] Hall also popped up during Garrison's investigation, leading the probe nowhere.[104] But what did Hall have to do with the assassination? What were his motives?

Hall had been arrested near Key Largo, Florida on September 2, 1963 for violations of the Neutrality Act. Two days later, after being released from custody, he flew to Los Angeles, California and met Cuban exiles Lawrence Howard and Celio Castro there on September 11.[105] A week later Hall retrieved a 30-06 Johnson semi-automatic rifle with a variable powered scope from a P.I. and soldier-of-fortune named Dick Hathcock. Hall, along with Gerry Patrick Hemming, had borrowed $100 from Hathcock and left the rifle, along with some golf clubs, with Hathcock as a security. On September 18, 1963, Hall paid Hathcock $50 and took back the rifle.[106] Hathcock's associate Roy Payne was later quoted as saying the weapon, if properly sighted, "would put a hole in a dime at 500 yards." Hall told Hathcock he was going to Dallas.[107]

Hall, along with Lawrence Howard and Celio Castro, arrived in Dallas on September 28, 1963 with a trailer full of arms and medicine, which they left in Dallas before getting on a bus for Miami on October 4. Hall returned to Dallas, with William Seymour, on October 12. They were about to go back to Florida with the weapons and medicine when they were arrested for drug possession on October 17. The pair finally managed to leave two days later for the Florida Keys.[108]

Loran Hall was again arrested, this time for illegal possession of arms, on October 31. Tired of his constant trouble with the authorities, Hall went back to Los Angeles ten days later.[109] He had with him the Johnson 30-06.[110] During an interview by Dick Russell in 1976, Gerry Patrick Hemming said that Hall had been in Dallas on the day of the assassination. "Yes, on the day of the assassination, I made a call from Miami to Texas," Hemming said. "And I pointedly asked, 'Is Lorenzo Hall in Dallas?' I made the call about 1:30 p.m. or 2:00 p.m. He was there. My contact had seen him in Dallas the day before."[111]

Apparently, Jim Garrison himself had developed evidence that Hall had left Los Angeles for Dallas prior to the assassination.[112] For his part, Hall claimed Hemming had been responsible for his arrest in Dallas in October 1963 on drug charges. "I was being set up for the Kennedy killing. Not as a conspirator or a patsy, but as a smoke screen. My arrest was for the records. To show that Loran Hall was in Dallas just before the President was killed."[113] But under questioning by HSCA Deputy Chief Counsel Robert Tanenbaum, Hall was evasive.

> *Tanenbaum: Mister Hall, were you in Dallas, Texas on November 22, 1963?*
>
> *Hall: I respectfully and regretfully invoke my rights under the Fifth Amendment under the Constitution to refuse to answer the question on the grounds that it may intend to incriminate me.*[114]

"As it stands right now," Hall told an interviewer after his questioning by the Committee, "there's only two of us left alive—that's me and Santo Trafficante. And as far as I'm concerned we're both going to stay alive—because I ain't gonna say shit."[115] The reader will recall that Trafficante had been a key Mob figure in the CIA-Mafia assassination plots against Castro. All this information gains monumental importance when one considers that documents recently released by the ARRB reveal that a 30-06 semi-automatic Johnson rifle identical to the one described by Dick Hathcock was found in Dealey Plaza shortly after the shooting.[116]

Thomas Beckham

Thomas E. Beckham had come up during the Garrison investigation, in connection with a man called Fred Lee Crisman and the Old Catholic Church of North America that David Ferrie and Jack Martin had been involved in. Beckham had been called to testify before the Grand Jury, and refused. Garrison went to court to have him extradited from Nebraska. On January 30, 1968, the extradition was granted and Beckham went to Louisiana. The next month, Beckham appeared in court, along with three gun-toting men acting as "bodyguards," to request a delay in his testimony. The request was granted until February 15. A few days before that, Beckham announced to the media that he was seeking election to a congressional seat in Nebraska. Finally, Beckham testified before the Grand Jury where he spent some six hours making various wild accusations (i.e. that he was being framed by Garrison and Martin). Having contributed nothing to Garrison's investigation, Beckham was cut loose.[116]

When HSCA investigators L.J. Delsa and Bob Buras began looking for Beckham in 1977 he was on trial in Mississippi for a minor charge on which he was acquitted. The resulting minor publicity of the trial made him easy to find. Having been located, Beckham proceeded to tell Delsa and Buras a much larger story than he told Garrison. In 2000, Delsa recounted to the author his first impression of Beckham:

*He was an interesting boy. He was a young kid that...there was a crew around in New Orleans that certain people used as...back during that era, it was the new era of James Bond, you know, the spy things were really intriguing to him and **they were using him**. This kid Beckham was a really intelligent guy.*[118] *[My emphasis.]*

Beckham said he had been involved in an organization that, in 1962-63, was involved in the raising of funds for anti-Castro activities via what Garrison biographer Joan Mellen would call an "odd church," registered under the Old Orthodox Catholic Church of North America.[119] Beckham's claim is confirmed by FBI records of that era.[120] According to Beckham, it was during this time that he and F. Lee Crisman became involved in a plot to assassinate President Kennedy. Beckham described a meeting in Algiers, Louisiana attended by David Ferrie, Sergio Arcacha Smith, G. Wray Gill, Vincent Marcello, Anna Burglass, a man named Charlie Morello and Clay Shaw, where the details of the assassination were plotted. Beckham said the motive for the crime was "the Cuban issue."[121] Beckham was given a package to deliver to the aforementioned Lawrence Howard at the Executive Inn in Dallas, and he did so—approximately two weeks before the assassination.[122]

Beckham also disclosed his association with F. Lee Crisman, who Beckham described as a CIA agent involved in Beckham's anti-Castro "Organization" who helped Beckham deflect Garrison's investigation away from "the Organization." [Ibid.] The only documentary evidence, however, that Crisman had something to do with the Agency is a document known as the "Easy Papers." The "Easy Papers" purport to be a history of Crisman's intelligence work compile from the CIA's "Central Records Dispatch, Davenport, Iowa." They were apparently given anonymously to researcher Mae Brussel, and their veracity is highly questionable.[123] Oddly enough, Crisman was once believed by some researchers to have been one of the three "tramps" arrested by Dallas police in Dealey Plaza in the aftermath of the assassination. Even Garrison subscribed to this view at one point.[124] Forensic anthropologists working for the HSCA examined photos of the "tramps," comparing them with photos of individuals believed to have possibly been the "tramps," and found that Crisman's face was consistent with one of the "tramps."[125] However, at the time of the assassination Crisman had been employed teaching high school in Rainier, Oregon. The HSCA obtained affidavits from three teachers, Marva Haris, Norma Chase, and Stanley Perloom, who testified that Crisman had been teaching school on November 22, 1963.[126]

At the outset Buras and Delsa found Beckham's story convincing, so they had him subjected to a polygraph exam that he passed with flying colors.[127] When Chief Counsel G. Robert Blakey learned this, he went mad and destroyed the New Orleans investigative team, informally suspending Buras and Delsa while removing Jonathan Blackmer completely. New people—even some from the MLK side of the investigation—who were not familiar with the Kennedy case were brought in.[128] Several researchers have expressed doubts in Beckham's credibility despite the results of the polygraph exam. Pro-Garrison researcher William Davy described Beckham's story as "mushy." Gus Russo interviewed Beckham prior to his death and didn't believe him either. Dave Reitzes has attacked Beckham's credibility, saying:

> [In my opinion], his only connection to the case is what Garrison would have called propinquity—he hung out with Jack Martin, who introduced him to Guy Banister and (one occasion, in G. Wray Gill's office) to Dave Ferrie, and he ran a few errands for Banister. Oh, and he knew Fred Lee Crisman, who was named in an anonymous letter to Big Jim as a CIA agent and friend of Clay Shaw's, neither allegation being true.[129]

Indeed, several of Beckham's claims are verifiable falsehoods. For instance, in his interview with L.J. Delsa, Beckham said he had spoken to Oswald in New Orleans *after* Oswald returned from Mexico City. We know Oswald did not return to New Orleans after Mexico City—he stayed in Texas.[130] All things considered, documentary researcher Larry Hancock has offered what is probably the best explanation to date of Beckham's role in the assassination:

> *He knew some key people in New Orleans. He was on the periphery of the conspiracy that set up Oswald and knows who was playing with him. He was paid to be a disinformation agent and take a heavy risk to block investigation of the right trail—paid by people who did give him enough information to make it good disinformation. Beckham could name the names that would solve a good part of this case but they would be the names of the folks who used him and not too much more I think. There is of course a wild possibility that he did indeed serve as a courier carrying maps and instructions to Dallas. I could almost believe that part, which would make a great lock on him and enable blackmailing him into being a potential sacrifice to the HSCA.*[131]

Obviously Thomas E. Beckham was a lead that the HSCA should have explored more fully—a lead that goes right back to the very same cast of characters in New Orleans that Jim Garrison looked into in 1967.

The Plotters

With all the information available in the new files about the assassination, it is now possible to make an educated guess at who might have been responsible for the plot to kill Kennedy. Not to identify the shooter, or some of the conspirators involved—the man who masterminded the crime of the century. The evidence is circumstantial, but the author believes a good case can be made that the man behind the murder of President John F. Kennedy was James Jesus Angleton.

It was Angleton's CIA Counterintelligence Staff that were responsible for the Mexico City deception, specifically the elite CI/SIG (Counterintelligence Special Investigations Unit) which was made up of only four to five people, including Birch D. O'Neal, Newton "Scotty"

Miler, and Ann Egerter who opened Oswald's 201 File in the first place.[132] But why did CI/SIG open a 201 file on Oswald?

The HSCA's Michael Goldsmith queried Angleton associate Raymond Rocca on this point:

> *I would imagine that they would have had that occasion whenever a question arose that concerned people that came within the purview of the mission that I have described, namely, the penetration of our operations or the advancement of our particular interests with respect to the security of those operations.... I mean, there were many sensitive areas that involved aspects, that involved sources and access to materials that were of higher classification than what you have shown me.*[133]

When Goldsmith asked Rocca about Oswald specifically, Rocca's answer was highly suggestive:

> *Rocca: Let me go back and open a little parenthesis about this. What I regard now, in the light of what you said, is probably a too narrow view of what SIG was interested in. They were also concerned with Americans as a security threat in a community-wide sense, and they dealt with FBI cases, with the Office of Security cases, and with other cases on the same level, as they dealt with our own, basically.... It would be with respect to where and what had happened to DDP materials with respect to a defection in any of these places.*
>
> *Goldsmith: Again, though, Oswald had nothing to do with the DDP at this time, at least apparently.*
>
> *Rocca: I'm not saying that. You said it.*[134]

Goldsmith also questioned Ann Egerter, the CI/SIG official who opened Oswald's 201 file. Once again, the answers are suggestive of an actual intelligence relationship between Oswald and the CIA:

Goldsmith: So, one purpose would be for CI/SIG to work with the Office of Security in investigating Agency employees who were under suspicion, possibly for becoming agents of the other side, is that right?

Egerter: Yes.

Goldsmith: What would be another purpose?

Egerter: I think that was the main purpose of the office. We were charged with the investigation of Agency personnel who were suspected one way or another.[135]

Goldsmith continued, surely realizing the importance of what Egerter was saying:

Goldsmith: Please correct me if I am wrong. In light of the example that you have given and the statements that you have made it seem that the purpose of CI/SIG was very limited and that limited purpose was being to investigate Agency employees who for some reason were under suspicion.

Egerter: That is correct.[136]

But why would CI/SIG open a 201 file on someone?

Egerter: Well, the 201 file is opened very generally on people on whom there are several documents. Inasmuch as any time there were several documents on an individual, why that person would have been of interest to whatever office opened the 201 file.

...

Goldsmith: When a 201 file is opened does that mean that whoever opens the file has either an intelligence interest in the individual, or, if not an intelligence interest, he thinks that the individual may present a counterintelligence risk?

Egerter: Well, in general, I would say that would be correct.[137]

So far, Egerter seems to be saying that the Agency *must* have had some kind of operational intelligence interest in Oswald. Goldsmith gave her one further chance to equivocate:

Goldsmith: Would there be any other reason for opening up a file?

Egerter: No, I can't think of one.[138]

Clearly, one capable of masterminding the assassination using Agency resources would have to be capable of hiding it. Angleton was one of the few men who could have done this, due to his influence of the CIA's Staff D, the unit that monitored the intelligence output of the super-secret National Security Agency. Angleton was the man who approved who got clearances to work in Staff D, and who did not.[139] According to David Wise, "D was the perfect cranny in which to tuck a particularly nasty piece of business like ZR/RIFLE," William Harvey's Executive Action project.[140] Harvey's own notes on the project include the following:

"Never mention word 'assassination'"

"no projects on paper."

"strictly person-to-person, singleton ops."

"planning should include provisions for blaming Sovs or Czechs in case of blow."

"no chain of connections permitting blackmail"

"Should have phony 201 in RG [Central Registry] to backstop this, all documents therein forged and backdated."

"Should look like a CE [counterespionage/counterintelligence] file."

[Executive action would] "require most professional, proven operationally competent, ruthless, stable, CE-experienced ops officers."

"[talk to] Jim A"[141]

One person who worked on Staff D, Anne Goodpasture, was one of the authors of the misleading CIA cable that went out to the FBI describing Oswald as a 35-year-old with a receding hairline. Goodpasture was close with Bill Harvey and David Atlee Phillips, who has appeared numerous times in the assassination saga—from New Orleans to Dallas to Mexico City.[142] It is interesting to note that CIA projects under cryptonyms beginning with the letters "ZR" were run from Staff D. We saw earlier how David Ferrie and possibly Clay Shaw had utilized or supported the resources of the ZR/CLIFF project.[143]

Suspiciously, Angleton would go on to promote the theory of a Soviet conspiracy endlessly after the assassination. John Whitten, a CIA officer in Mexico City, was assigned by Richard Helms to write a report on Oswald's movements leading up to the assassination. Whitten encountered vehement opposition from Angleton in writing his report, which rejected the idea of a Soviet plot. Whitten's report was submitted to Angleton on December 13, 1963, but Whitten was unaware that only three days before Raymond Rocca had received a report based on an early draft of Whitten's from an unknown author that departed severely from Whitten's conclusions. The Rocca memo contained the said that "while it is unlikely that Oswald's contacts with the Soviet Embassy had a more sinister purpose, *it cannot be excluded.*"[144] [My emphasis.] The Rocca memo also included a paragraph found nowhere in Whitten's report alleging that Gustav Vlahov, the Yugoslav Ambassador to Mexico, had foreknowledge of the assassination.[145]

Angleton would later try to embarrass Whitten in front of Helms in retaliation for the report. As Whitten recalled to the HSCA,

> *Whereupon Helms—Angleton started to criticize my report terribly— without pointing out any inaccuracies, it was so full of wrong things, we could not possibly send it to the Bureau, and I just sat there and I did not say a word. This was a typical Angleton performance. I had*

*invited him to comment on the report and he had withheld all of his
comments until he got to the meeting whereupon Helms turned the
operation, the investigation, over to Angleton's staff.*[146]

Angleton's attack on Whitten would be repeated on a larger scale and
with horrific results when KGB defector Yuri Nosenko said in 1964 that
the KGB had had no interest whatsoever in Oswald.[147] As payment for
telling the truth about Oswald, Angleton, now supported by Helms,
placed Nosenko in solitary confinement in the basement of a CIA building where he was held and interrogated for more than three years. During
his interrogation, Nosenko had several of his teeth knocked out.[148]
Nosenko was also not allowed to brush his teeth for two years and lost several more to decay. Add to this Nosenko's starvation and drugging at CIA
hands, and it was miracle that Nosenko survived at all—let alone stuck to
his story.[149]

Before Nosenko was given a polygraph test he was drugged with a substance he believed was LSD. Immediately prior to the polygraph, Nosenko
was subject to a rectal exam in which a CIA doctor inserted a finger in
Nosenko's anus for some ten minutes. Nosenko believed the purpose of
the exercise was to arouse him sexually and traumatize his system in order
to throw off the results of the polygraph. The polygraph examiner was
intentionally antagonistic, calling Nosenko a "liar" and a "homosexual." It
is no wonder Nosenko failed the test.[150] Despite Angleton's tactics, the
imprisonment of Nosenko was a divisive, controversial subject within the
Agency. Helms finally ordered a non-threatening interrogation of
Nosenko, which was followed up with another polygraph exam minus the
Nazi-esque tactics. Nosenko passed and was at last freed.[151] In recognition
of his suffering, the CIA bought Nosenko a house in North Carolina, got
him American citizenship and provided him with a $30,000 annual
allowance in return for his silence.[152]

As we saw earlier, it was Angleton's Counterintelligence office that
spied on Garrison witness Dr. John Nichols and compiled a dossier on the

Shaw trial jurors (the only conceivable purpose of which would be to facilitate jury tampering). In his HSCA deposition, John Whitten revealed that CI was keeping track of Garrison's investigation:

> *Mr. Goldsmith: Once Angleton and his staff took over the investigation, did you have any involvement at all?*
>
> *Mr. Whitten: From time to time Ray Rocca would call me up and I would go down and see them and we would discuss certain aspects of the case. **Particularly when Garrison, in New Orleans, started his fandango.** Rocca could not believe that there had not been any information in the initial reports about Clay Shaw and all of the other oddballs whom Garrison dragged in the case.*
>
> *Mr. Goldsmith: To your knowledge, did the CIA monitor closely the Garrison investigation of the Kennedy assassination?*
>
> *Mr. Whitten: **Rocca paid attention to it.***
>
> ...
>
> *Mr. Goldsmith: Did he [Rocca] ever indicate to you that the Agency might have been infiltrating the Garrison investigation?*
>
> *Mr. Whitten: No. If he had known it, **he would not have told me.**[153]* [My emphasis.]

But times change, and by 1974, so had the Agency. William Colby was now DCI and knew that it was time for Angleton's reign of terror to come to an end. That December, Colby admitted to journalist Seymour Hersh that Angleton's CI unit had conducted illegal domestic operations (an admission that would help lead to the Rockefeller Commission and Church Committee investigations), then fired Angleton, along with CI gurus Ray Rocca, Newton Miler and other Angletonites.[154] Angleton then took the offensive, threatening blackmail. In a statement recorded by the *New York Times*, Angleton said cryptically, "A mansion has many rooms…I'm not privy to Who Struck John." During a deposition in the case of Hunt v. Liberty Lobby, Angleton tried to explain. "It had nothing, the 'John' does not refer to John F. Kennedy," he said. No one asked if it did.[155]

An anti-Semitic newspaper called *The Spotlight* ran an irresponsible story by former Helms aide Victor Marchetti in 1978. The article described a 1966 Angleton memo to Helms explaining that the Agency needed to come up with a story to explain the presence of E. Howard Hunt in Dallas on November 22, 1963, and claimed that the CIA would attempt a "limited hangout" by hanging Hunt out to dry for his involvement in the assassination. This never happened, and Hunt successfully sued the Liberty Lobby, publishers of *The Spotlight*, for defamation. *Spotlight* owner Willis Carto asked Mark Lane to take the case, and the pair successfully appealed for a new trial. The trial became the subject of Lane's best-selling book *Plausible Denial*. Lane defended the Liberty Lobby by making the case that Hunt *had* been involved in the assassination. Lane did manage to convince the jury who found for his client that at the very least Marchetti's article did not represent actual malice against Hunt. And while Lane managed to impeach Hunt and the majority of Hunt's witnesses in cross-examination, Lane's own case was built on the weak foundation of perjurer Marita Lorenz.[156]

One important piece of evidence did come from Lane's show-trial: the memo described by Marchetti was real. Lane has a real problem since Marchetti did not see the memo himself—his sources were William Corson and the infamous "garbologist" A.J. Weberman.[157] Lane salvaged Liberty Lobby's case by locating a CNN journalist named Joseph Trento who in 1978 had written an article for the *Sunday News Journal* describing the exact same memo. Not only that, but Trento had *seen* the memo with his own eyes![158] At the time, Trento would not reveal who had showed him the memo but after the trial in Hunt v. Liberty Lobby and several years after Angleton's death, Trento admitted that his source had been Angleton himself.[159] Trento had been having lunch with Angleton (the pair had been friends for several years) at the Army-Navy Club when Angleton had asked, "Did you know Howard Hunt was in Dallas on the day of the assassination?" Angleton made arrangements for Trento to see the document and—again pushing the Soviet plot theory—that he believed Hunt had been sent to Dallas by a Soviet mole in the Agency. Trento said Angleton had the memo given both to him and the HSCA by Howard Baker. Trento didn't buy Angleton's story, however, as he would later tell author Dick Russell:

> *I later came to conclude that the mole-sent-Hunt idea was, to use his phrase, disinformation; that Angleton was trying to protect his own connections to Hunt's being in Dallas…. My guess is, it was Angleton himself who sent Hunt to Dallas because he didn't want to use anybody from his own shop. Hunt was still considered a hand-holder for the Cuban exiles, sort of Helms' unbroken pet.*[160]

Consider also the testimony of Richard Helms himself in the case of Hunt v. Liberty Lobby. Helms was asked if it was possible that Angleton could have arranged the Kennedy assassination without the knowledge of his superiors in the Agency. Helms replied, "I don't believe it is likely that Mr. Angleton (a) would have wanted to assassinate President Kennedy, or (b) that he would have taken off from the agency and done this without anybody's being aware of it." In the words of Mark Lane, "Ringing denials were absent that day."[161]

Epilogue

Unanswered Questions

Was Clay Shaw guilty? This is an odd question to be posing in a book defending Garrison's case, but it is nevertheless one worth asking. Certainly Perry Russo was telling the truth as he knew it, but it was only the truth *as he knew it*. Let us examine some of the things Russo must have gotten wrong.

First of all, was Lee Harvey Oswald really the "Leon Oswald" Russo saw at Ferrie's apartment? The answer appears to be no. Russo only identified Oswald as "Leon Oswald" after whiskers were drawn on the Oswald photo. Was Oswald ever as unkempt as Russo remembered? From an interview with Oswald's landlady Jessie Garner:

> *Q. I'm going to read a description given by Perry Russo of a man that he saw in the apartment of David Ferrie. He described this man as having a bushy beard, being cruddy—very, very dirty. In your opinion, could that description have fit the Lee Harvey Oswald that you knew?*
>
> *A. I don't see how that would fit him, because I've never seen him like that.*

Ruth Paine was asked the same question.

> *When I came to New Orleans, about September 20th, he was clean-shaven then, and I never saw him with a beard. I don't believe he had one, to my knowledge. I think Marina would have mentioned it. And he was also neat when he dressed, and clean, it seemed to me. I just feel that Mr. Russo must have seen someone else that he thinks was Lee Oswald.*

On February 24, 1967, Russo had been interviewed by Jim Kemp of
WDSU-TV:

> *Q: Did he ever mention Lee Harvey Oswald's name?*
>
> *A: No.*
>
> *Q: No conversation at all about —*
>
> *A: No. I had never heard of Oswald until the television of the assassination.*

Russo explained his comments at the Clay Shaw preliminary hearing:

> *Q. Did you recognize the alleged assassin as the man whom you had known?*
>
> *A. I gave it thought and said it was possibly the man, and I said I am not sure at that time, and then I got involved with other things.*

So Russo was not really sure "Leon" Oswald and Lee Harvey Oswald
were the same man. Niles "Lefty" Peterson also remembered "Leon"
Oswald at Ferrie's party. But from his description of the roommate on the
June 1967 NBC special, we can see that he is not describing Lee Harvey
Oswald:

> *Q. Describe his height, his general build, and...*
>
> *A. He's about 6 or 6'1", about 170 pounds, I'd say. 165, 170 pounds.*
>
> *Q. Was he quite a bit taller than you?*
>
> *A. Oh, yeah, he was taller than me, yeah.*
>
> *Q. How tall are you?*
>
> *A. 5'9".*

Q. So how much taller than you would he have been?

A. About two or three inches.

Lee Harvey Oswald was 5 feet, nine inches-the same height as Peterson. Ferrie's friend Layton Martens offered a clue as to who "Leon" Oswald may have actually been.

Q. There has been testimony recently about a roommate of Ferrie's who was unkempt or wore a beard. Do any of the people you knew and who knew Ferrie fit this description?

A. James Lewallen could possibly fit that description very well. I remember at that time Lewallen did have some sort of beard, and I wouldn't necessarily call him unkempt, but to some people this might represent being unkempt. But one of the things I've noticed, remembering Lewallen, he bears a striking resemblance to this mock picture of Oswald [sketched by the NODA at Perry Russo's direction].

Q. Could he have been considered a roommate of Ferrie's?

A. Yes, he could have, possibly, I think he and Ferrie did room together sometime maybe prior to that, maybe around that time.

Q. Did you know anyone at the time associated with Ferrie by the name of Leon?

A. Well, Jim Lewallen's last name, sometimes people would address him as, "Hey, Lou," "Lee," or something like that.

And what about Clay Shaw? Russo's certainty as to his identification of Shaw as the man at the party went through phases as the period after Shaw's arrest wore on, but Shaw is the only man we know to be Clay Bertrand. In all likelihood, he *was* there at Ferrie's apartment. But did Shaw, Ferrie and Oswald/Lewallen's discussion amount to conspiracy? Going back to Russo's testimony at the Shaw trial, we find:

Q: As a matter of fact, Mr. Russo, isn't it a fact that you did not really take this seriously what you heard up there on Louisiana Avenue Parkway?

A: Initially you could not believe Ferrie and you could not believe him, from the first encounter I had with him he was just prone to the spectacular.

Q: I see. Did this not have all the characteristics of a bull session that you had related?

A: Every characteristic of it.

Q: It did?

A: Yes.

. . .

Q: Did anyone there swear you to secrecy or threaten to do anything to you if you should tell about this meeting?

A: No.

Q: Never did. And actually, Mr. Russo, you left the premises that night not knowing whether it was just a bull session or what it was. Is that correct?

A: Right.

But the contents of this bull session are eerily reminiscent of what actually happened—Ferrie in Hammond, Shaw in San Francisco and his bizarre behavior in front of J. Monroe Sullivan. Shaw's reluctance to tell the truth about his involvement with Ferrie, Oswald and the Cuban exiles does not have to be sinister. In fact, it would be quite logical for a community figure, especially a homosexual one, to hide his participation in the New Orleans underworld and the CIA's secret ops against Castro's

Cuba. Can we ever be certain if Shaw was guilty or not? It is this uncertainty that has led numerous reputable researchers such as Martin Shackelford and Larry Hancock to simultaneously acquit Garrison's investigation *and* Shaw. Indeed, it seems that the jury's verdict may have been the correct one historically and probably the only choice legally.

In the words of Louisiana historian Michael L. Kurtz:

> *Assuming one believes the witnesses that Garrison brought forth, I think you could make the case that Clay Shaw knew Lee Harvey Oswald, David Ferrie, knew each other—maybe drove around together in a black limousine. To jump from there to saying that there was an actual plot to assassinate John F. Kennedy that Clay Shaw was a part of is carrying, to me, a question of guilt by association to its extreme degree.*

The best possible case Garrison could make was Shaw as an accessory after the fact. There is simply not enough evidence to warrant the conspiracy allegation, which Garrison would likely never have made had it not been for the untimely death of David Ferrie. But as time went on, the stakes grew, and Jim Garrison did not want to be made to look like a fool. If he ever had doubts about Shaw he never acknowledged them, and furthermore never considered backing down.

Was Garrison guilty? And what of Jim Garrison? I have stressed repeatedly throughout this book that he was not perfect, but what did he get wrong? There are unsubstantiated allegations (detailed in Patricia Lambert's False Witness) that Garrison molested a young boy at the New Orleans Athletic Club. Like many researchers, I believe in the existence of the allegation, which was made anonymously. I will not, however, vouch for its accuracy nor do I feel that Garrison's personal life—criminal or otherwise—is relevant to the study of the assassination. Perhaps Joan Mellen's upcoming biography of Garrison well shed more light on this incident. Garrison, as we saw in Chapter Seven, never violated the rights of his defendants by discussing their cases in the media. But Garrison did not restrain himself from discussing the assassination. In Chapter Four we saw how Garrison made a fool out of himself and his probe on a number of occasions. Journalist William Turner described one of these incidents in his 2001 book *Rearview Mirror*:

> *Although the media ganged up on Garrison, it must be said that he fed them lunch through his lack of understanding of their appetite.... One of his first encounters with the fourth estate was a disaster. After working all night on the case, he was accosted by a gaggle of reporters demanding to know what progress he was making, to which he replied, "No comment." On the elevator going down, one reporter persisted, "When are the arrests going to be made?" Garrison had previously stated that everyone implicated would eventually be arrested, but that event might be a long way off. Fearful that the reporter had misinterpreted his confidence that the case would in time be solved, he reiterated, "Of course there will be arrests." The reporter escalated the question by asking, "You mean you've solved the case?" "Of course. We solved it weeks ago in the essentials," Garrison shot back defensively. As it came out in the local newspapers, there was an old photo of the DA grinning with the caption, "CASE SOLVED SAYS GARRISON." The story was flashed over the wires to the rest of the world."*

Garrison's off and on again publicity stunts did much to hurt the probe's reputation and lend substance to the charges against it.

Another of Garrison's malfeasances was the use of non-credible witnesses like Vernon Bundy and Charles Spiesel to make his argument. Later, in his book On the Trail of the Assassins, Garrison used Richard Case Nagell to bolster his case against Shaw. Researcher Dave Reitzes makes a good case for Nagell's mental illness in his article "Truth or Dare." (Available on-line at http://www.jfkassassination.net/nagell1.htm) Garrison often lost track of his focus as well, going off on investigative tangents and sometimes making only a half-hearted effort to prove Shaw's guilt. Richard Billings recorded the following in March 1967:

> *The following day Acoca and I paid a visit to the Criminal Courts Building, where we had a talk with Alcock. A word on Alcock: here is an assistant district attorney who must present the case to the jury in September against Shaw. Now, Alcock is a level-headed guy, he believes in the case, he's loyal to Garrison, but he admits that all the evidence he's got comes from Perry Raymond Russo. There is nothing else to support a case against Shaw, and he knows it, and he says it, privately. He says that he would not be embarrassed to go before a jury, but he damn well wishes that Garrison would get off the numbers game and would stop flailing at the CIA and would get down to cases, but he admits and knows, and though he almost reveres this boss of his for, I suppose, ambitious reasons, he says Garrison knows little and cares less about the law. Well, we've known that for some time. Anyway, we discussed with Alcock ways of trying to pin down the evidence, making it clear to him that if he could do that, we would rather write a story about the case and not become so damned concerned about Garrison's misbehavior.*

By not focusing and by not making his best possible case against Clay Shaw, it could be argued, Garrison violated Shaw's rights to a full and fair prosecution. At the very least, he didn't try as hard as he should have.

How then do we reconcile these gray areas? Perhaps we should stop trying. An accurate understanding of the Kennedy assassination requires more than waxing eloquent over the nature of the conspiracy, the political forces involved and the misapplication of propinquity (something Garrison was quite guilty of from time to time). John Kennedy was not murdered by forces, powers, principalities, or nebulous groups liked "the Military-Industrial Complex" or "the Power-Elite." He was killed by specific individuals. It was not a "conspiracy of one" or a "conspiracy of many"—it was a conspiracy of a finite number.

James Jesus Angleton is dead. So is Kerry W. Thornley. Neither, if they were guilty, will receive any kind of Earthly justice. The assassination, especially since September 11, is now a historical event (albeit one in living memory). For the truth to be accepted the assassination *must* be looked at as a historical event, not a philosophical discussion. If the critical community can elevate the dialogue to that level, one day another name (perhaps Angleton) will replace that of Oswald in historical consciousness.

> *The American people have suffered two tragedies. In addition to the assassination of the President by dishonorable men, our national integrity is now being assassinated by honorable men. It does not matter what the rationale is—whether to calm the public or protect our image—the fact remains that the truth is being concealed.*

Those were the words of Jim Garrison. Since November 22, 1963, the faith of Americans in their government has been irrevocably eroded. This cynicism is entirely justified—after all, the president is dead and the Warren Commission lied. Presidents from Johnson on through Clinton have continued to lie, be it about Watergate, Vietnam or the conflict in Kosovo. But what is the price of this cynicism?

Politicians continue, and will continue, to philander because they have been allowed to. And a large segment of the population now questions all claims and actions of the federal government, whether that suspicion is justified or not.

Thankfully this regrettable trend is beginning to reverse itself. In the aftermath of the War on Terrorism, and the Bush administration's restoration of integrity to the White House, pollsters are finding for the first time since the mid-60s that people are beginning to trust government once more. More than 38 years after it happened, we can now begin to consider the assassination a historical event rather than an unsolved crime.

The price of our post-assassination cynicism was a loss of perspective. The crimes of the elite, from Watergate to Iran-Contra and beyond, reinforced a vague idea of the helplessness of the average American. But we are not helpless. This country is still a country of the people, by the people, and for the people—as long as we have the courage to get out and vote and say what we believe.

That unique period of pessimism that pervaded American from November 22, 1963 to September 11, 2001 is over, forever consigned to the ages. America's self-doubt grew because there was no War on Conspiracies to right the wrongs wrought by the snipers in Dealey Plaza. The Commission ignored the evidence, Garrison was stopped in his tracks and the House Select Committee was watered down by bureaucracy. When the smoke cleared from the attacks on the World Trade Center and the Pentagon, America rose from the ashes. President Bush summoned forth our armed forces and we were ready to wage war—however long, however costly it might be—against al-Qaeda and the forces of evil. And by December 2001, the Taliban had followed facism, Nazism and totalitarianism straight to "history's unmarked grave of discarded lies," just as President Bush promised on September 20. Al-Qaeda is not far behind.

Just imagine what it would have been for the country if the conspirators had received indictments as swiftly as the terrorists received cluster bombs?

As the period following the assassination passes into history, the assassination itself is passing from a question of resolution to a question of understanding. What factors contributed to the social, political and spiritual downturn that came with Kennedy's murder? And why?

The more we understand this period of history, the more we understand Jim Garrison. Garrison was no saint; yet, we find that that fact is unconnected to the strength or weaknesses of his case against Clay Shaw or Kerry Thornley (Does Mark Furhman being a racist make O.J. less guilty?). Garrison made his mistakes. He was human. He made far fewer than either the Warren Commission or the House Select Committee, yet he was subject to far more scrutiny. Garrison wrote a self-serving memoir. Students of military history know he is not alone—nearly every Civil War commander that wrote a book wrote a vain, subjective one. In the end, Garrison should be remembered as a patriotic prosecutor trying to do his duty as best he saw it. It is high time we stop cross-examining Garrison's good name, and start taking a serious look at the evidence.

The American Republic cannot wait.

About the Author

Joe G. Biles' work on the assassination includes a half-dozen published articles, a website and a successful monograph, *The Arrogance of Ignorance: A New Look at the JFK Cover-Up*. *In History's Shadow* is his first full-length book. Biles' work on the Garrison investigation and his record of community service earned him the JFK Lancer Student of the Year Award in 2001.

Born near Burnet, Texas, Joe grew up in Mineral Wells where he graduated Mineral Wells High School in 2002 as president of the senior class. In his spare time, Biles enjoys music, soccer and reading. He is currently an undergraduate student at Texas Tech University where he is working toward a Bachelor's Degree in History and a military commission from the Air Force ROTC program.

Biles is a cadet lieutenant colonel in the Civil Air Patrol (U.S. Air Force Auxiliary) where he currently serves as cadet commander of Lubbock Composite Squadron, as well as Cadet Programs Advisor for Texas Wing Group 1, an area spanning the entire Texas panhandle. Biles holds the coveted Gen. Ira C. Eaker Award and is a graduate of Cadet Officer School at Maxwell AFB, Alabama.

Joe's next project is an untitled work on the Afghan Civil War, circa 1996-2001.

Appendix A
Warren Commission Exhibit 92, an essay by Lee Harvey Oswald

The lives of Russian workers is governed, first and foremost, by the "collective," the smallest unit of authority in any given factory, plant, or enterprise. Sectional and shop cells form a highly organized and well supported political organization. These shop committees are in turn governed by the shop and section party chiefs who are directed by the factory or plant party secretary. This post carries officially the same amount of authority as the production director or president of the plant, but in reality it is the controlling organ of all activities at any industrial enterprise, whether political, industrial, or otherwise personal relations. The party secretary is responsible for political indoctrination of the workers, the discipline of members of the Communist party working at the plant, and the general conduct and appearance of all members.

The Minsk Radio and Television plant is known throughout the Union as a major producer of electronics parts and sets. In this vast enterprise created in the early 50's, the party secretary is a 6'4" man in his early 40's—has a long history of service to the party. He controls the activities of the 1,000 communist party members here and otherwise supervises the activities of the other 5,000 people employed at this major enterprise in Minsk, the capital of the 3rd ranking Republic Belorussia.

This factory manufactures 87,000 large and powerful radio and 60,000 television sets in various sizes and ranges, excluding pocket radios, which are not mass produced anywhere in the U.S.S.R. It is this plant which manufactured several console model combination radio phonograph television sets which were shown as mass produced items of commerce before several hundreds of thousands of Americans at the Soviet Exposition in New York in 1959. After the Exhibition these sets were duly shipped back to Minsk and are now stored in a special storage room on the first floor of the Administrative Building—at this factory, ready for the next international Exhibit.

I worked for 23 months at this plant, a fine example of average and even slightly better than average working conditions. The plant covers an area of 25 acres in a district one block north of the main thoroughfare and only two miles from the center of the City with all facilities and systems for the mass production of radios and televisions; it employees 5,000 full time and 300 part time workers, 58% women and girls. This factory employs 2,000 soldiers in three of the five mainshops, mostly these shops are fitted with conveyor belts in long rows, on either side of which sit the long line of bustling women.

500 people, during the day shift, are employed on the huge stamp and pressing machines; here sheet metal is turned into metal frames and cabinets for televisions and radios.

Another 500 people are employed in an adjoining building for the cutting and finishing of rough wood into fine polished cabinets. A laborer's process, mostly done by hand, the cutting, trimming, and the processes right up to hand polishing are carried out here at the same plant. The plant also has its own stamp making plant, employing 150 people at or assisting at 80 heavy machine lathes and grinders. The noise in this shop is almost deafening as metal grinds against metal and steel saws cut through iron ingots at the rate of an inch a minute. The floor is covered with oil used to drain the heat of metal being worked so one has to watch one's footing; here the workers' hands are as black as the floor and seem to be eternally. The foremen here looks like the Russian version of "John Henry," tall and as strong as an ox. He isn't frilly, but he gets the work out.

The plant has its electric shop, where those who have finished long courses in electronics work over generators, television tubes, testing experiment of all kinds. The green work tables are filled high here. Electric gadgets are not too reliable, mostly due to the poor quality of wires, which keep burning out under the impact of the usual 220V____ voltage. In the U.S. it is 110V.

The plastics department is next. Here 47 women and three physically disabled persons keep the red hot liquid plastic flowing into a store of odd presses, turning out their quota of knobs, handles, non-conducting tube bases, and so forth. These workers suffer the worst condition of work in the plant, an otherwise model factory, for the Soviet Union, due to bad fumes and the hotness of the materials. These workers are awarded 30 days vacation a year, the maximum for workers. Automation is now employed at a fairly large number of factories, especially the war industry. However, for civilian use, their number is still small.

At this plant at least one worker is employed in the often crude task of turning out finished, acceptable items. Often, one worker must finish the task of taking the edge of metal off plastic and shaving them on a foot driver lathe. There is only so much potentiality in presses and stamps, no matter what their size.

The lack of unemployment in the Soviet Union may be explained by one of 2 things. Lack of automation and a Bureaucratic corps of 16 workers in any given factory. These people are occupied with the tons of paperwork which flow in and out of any factory. Also the number of direct foremen is not small to the ratio of workers in some case 1-10, in others 1-5, depending on the importance of the work.

These people are also backed by a small array of examiners, committees and supply checkers and the quality control board. These people number (without foremen) almost 300 people, total working force 5,000—3-50 without foreman.

To delve deep into the lives of the workers, we shall visit most of the shops one after another and get to know the people. The largest shop employs 500 people; 85% women and girls; females make up 60% of the work force at this plant.

Here girls solder and screw the chassis to the frame attaching, transistors, tubes and so forth. They each have quotas depending upon what kind of work they are engaged in. One girl may solder 5 transistors in four minutes while the next girl solders 15 wire leads in 13 minutes. The pay scales here vary but slightly with average pay at 80 rubles without deductions. Deductions include 7 rubles, general tax, 2.50 rubles for bachelors and unmarried girls and any deductions for poor or careless work the inspectors may care to make further down the line. They start teams of two mostly boys of 17 or 18, turning the televisions on the conveyor belts right side up, from where there has been soldering to a position where they place picture tubes onto the supports. These boys receive for a 39 hour week, 65-70 rubles, not counting deductions. Further on, others are filling tubes and parts around the picture tube itself, all along the line there are testing apparatus with operators hurriedly affix shape type testing currents, and withdrawing the snaps that fitting out a testers card, pass the equipment back on the conveyor, speed here is essential.

The Communist party secretary here, as in most shops, has promised to increase production by 2% in honor of the coming end of the third year of the current 7 year plan. Now the televisions are carried around the convey to go back down the line where others sit to complete the process, the smoke from the careful soldering doesn't keep the girls from chattering away and that, coupled with the boys at the end of the line, testing the loudspeakers, makes for a noisy but lively place, with the laughter of girls mixing with music and occasional jazz programs, which the testers favor for purely personal reasons until the foreman looks his way.

As we go out we see crates of the finished product with the well known, "made in Belorussia," stamp.

One of the most interesting things in observing Russian life and conventions, is the personal relationship to each other; there exists a disciplined comradeship springing from the knowledge that in Soviet Society the fundamental group is the "Kollective" or intershop group. These groups with the shop or section party chiefs and foremen, are the worlds in which the Russian workers live. All activities and conduct of members is dependent upon the will of the "Kollective."

In the shop where I worked, the experimental shop, of the Minsk Radio and Television factory, there were 58 workers, including the party shop secretary, who is a Communist worker assigned into the shop by the factory Party Secretary, the Master Foreman, assigned by the Shop production head who is assigned in turn by the Director of the Factory.

The key person in the shop, as every one appreciates, is Comrade Lebizen, 45 years old, the party-secretary. His background is that after serving his alloted time in the Young Communist League before the war, he became a member in good standing of the Communist Party of the Soviet Union CPSU. During the war, he was for a short time, a tankest, but his talents seemed to have been too good for that job so he was made a military policeman, after the war, starting at this newly built factory. He was appointed by the factory Communist party chief, as shop secretary, responsible for shop discipline, party meetings, distribution of propaganda, and any other odd "jobs" that might come up, including, seeing to it that there always enough red and white signs and slogans hanging on the walls. Lebizen holds the title (besides Communist) of "Shock worker of Communist Labor," this movement was started under Stalin a decade ago, in order to get the most out of the extreme patriotism driven into Soviet children at an early age. Indeed, Lebizen is a skilled mechanic and metal worker and for his work he receives 130-140 rubles– month minus deductions. This shop party secretary, together with the section party chief, usually selects workers for the title "shock worker of Communist Labor." These people are not necessarily Communist party members, although it helps in the same way party membership helps in any facet of life in the U.S.S.R.

Factory meetings of the "Kollectives" are so numerous as to be staggering.

Take for instance during one month the following meetings and lectures are scheduled: 1 prof. Union; which discusses the work of the prof. union in collecting dues, paying out receipts on vacations orders, etc. (pg 24), political information (4) every Tuesday on the lunch hour, Young Communist Meetings (2) on the 6th and 21st of every month, production commitees (1) made up of workers, discussing ways of improving work, Communist party meeting (2) a month called by the section Communist party sec.; the school of Communist labor meeting (4) compulsory) every Wednesday, and sport meeting, 1 a month, non-compulsory, a total of 15 meetings a month, 14 of which are compulsory for Communist party members and 12 compulsory for all others. These meetings are always held after work or on the lunch hour. They are never held on working time. Absenteeism is by no means allowed. After long years of hard discipline, especially under the Stalin regime, no worker will invite the sure disciplinary action of the party men and inevitably the factory party committee because of trying to slip out of the way or giving too little attention to what is being said.

A strange sight indeed is the picture of the local party man delivering a political sermon to a group of usually robust simple working men who through some strange process have been turned to stone. Turned to stone all except the hard faced Communists with roving eyes looking for any bonus-making catch of inattentiveness on the part of any worker; a sad sight to anyone not used to it, but the Russians are philosophical. "Who likes the lecture?" "Nobody, but it's compulsory." Compulsory attendance at factory meetings isn't the only way to form spontaneous demonstrations and meetings. The "great October revolution" demonstrations, the May day demonstrations are all formed in the same way. As well as spontaneous meetings for distinguished guests. The well organized party men mark off the names of hundreds of workers approved to arrive at a certain place at a given time. No choice, however small, is left to the discretion of the individual.

Part II The Experimental Shop

For a good cross section of the Russian working class, I suggest we examine the lives of some of the 58 workers and 5 foremen working in the experimental shop of the Minsk radio plant. This place is located in the midst of the great thriving plant which produces some of the best known radios and TV's in the Soviet Union.

The shop itself is located in a two story building with no particular noticeable mark on its red brick face. At 8:00 sharp, all the workers have arrived and at the sound of a bell sounded by the duty orderly, who is a worker whose duty it is to see to it that the workers do not slip out for too many smokes, they file upstairs, except fot 10 turners and lath operators whose machines are located on the first floor. Work here is given out in the form of blueprints and drawings by the foreman Zemof and Jr. foreman Lavcook, to workers whose various reliability and skill calls for them, since each worker has with time acquired differing skills and knowledge. Work is given stricty according to so-called "pay levels", the levels being numbered 1-5 and the highest level "master". For level one (1) a worker receives approximately 68 rubles for work, level (2) a worker receives 79.50, for three, 90 rubles, for four, 105 rubles, for 5, 125 rubles, and for masters about 150. These levels of pay vary slightly because workers receive a basic pay of, for 1st level 45 rubles and bonuses bringing the total to 68 rubles, including reductions for taxes, the basic pay of a master is 90 rubles. Except in instances for poor quality work, bonuses are always the same, giving use to a more or less definite pay scale. A worker may demand to be tested for a higher pay level at any time. Only skill is "a barrier" to higher pay. The foreman and shop head all receive about 120 rubles basic pay but much higher bonuses are awarded to the best shops by the factory committee for good production standards.

Our shop head Shephen Tarasavich Velchok is a stout, open faced, and well skilled metal worker who, although he hasn't got a higher education, which is now a prime requisition for even a foreman's job, he managed to finish a 4 year night school specialty course and through the help of the director of the factory, Mr. Ukayvich, became shop head in an important segment of this large plant, employing 5,000 people. Shephen has an almost bald head except for a line of hair on the left side of his head, which he is forever combing across his shiny top. Aged 45, he is married with two children aged 8 and 10. It may be explained that the Russians seem to marry much older than their American counterparts, perhaps that can be explained by the fact that in order to receive an apartment, people often must wait for 5 or 6 years and since security is so unstable, until a commonly desired goal is reached, that is an apartment for oneself, most Russians do not choose to start families until later in life. Shephen is responsible to the factory committee and director for the filling of quotas and production quantity. His foreman Zemof is 38 years old, has a wife and 15 month old baby, not too long ago moved out of his one room flat without kitchen or private toilet, into a newly built apartment house and flat of two small rooms, kitchen and bath, a luxury not felt by most Russians. A tall thin man with dark creases in his face, his manner, nervous, spontaneous and direct, betrays his calling. His job, keep the working on the premises going as quickly and efficiently as possible. His Assistant, Jr. Foreman Lavcook, is much younger, ten year younger, enigmatic, handsome, quick, he climbed to his post through a night school degree and a sort of rough charm, which he instinctively uses in the presence of superiors. The shop's mainstay is composed of 17 so-called "Shock workers" whose pictures hang on a wall near the stairs so that all might strive to imitate them.

Usually of the 5 level or master class of workers, they are experienced at work and politics.

Most shock workers are men of the older aged groups, 40-50, not always members of the communist party, they carry the production load and most of the responsibility of the interlife of the "Kollective".

The remaining 41 workers are divided about half into 18-22 year olds, now metal workers, trying to fulfill their obligatory two years at a factory, before going on to full time day studies at a local University, or one of the specialized institutes, and older workers who have been working at the plant for 4-6 years and occupy the middle number worker levels, 3, 4,; these workers are aged about 24-30 and form the mass of laborers at the factory. 70% have families, apartments are few, most occupy rooms belonging to relatives or rooms let to rent by holders of two or three room apartments, often for as high as 20 rubles a month, although rent in the Soviet Union is paid by the square meter and 3, 15 meter rooms with kitchen and bath cost about 32 rubles a month. The housing shortage is so critical that people count themselves lucky to even find a person willing to let his room, room renting also is the most common form of speculation in the USSR. Often it reaches heights all out of proportion with reality, such as the man who derived 60 rubles a month from letting his room in the summer while he himself was living in a summer house or "Dacha," in the country. Such speculation is forbidden and carries penalties, including deportation to other economic areas of the USSR for terms of up to 6 months. Still these are the most common instances. Most workers in Minsk come from peasant stock, which repopulated the city at the end of the 2nd WORLD WAR. Like most Russians they are warm hearted and simple but also stubborn and untrustworthy.

The life of the "Kollective" or rather inter-life, since it often touches upon more than just the work, is the most reflective side ot the complex working of the Communist party of the USSR. It is the reflection of mass and organized political activity, deciding the actions of every individual and group, placing upon society a course, so strict, so disciplined, that any private deviation is interpreted as politcal deviation and the enforced course of action over the years has become the most comprehensible educational and moral training probably in the history of the world.

To understand the work and workings of the "Kollective" one must first ask who controls, who leads the "Kollective". The answer to that is a long one; all plants and factories in the Soviet Union have party committees, headed by one graduate of a higher party schools whose function is to control discipline members of the Communist party, and who, working in conjunction with the directors of the factory, controls all factors pertaining to the work, alterations, and production of any given line. It must be noted that officially the party men occuppies a position exactly equal to the head of any factory; however the facts point out that he has, due to the fact that Communist hold the leading positions in plants, considerable more sway over the activities of the workers than anyone else. No suggestion of the party man is ever turned down by the directors of our factory, that would be president to treason. The party man is appointed by the H.Q of the central committee of the Communist Party and in turn the party man designates who shall be shop and section party secretaries, a post well coveted by employed Communists. These Communists in reality control every move of "Kollectives." They are responsible for the carrying out of directives pertaining to meetings, lectures, and party activities in the local cells.

These meetings or "Sabranias" are almost always held at the lunch hour or after working hours. The number of meetings of a strictly political nature is not small, considering that on an average 8 meetings are held a week and of these you have "young Communist, party communist meeting," "political information" and the "school of Communist labor." These are every week and are compulsory for all workers. Also monthly meetings, include "Production meeting," "General trade Union," "Shop Committee," and "Sport Meeting," none of these are compulsory. The numbers of meetings held a month average 20. 50% of these are political or by-political meetings. Meetings last anywhere from 10 minutes to two hours; usually the length of "Political information meetings" held every Tuesday is 15 minutes. An amazing thing in watching these political lectures is that there is taken on by the listeners, a most phenomenal nature, one impervious to outside interference or sounds. After long years of hard fisted discipline, no worker allows himself to be trapped and called out for inattentiveness by the ever present and watchful party secretary and members of the Communist party. This is mostly seen in political information of Central Committee party directive readings. At these times it is best to curb one's natural boisterous and lively nature. Under the 6' by 6' picture of Lenin, founder of the Soviet State, the party section secretary stands. In our section a middle aged poched man by the name of Sobakin, an average looking man wearing glasses, his wrinkled face and twinkling eyes give one the impression that any moment he's going to tell a racy story or funny joke, but he never does. Behind this man stands 25 years of party life. His high post, relatively speaking for him, is witness to his efficiency. He stands expounding from notes in front of him, the week's "Information", with all the lack of enthusiasm and gusto of someone who knows that he has no worries about an audience or about someone getting up and going away.

Appendix B
NODA Affidavits of Witnesses Against Thornley

HSCA Record #: 180-10088-10486
AGENCY FILE #: 007271 [2 OF 6]

STATE OF LOUISIANA
PARISH OF ORLEANS

AFFIDAVIT

BEFORE ME, the undersigned authority, personally came and appeared:

BARBARA REID

who, after first being duly sworn, did depose and say:

I can remember walking into the Bourbon House one afternoon around 3:30 P.M. around the middle of September in the year 1963. I noticed Kerry Thornley sitting alone at one of the tables in the Bourbon House and I told him hello and sat down at the table next to him.

I can also recall that Peter Deageano was sitting at the table with me eating a hamburger. I struck up a casual conversation with Pete and Kerry. A short time later a person walked into the Bourbon House and joined Kerry Thornley at his table. I recall associating a sense of familiarity with this individual as the same individual who had received some publicity as a Communist because of his earlier activity of distributing Fair Play for Cuba leaflets in front of the International Trade Mart in New Orleans.

Also, I associated him as the person who was interviewed by Bill Stuckey of WDSU.

We engaged in casual conversation for a short period of time and then approximately ten to fifteen minutes later, I left the Bourbon House.

HSCA Record #: 180-10088-10485
AGENCY FILE #: 007271 [2 OF 6]

STATE OF LOUISIANA
PARISH OF ORLEANS

AFFIDAVIT

BEFORE ME, the undersigned authority, personally came and appeared

PETER DEAGEANO

who, after first being duly sworn, did depose and state:

I can remember being in the Bourbon House after the assassination of President Kennedy when a picture of Lee Harvey Oswald appeared on the television screen. As soon as I saw his picture on television I immediately recognized his face and remarked to someone that I had seen him before in the Bourbon House. The first thing I remember about him was that I saw him handing out leaflets on Canal Street some time before the assassination. I was coming back from a bid in connection with my job and I was walking on Canal Street and as I passed in front of McCrory's

Department Store in the 1000 Block of Canal Street, I saw him handing out leaflets in that vicinity. I recognized him as the same person that I had seen a few days earlier in the Bourbon House and I walked up to him to say hello and to see what he was doing. When he saw me he handed me one of his leaflets.

I looked at it and when I saw that it said something about helping Cuba, I just threw it down and walked off. I then remembered that I also saw him a few days before this incident in the Bourbon House. It was between 2:00 and 4:00 o'clock in the afternoon either in August or September of 1963. I was sitting at a table in the Bourbon House eating a hamburger. There weren't too many people in the Bourbon House and as I looked around I noticed Kerry Thornley, Jeanne Hack and him sitting at a table close to me. I looked at them and said hello and either Kerry Thornley or Jeanne Hack introduced him to me. I cannot remember how he was introduced or any of the conversation that we may have had as it was a very casual meeting. However, I remember thinking to myself that he might be related to Kerry Thornley as he resembled him quite a bit. I don't remember how long they stayed in the Bourbon House that afternoon, but they left together while I was still in there. After the assassination of President Kennedy a picture of Lee Harvey Oswald appeared on television and I immediately recognized him as being identical to the person I had seen handing out leaflets on Canal Street, and identical to the person that I saw sitting in the Bourbon House with Kerry Thornley and Jeanne Hack.

HSCA Record #: 1801007610180
AGENCY FILE #: 008269 [PT. 13]

MEMORANDUM
March 14, 1968
TO: JIM GARRISON, District Attorney

FROM: ANDY SCIAMBRA, Assistant District Attorney
RE: KERRY THORNLEY

On the night of March 12, 1968, Harold Weisberg and I interviewed BERNARD GOLDSMITH. GOLDSMITH repeated essentially what he had previously told Gary Sanders, however, upon further prodding by Weisberg and myself he made a few additional comments concerning THORNLEY. He repeated that THORNLEY was a right-winger and so set in his political beliefs that he, GOLDSMITH, and THORNLEY made an agreement not to talk politics. He says he can never remember THORNLEY mentioning BRINGUIER or KENT COURTNEY's name. He said that THORNLEY and LOVIN were friends (LOVIN told him that he was in the Bay of Pigs Invasion). GOLDSMITH said that he remembers being in the Bourbon House on the night after the assassination and THORNLEY remarking to him that he had known OSWALD in that OSWALD had lived on Exchange Place. THORNLEY also told him that OSWALD was not a communist. GOLDSMITH said that THORNLEY did not specify as to the time when he had known OSWALD but only stated that he had known OSWALD. GOLDSMITH does not recall him ever saying specifically that he knew OSWALD when OSWALD was in New Orleans.

GOLDSMITH also says that he vaguely remembers ROGER LOVIN telling him that he, LOVIN, was a roommate of OSWALD at one time and GOLDSMITH said that he seems to remember LOVIN saying this in connection with a conversation about LOVIN's Cuban activities.

GOLDSMITH also said that JOHN EFFERSON and TIM SOHR were friends of THORNLEY's. SOHR is presently serving time at Angola.

Barbara and I will make further attempts to talk to GOLDSMITH who may know some additional information.

Notes

A Note on Sources

I have adopted certain conventions when referring to commonly cited source materials. *WCR x* refers to page "x" of the Warren Commission Report (Washington, D.C: U.S. Government Printing Office, 1964). Likewise does *HSCR x* refer to the report of the U.S. House of Representatives Select Committee on Assassinations (Washington, D.C: U.S. Government Printing Office, 1979). 2 WCH 374 means page 374 of Volume II of the Warren Commission's hearings and exhibits. CE 399 is Commission Exhibit 399, in this case the "Magic Bullet" itself. WCD 347 is Warren Commission Document 347, a memo on Oswald's visit to Mexico City. The Commission Documents were classified and hence not published. The vast, vast majority have since been released and are held in the National Archives. 10 HSCA 321 refers to page 321 of Volume X of the House Select Committee's printed hearings and exhibits. Lastly, NODA means those documents held by the New Orleans District Attorneys Office and NARA is the National Archives and Records Administration.

As far as the sources cited, I have divided my text into two types of material. With text dealing with facts or subjects already adequately explored by other authors I generally cite from secondary sources (three excellent and commonly cited ones are William Davy's *Let Justice Be Done*, James DiEugenio's *Destiny Betrayed*, and Patricia Lambert's *False Witness*); with text examining new evidence and topics I refer to primary sources. Wherever possible I have included the notation "*NARA# xxxxxx*," giving the actual number the document is stored under in the National Archives so the interested reader can order the document themselves. For documents obtained from other researchers, it is sometimes not possible to give an NARA Record Information Form (RIF) number. Many of these documents are also available from the Assassination Archives and Research Center (AARC) in Washington, D.C, which can be reached at (202) 393-1917.

Preface

1. DiEugenio 128-129

2. A good example of this effect is the way the media treated the D.B. Thomas study of the JFK acoustics evidence earlier this year. For about a week, it was reported that the acoustics had been re-evaluated and that they reveal to a 96.3% certainty that there was a shot fired at the president from the Grassy Knoll. (Actually, they reveal that the odds of the acoustical impulses being mere random static are just 3.7%, but we're talking about the media here—not scientists.) After this news was no longer new, the media went right back to referring to Oswald as the lone assassin whenever mention of the murder came up.

Chapter One

1. Garrison 13

2. Ibid 13-14

3. Turner, William. "The Garrison Commission on the Assassination of President Kennedy," Ramparts, January 1968.

4. Davy 1

5. Ibid 279 n.1

6. 10 HSCA 130

7. FBI Document #89-69-169. The evidence of Oswald's 1963 association (it is no longer questioned that they had met in 1955 in the Civil Air Patrol) with David Ferrie is plentiful and well-documented. In addition to Garrison's witnesses, a young man named Van Burns saw Ferrie and Oswald together at the Pontchartrain Beach amusement park. Burns was introduced to the pair by a mutual friend, who told burns about Ferrie's involvement in "missions" to Cuba. (Kurtz *xxxix-xl*) Oswald and Ferrie

were frequently seen together in the Napoleon House where they would debate Kennedy's foreign policy with college students. They also traveled to Baton Rouge at one point where they virulently criticized Kennedy's policies. (Kurtz 203)

8. Ferrie's anti-Castro activities in James and Wardlaw 45; Oswald information from Scott 20.

9. Davy 2

10. Lambert 24

11. Ibid 29

12. Davy 2

13. Lambert 25. Martin would later resurrect certain parts of this story (that Ferrie had flown Oswald to Dallas) to the NODA in December, 1966. These were then recanted.

14. James and Wardlaw 48

15. DiEugenio 123. Information on the passports in Ferrie's apartment from James and Wardlaw 44.

16. FBI Interview of David Ferrie, 11/25/63. WCD 75.

17. Davy 48

18. Qtd. in Ibid.

19. Ibid 46

20. Ibid.

21. Ibid 46-47. Patricia Lambert claims Ferrie *did* skate that day, just to prove to Beaubouef that "he could do it," citing Rolland's testimony, Ferrie's FBI interview and a Beaubouef interview. Rolland did not see Ferrie put on skates, and Ferrie's FBI interview lacks the "he could do it" quote, leaving the Beaubouef interview as Lambert's source. Beaubouef would later show up claiming Garrison's men had tried to bribe him for perjured testimony and threatened his life, offering a forged transcript of a recording of the discussion to prove it. Beaubouef retracted his claim. See Chapter Five.

22. Garrison 11

23. 10 HSCA 123

24. Davy 37
25. Warren Commission Report (hereinafter cited as WCR) 23
26. Garrison 51
27. WCR 388-390
28. Garrison 51
29. 8 WCH 233
30. Ibid.
31. Ibid.
32. Ibid 233-235
33. Garrison 53
34. 11 WCH 83
35. Ibid 86

Chapter Two

1. Qtd. in Marrs 111
2. Marrs 103
3. 8 WCH 317. Lee Harvey Oswald's brother was named Robert Edward Lee Oswald. Ironically, the Dallas policeman Oswald allegedly murdered was Jefferson Davis Tippet.
4. Ibid 318
5. Ibid 266
6. Ibid 276
7. Ibid 285-286
8. Ibid 317
9. Ibid 318
10. Ibid 321
11. Ibid.
12. Qtd. in Marrs 110
13. 8 WCH 307
14. Garrison 25
15. 8 WCH 321
16. Qtd. in Scott 10

17. Garrison 25
18. 8 WCH 322
19. Ibid.
20. Ibid 322-323
21. Marrs 111

Chapter Three

1. Marrs 118
2. Ibid.
3. Ibid 119
4. Ibid.
5. Ibid.
6. Ibid.
7. Ibid.
8. Ibid 122-123
9. Qtd. in Weisberg 132
10. Marrs 124
11. alt.assassination.jfk post by Stuart Wexler, July 20, 2001.
12. Ibid.
13. alt.conspiracy.jfk post by Jim Hargrove, July 19, 2001.
14. 16 WCH 287-336
15. Marrs 200
16. Davy 200-201

Chapter Four

1. alt.assassination.jfk post by Matt Allison, January 19, 2001.
2. Garrison 26
3. Davy 37
4. Ibid 60. The DRE was created by the CIA under the codename AMSPELL.
5. Ibid 61
6. Ibid 58

7. Ibid 61

8. Ibid 40-41. Other witnesses to Oswald's presence at 544 Camp Street include Vernon Gerdes, Delphine Roberts, Dan Campbell, Allen Campbell, William Gaudet, Michael Kurtz and Carlos Quiroga. I do not mention them in the main text due to the fact that they never talked to Garrison. Salvatore Panzeca, a member of the Clay Shaw defense team, interviewed Gerdes in early 1967. He said that he had seen Ferrie, Oswald and Banister together in Banister's office. New Orleans Attorney Stephen Plotkin told Panzeca that Gerdes was "reliable." Delphine Roberts told the House Select Committee on Assassinations that Oswald had been one of Banister's agents and was "on familiar terms with Banister and with the office." Dan and Allen Campbell both recalled seeing Oswald in Banister's office, and when Allen mentioned Oswald's pro-Castro leafleting he was told by Banister, "Don't worry about him....He's with us, he's associated with the office." Both the Campbell brothers first came forward in interviews with Anthony Summers. Gaudet told Summers that, "I did see Oswald discussing various things with Banister at the time."

Perhaps the most compelling witness to an Oswald/Banister relationship is journalist Michael Kurtz. His testimony is not compelling in that he supports Garrison's assertions; rather, it is credible because he *doesn't*. Kurtz is quick to denounce both the Shaw prosecution and Stone's "JFK." He says that there is no question that Oswald knew both Banister and Ferrie, yet attaches no importance whatsoever to those facts. Kurtz was no friend of Garrison's and had no reason to lie to support him. Even Garrison critic Dave Reitzes finds him credible. In the May of 1963, Kurtz was a student at Louisiana State University, then the first fully integrated university in the country. It was during this month that an informal debate occurred on campus concerning the issue of civil rights. What was unusual about this debate was that one W. Guy Banister was one of the debaters! This really isn't all that unusual; Banister was known to have his investigators infiltrate left-wing groups on college campuses. On this occasion the aforementioned George Higginbotham, also a student at LSU, introduced Banister. Banister, however, had a guest—Lee Harvey Oswald. According to Kurtz, Banister even introduced Oswald to the group by name. In the course of the debate, Banister virulently criticized Kennedy for his failure to provide air cover for the exiled Cubans in the Bay of Pigs invasion. This was not Banister's last appearance at LSU; Kurtz says he saw him there several times by himself. Kurtz also says that George Higginbotham told him that Banister later returned with Oswald for another debate.

Later that summer, Kurtz worked for a newspaper in an office across the street from Banister's office at the Newman building. One day Kurtz went to Mancuso's (a restaurant on the bottom floor of the building) for coffee at lunch, and it was there that he saw—again—Oswald with Banister, this time having lunch. Banister reportedly recognized Kurtz from the LSU debate and waved. After the assassination, he called the FBI about Oswald and Banister only to be rebuffed. As we have seen, this pattern of official ignorance is sad but predictable. Dave Reitzes says of him, "I briefly talked to Kurtz twice by telephone in the fall of 1998, and I found him to personally seem very credible....[The] apparent inconsistencies in his story are superficial and easily explained." Kurtz, a professional historian, testified about what he saw, in addition to offering suggestions on avenues of evidence to explore, to the Assassination Records Review Board during the mid-1990s.

Carlos Quiroga actually denied that Oswald knew Banister and that Oswald was in fact part of an "anti-Castro operation," but failed an April 1967 polygraph test on these points.

9. Ibid 41

10. DiEugenio 131. Statements made by Jack Martin in January of 1967 indicate that Lewis was lying (see Lambert 54). Lewis did get cold feet after the truth about the supposed armed attack against him was exposed, and disappeared, meaning no one ever had the opportunity to cross-examine him on this point. I mention his accusation in the text because on its face it confirmed Garrison's suspicions about 544 Camp

Street, because Quiroga may have been involved judging from his poor polygraph performance (see note 8: Quiroga was also lying when he answered no to the question, "Prior to the assassination of the President, did you ever see any of the guns which were used in the assassination?"), and because Garrison later developed conspiratorial evidence against Arcacha Smith. See DiEugenio, James. "Rose Cheramie: How She Predicted the JFK Assassination." *Probe* v.6#5 (Jul./Aug. 1999).

11. Journal of *Life* editor Richard Billings (January 22, 1967).

12. 11 WCH 331-337. Oswald's presence in Andrews' office was confirmed by one of his employees, R.M. Davis. From a memo by FBI Agent Regis Kennedy: "He advised that he recalls OSWALD visiting ANDREWS' office and ANDREWS had mentioned to him that OSWALD was desirous of obtaining a hearing on his bad conduct discharge from the U.S. Marine Corps." See Weisberg 137.

13. Davy 191-192

14. Louisiana v. Clay Shaw, February 17, 1969.

15. FBI memo by Richard Bucaro, December 5, 1963. Contained in NARA# 1801003010064.

16. Lambert 297 n.31

17. Ibid 47

18. Garrison 95

19. Davy 63-64

20. Ibid.

21. Turner 179

22. Davy 90

23. Vea 6

24. Davy 64

25. Lambert 51

26. Ibid 52

27. Davy 21

28. Ibid 22-23

29. Ibid 25

30. Ibid. Mancuso described Novel as "a manipulator pretending to be a nice guy, but actually a man with a violent streak who always had to dominate everyone." Mancuso also said Novel had business dealings with Shaw. It was Mancuso and Ehlinger who informed the NODA of Novel's association with Dean Andrews and Shaw.

31. Ibid.

32. Ibid 284 n.15

33. Ibid 26

34. DiEugenio 135

35. Pease, Lisa. "James Jesus Angleton and the Kennedy Assassination, Part I." *Probe* v.7#5 (Jul./Aug. 2000).

36. Airtel from SAC, NO to DIRECTOR, FBI 2/23/67, FBI #62-106060-4741

37. DiEugenio 136

38. Legal theory on breaking a conspiracy in court dictates that the preferred method is to isolate one of the conspirators from the others and offer some kind of deal in exchange for testimony against his or her co-conspirators. Although there is no evidence Novel knew anything about the assassination, he could have been used in this fashion to prove Shaw and Ferrie were with the CIA.

39. Qtd. in DiEugenio 137-138

40. Ibid 135

41. Ibid.

42. Davy 145, 306 n.93

43. Ibid 65-66

44. Ibid.

45. Qtd. in DiEugenio 149

46. Davy 65-66

47. Memo from Sciambra and Ivon to Garrison, February 28, 1967.

48. Ibid.

49. Ibid.

50. Ibid.

51. Ibid.

52. Ibid.

53. Davy 66

54. Ibid.

55. Vea 7

56. Ibid.

57. Davy 66

58. Ferrie was born March 18, 1918.

59. Davy 67

60. Ibid.

61. Tyler video, *He Must Have Something.*

62. Vea 14

63. News story of Febuary 25, 1967. "Local Man Says He Recalls Remark by David Ferrie About Getting JFK," *Baton Rouge Morning Advocate.*

64. Ibid.

65. Davy 121

66. FBI memo from New Orleans office to Director, February 25, 1967.

67. Memo to Jim Garrison from Andrew J. Sciambra, RE: Interview With Perry Raymond Russo.

68. Ibid.

69. Ibid.

70. Davy 121

71. DiEugenio 144

72. Ibid.

73. Interview with Perry Raymond Russo at the Mercy Hospital on February 27, 1967.

74. DiEugenio 145

75. Davy 121

76. Memo to Jim Garrison from Andrew J. Sciambra, RE: Interview With Perry Raymond Russo.

77. Davy 121

78. The "Get Russo to New Orleans" order was described in the rebuttal argument of James Alcock, Louisiana v. Clay Shaw, February 28, 1969.

79. Garrison: DiEugenio 145-146, Chetta: Davy 176, also, journal of *Life* editor Richard Billings (March 2, 1967).

80. William Davy interview of Niles Peterson. Also, DiEugenio 144, citing Popkin, Richard H. "Garrison's Case." *New York Review of Books* (September 14, 1967).

81. Lambert 3-4

82. Ibid. The two other witnesses Sciambra mentioned were Niles "Lefty" Peterson and Sandra Moffett, two of Russo's friends who he said had accompanied him to the party at Ferrie's. Moffett originally agreed to testify and had been scheduled to go before the Grand Jury in April of 1967. She then had a change of heart, and fled to Iowa to avoid extradition. Peterson did not recall Shaw's presence at the party, but did remember a 'Leon' Oswald being there.

83. Davy 122-123

84. Garrison 175

85. James and Wardlaw 69-72

86. Ibid 76

87. Ibid 76-77

88. Ibid 79

89. James and Wardlaw 87

90. Ibid 88

91. Ibid.

92. Lambert 99-100

93. Ibid.

94. Ibid 101

95. Ibid.

96. James and Wardlaw 82

97. Lambert 95-102

Chapter Five

1. Memo from Harold Weisberg to Jim Garrison, April 9, 1968. NARA# 1801007610190.

2. Louisiana v. Clay Shaw, February 26, 1969. Sciambra recalled finishing the memo seven to ten days after starting it, therefore completing it around March 6-9. However, Phelan received his copy from Garrison *on* March 6, so Sciambra had to be mistaken. No one as ever claimed Sciambra finished the memo earlier. William Gurvich told Phelan, "This little son of a bitch, this [memo] was his little magnum opus...Man, he worked that memo over and polished it and repolished [Sic] it." This does not sound like Sciambra finished the memo on February 27. Regardless of the date, the import of the Lou Ivon affidavit is the same.

3. Qtd. in Weisberg 230-231

4. NODA Memo from Sciambra to Garrison, February 28, 1967.

5. Louisiana v. Clay Shaw, February 26, 1969.

6. Ibid.

7. Louisiana v. Clay Shaw, February 28, 1969.

8. Louisiana v. Clay Shaw, February 6, 1969.

9. Louisiana v. Clay Shaw, February 26, 1969.

10. Ibid.

11. Davy 122

12. Ibid 131

13. Ibid 131-132

14. Ibid.

15. Ibid 133

16. Ibid 134

17. Qtd. in Ibid 134-135

18. Ibid.

19. Ibid 136

20. Ibid.

21. Ibid 124

22. Qtd. in Ibid 125

23. DiEugenio 161. In addition, a friend of Shaw's named Nina Sulzer had threatened Bundy's life and told him he was "riding the wrong horse" and that he was "on a losing team." See Davy 125-126. All this is ironic, considering that Bundy probably actually was lying. See Chapters Four and Six.

24. NODA Affidavit of Fred Leemans, reprinted in *Probe* v.4#4 (May./Jun. 1997) p.10

25. DiEugenio 168

26. Lambert 120

27. DiEugenio 184

28. Ibid 185

29. Lambert 120-121

30. August 14, 1967 UPI Report–GARRISON WINS PERJURY CASE

31. Lambert 298 n38

32. Davy 290 n.28

33. August 14, 1967 UPI Report–GARRISON WINS PERJURY CASE

34. Garrison 94-95. In addition to the previously cited Garrison quote, in an August 5, 1967 memo from Louisiana State Trooper Sergeant John Buccola to Lou Ivon, the author wrote:

> "On Weds. night April 12, 1967, Lt. Casso and myself entered the '544' Bar on Bourbon St. and noticed Dean Andrews seated at the bar. As a result of our lifetime acquaintance, our conversation was casual and intimate...I explained to him that my opinion was that no DA prosecuted a perjury charge—that said charge was to force the individual to tell the truth, and that if he would identify Bertrand, I was sure the perjury charge would be dropped. Andrews replied that he would rather pull five years than identify Bertrand because these people played for keeps, and that five years was better than being dead."

35. Lambert 298

36. Qtd. in Weisberg 140

37. Summers 241

38. Dave Reitzes interview with Harold Weisberg, December 3, 1998.

39. August 14, 1967 UPI Report–GARRISON WINS PERJURY CASE

40. Lambert 122

41. Garrison 284

42. Lambert 176

43. Lifton, David. "Is Garrison Out of his Mind?" *Open City* (May 31-June 6, 1968).

44. Ibid.

45. Ibid.

46. Ibid.

47. Ibid.

48. James Alcock interview with David Logan, April 13, 1968.

49. Lambert 228

50. Lifton, David. "Is Garrison Out of his Mind?" *Open City* (May 31-June 6, 1968).

51. Lambert 230

52. Lifton, David. "Is Garrison Out of his Mind?" *Open City* (May 31-June 6, 1968).

53. Ibid.

54. NODA Affidavit of Peter Deageano, NARA# 180-10088-10485. Also see Vea 31.

55. Ibid.

56. Vea 31

57. NODA Affidavit of Barbara Reid, NARA# 180-10088-10486.

58. Vea 33

59. NODA memo from Sciambra to Garrison, March 12, 1968. NARA# 1801007610180.

60. Ibid.

61. NODA memo from Sciambra to Garrison, November 6, 1967. NARA# 180-10109-10089.

62. Ibid.

63. Alderson/Farrell FBI Interview with Kerry Wendell Thornley, November 25, 1963. NARA# 157-10003-10030.

64. FBI Telex from SAC, Dallas to Director and SAC, New Orleans, November 25, 1963.

65. NODA memo from Sciambra to Garrison, November 6, 1967. NARA# 180-10109-10089.

66. Ibid.

67. NODA memo from Sciambra to Garrison, April 2, 1968.

68. Telephone Interview of Cliff Hall by Richard V. Burnes, January 10, 1968.

69. Ibid.

70. Ibid.

71. Ibid.

72. Letter from John Schwegmann, Jr. to Jim Garrison, February 22, 1968.

73. 11 WCH 110

74. Ibid 336

75. Kennedy/Chlager FBI Interview of Kerry Wendell Thornley, November 27, 1963. NARA# 157-10003-10054.

76. Thornley Ex. 1, printed in 21 WCH 669.

77. Davy and DiEugenio, "False Witness: Aptly Titled." *Probe* v.6#4 (May./Jun. 1999).

78. Vea 39

79. 1976 Affidavit of Kerry W. Thornley, NARA# 180-10109-10087.

80. Ibid.

81. Davy 40

82. James DiEugenio interview with Dan Campbell, September 3, 1994.

83. February 22, 1968 New Orleans Times Picayune story–OSWALD MARINE BUDDY CHARGED: Perjury Laid to Thornley in Garrison Probe

84. Ibid.

85. Ibid.

86. Ibid.

87. Davy and DiEugenio, "False Witness: Aptly Titled." *Probe* v.6#4 (May./Jun. 1999).

88. Ibid. Thornley was referred to in the press as a "freelance writer." When I meet a freelance writer, I usually ask which restaurant he or she buses tables at. I even ask myself this question.

89. Lifton, David. "Is Garrison Out of his Mind?" *Open City* (May 31-June 6, 1968).

90. February 22, 1968 New Orleans Times Picayune story–OSWALD MARINE BUDDY CHARGED: Perjury Laid to Thornley in Garrison Probe

91. Davy 169-170

92. Ibid 171-172

93. Ibid 173

94. DiEugenio 367 n.21

95. Davy 61. Since the Garrison probe, Bethell has gone on to become an author and contributing editor to the conservative newsmagazine *National Review.*

96. One wonders why a conviction against Thornley wouldn't have done the trick. By January 1969, Garrison had already convicted Dean Andrews. Another conviction, even for perjury, would have put him at 2-0. If Garrison had spent a third the time in 1968 on Thornley that he spent of on Shaw, there is little doubt he could not have found and identified witnesses to Thornley's presence at 544 Camp Street. This would have elevated the case far above simple perjury—the Alger Hiss trial was just a little perjury case, wasn't it?—and hinted at the outline of the conspiracy. The Campbell brothers have stated that they would have been

willing to cooperate with Garrison. Author William Davy has argued that another strategy against Shaw would have made all the difference in the world. If Shaw had been questioned before the Grand Jury in 1967 about his associations with Oswald and Ferrie, his CIA employment, the Bertrand alias or the San Francisco trip he could have easily been convicted of perjury making him much easier to convict of conspiracy later on.

97. Jim Garrison, *A Heritage of Stone* (New York: Berkley Publishing Corp., 1970), p.18.

Chapter Six

1. This was extremely interesting, as Garrison did not personally believe Oswald had participated in the assassination. Garrison's pet theory was that Oswald had been involved with the group plotting the murder, and maybe believed he was infiltrating it—based on the account of Richard Case Nagell—but wound up being the scapegoat. Nevertheless, whether or not Oswald's heart was truly with the plotters, his actions as evidenced by Perry Raymond Russo could have been legally interpreted as conspiracy.

2. Davy 193

3. Davy and DiEugenio, "False Witness: Aptly Title." *Probe* v.6#4 (May/Jun. 1999).

4. William Davy interview with L.J. Delsa, April 5, 1995, and confirmed to the author by Delsa on September 5, 2000.

5. Fensterwald 476-477

6. Louisiana v. Clay Shaw, February 6, 1967.

7. Lambert 163 n., Davy 310 n.8

8. Ibid.

9. Ibid.

10. Vea 21

11. Davy 310 n.8

12. Lambert 163 n.

13. CLYDE JOHNSON KILLED, REPORT: Felled by Shotgun Blast, Sheriff Says," New Orleans Times-Picayune, July 24, 1969.

14. Davy 310 n.8

15. Louisiana v. Clay Shaw, February 6, 1967.

16. Ibid.

17. Ibid.

18. Ibid.

19. Ibid.

20. Ibid.

21. Ibid.

22. Ibid.

23. Ibid.

24. Ibid.

25. Louisiana v. Clay Shaw, February 7, 1967.

26. Ibid.

27. Kirkwood 224-229

28. Ibid 231-245

29. Ibid.

30. Davy 174

31. Tyler video, *He Must Have Something.*

32. Davy 174.

33. Tyler video, *He Must Have Something.*

34. DiEugenio, Jim. "Inside Clay Shaw's Defense Team: The Wegmann Files." *Probe* v.4#4 (May/Jun. 1997).

35. DiEugenio 194

36. Turner 182

37. Davy 185

38. Louisiana v. Clay Shaw, February 10-12, 1967.

39. Ibid.

40. Ibid.

41. Ibid.

42. DiEugenio 195-196

43. Louisiana v. Clay Shaw, February 12, 1967.

44. Ibid.

45. Ibid.

46. Ibid.

47. Kevin, Art. "The Jolly Green Giant: A Look Back at the Case Against Clay Shaw by D-A Jim Garrison." *Kennedy Assassination Chronicles* v.3#2 (Summer 1997). Available on-line at http://www.vegasradio.com/jolly_green_giant.htm.

48. Louisiana v. Clay Shaw, February 17, 1967.

49. Davy 173

50. Louisiana v. Clay Shaw, February 17, 1967.

51. Ibid.

52. Qtd. in Weisberg 212-213

53. Ibid.

54. Qtd. in Davy 191

55. Ibid.

56. Ibid 192-193

57. Ibid.

58. Ibid 9

59. Ibid.

60. Ibid 282 n.23

61. Orleans Parish Grand Jury Testimony of William Dalzell, November 2, 1967.

62. Davy 18. Indeed, Dalzell admitted to the HSCA that he had worked for the CIA (Davy 283 n.27, citing HSCA document #064559, December 9, 1977).

63. FBI memo by Richard Bucaro, December 5, 1963. Contained in NARA# 1801003010064.

64. FBI memo by Regis Kennedy, December 6, 1963. Contained in NARA# 1801003010064.

65. Davy 51

66. James and Wardlaw 152

67. Orleans Parish Grand Jury Testimony of Regis Kennedy, May 17, 1967.

68. Ibid.

69. Ibid.

70. Ibid.

71. Ibid.

72. 11 WCH 334

73. Ibid 333

74. If the feelings of Lambert and Reitzes are correct, the VIP room evidence bears similarity to another incident encountered during the Garrison probe—a library card under the name Clem Bertrand, with the business listed "International Trade Mart" and the home address given as 3100 Louisiana Avenue Parkway (two blocks or so from Ferrie's apartment). Garrison received it anonymously and wrote it off as a (bad) forgery. The signature was nothing like Shaw's and the address in question (at least presently) does not exist. It is likely someone meant to put Ferrie's 3330 address.

75. Handwritten note accompanying photos taken of the book by Clancy Navarre.

76. Davy 178

77. Lambert 145

78. Ibid 151-152

79. Ibid.

80. For more details on this issue, see Davy 181.

81. Ibid.

82. Louisiana v. Clay Shaw, February 24, 1967.

83. Reitzes, Dave. "Who was Clay Bertrand?" *Who Speaks for Clay Shaw?* Available on-line at http://www.jfkassassination.net/shaw2.htm

84. Lambert 156 n.

85. Louisiana v. Clay Shaw, February 24, 1967.

86. Ibid.

87. Ibid.

88. Ibid.

89. Rebuttal arguments of James Alcock, Louisiana v. Clay Shaw, February 28, 1969.

90. Louisiana v. Clay Shaw, February 28, 1969.

91. Louisiana v. Clay Shaw, February 24, 1969.

92. Reitzes "Who Speaks?"

93. Louisiana v. Clay Shaw, February 7, 1969.

94. DiEugenio, James. "Inside Clay Shaw's Defense Team: The Wegmann Files." *Probe* v.4#4 (May/Jun. 1997).

95. James DiEugenio has indicated to the author that both sides wanted an analyst of national reputation, and Appel and McCarthy both filled that role.

96. Reitzes, "Who Speaks?"

97. Louisiana v. Clay Shaw, February 26, 1969.

98. Ibid. The defense should have known better. Davis was essentially used in an attempt at proving a negative. As far as the other white man, the NODA had already learned his identity. He was Captain Henry C. Spicer. See Davy 180.

99. Davy 178

100. November 15, 1967 Memo from Lloyd A. Ray to DCS Director.

101. November 30, 1967 Memo from Lawrence Houston. Another portion of this memo reads that should Moran identify Shaw and Bertrand as different people that "we [the CIA] have means of getting this information on to Dymond for use in preparing Shaw case without involving Hunter or Agency."

102. Louisiana v. Clay Shaw, February 27, 1969. Other questions and responses included:

> *Q. Mr. Shaw, have you ever been known as Clay Bertrand?*
> *A. No, I have not.*
> *Q. Have you ever been known as Clem Bertrand?*
> *A. No, I have not.*

103. DiEugenio 199

104. Ibid.
105. Ibid 200
106. Louisiana v. Clay Shaw, February 19, 1969.
107. Ibid.
108. Ibid.
109. Ibid.
110. Ibid.
111. Ibid.
112. Ibid.
113. Ibid.
114. DiEugenio 200-201
115. Ibid.
116. Ibid 201-202
117. Ibid.
118. Davy 174-175
119. Joan Mellen e-mail to the author, April 27, 2001.
120. DiEugenio 200
121. Ibid 369 n.71
122. Ibid 369 n.81
123. Louisiana v. Clay Shaw, February 21, 1969.
124. Louisiana v. Clay Shaw, February 28, 1969.
125. Louisiana v. Clay Shaw, February 21, 1969.
126. Davy 182
127. Louisiana v. Clay Shaw, February 21, 1969.
128. Louisiana v. Clay Shaw, February 21 and 22, 1969.
129. Louisiana v. Clay Shaw, February 24 and 25, 1969.
130. 2 WCH 382
131. Louisiana v. Clay Shaw, February 26, 1969.
132. Louisiana v. Clay Shaw, February 27, 1969.
133. Louisiana v. Clay Shaw, February 28, 1969.
134. Ibid.
135. Ibid.

136. Ibid.

137. Ibid.

138. Ibid.

139. Lambert 163

140. Tyler video, *He Must Have Something*.

141. Lambert 163

142. Louisiana v. Clay Shaw, March 1, 1969.

143. Lambert 161. Of the verdict, Garrison later wrote, "As a district attorney I accept the verdict of the jury. However, to misconstrue this verdict as an acquittal of the federal government in its involvement in the assassination of the President and in its suppression of the evidence would be a serious mistake. Jim Garrison, *A Heritage of Stone* (New York: Berkley Publishing Corp., 1970), p.19.

144. Ibid 160-161

Chapter Seven

1. Tyler video, *He Must Have Something*.

2. Christenberry Decision.

3. DiEugenio 375 n.75

4. 09/18/67 Memo from Alcock to Garrison, NARA# 180-10076-10048

5. There has been some debate as to whether the presence of the alias in Shaw's CIA file might merely be something Shaw's superiors put in the file after hearing press reports about the alleged alias.

6. Tyler video, *He Must Have Something*.

7. Ibid.

8. Ibid.

9. E-mails to author from researchers William Davy and Dave Reitzes, dates unknown.

10. Ibid.

11. Christenberry Decision.

12. Davy 173

13. Christenberry Decision

14. Davy 115

15. Orleans Parish Grand Jury Testimony of Ross Yockey, July 12, 1967.

16. James DiEugenio interview with Perry Russo.

17. Memorandum from the files of Edward Wegmann, January 27, 1971.

18. Ibid.

19. William Davy interview with Niles Peterson. Also, DiEugenio 144, citing Popkin, Richard H., "Garrison's Case," New York Review of Books, September 14, 1967.

20. Christenberry Decision

21. James Alcock interview with David Logan, April 13, 1968. Available from the Jim Garrison papers at the AARC.

22. Ibid.

23. Affidavit of Henry Burnell Clark.

24. Louviere, Wagner, and Laurent from Davy 186; Clark from journal of *Life* editor Richard Billings (March 16, 1967).

25. Affidavit of Mrs. June A. Rolfe, NARA# 180-10096-10021.

26. Ibid.

27. DiEugenio 268

28. Ibid.

29. Qtd. In Garrison 316-317

30. DiEugenio 269

31. Garrison 318

32. DiEugenio 269

33. DiEugenio, James. "Connick vs. Garrison: Round Three." *Probe* v.2#5 (Jul./Aug. 1995).

34. DiEugenio, James. "Raymond vs. Connick: Round One." *Probe* v.2#5 (Jul./Aug. 1995).

35. Davy 188

36. Ibid 200

37. DiEugenio 269

38. DiEugenio, James. "The Sins of Robert Blakey." *Probe* v.5#6 (Sep./Oct. 1998).

39. Ibid.

40. Ibid.

41. Ibid.

42. Ibid.

43. Ibid.

44. DiEugenio, James. "The Probe Interview: Bon Tanenbaum." *Probe* v.3#5 (Jul./Aug. 1996).

45. DiEugenio, James. "The Sins of Robert Blakey." *Probe* v.5#6 (Sep./Oct. 1998).

46. Author interview with L.J. Delsa, September 5, 2000.

47. DiEugenio, James. "The Sins of Robert Blakey." *Probe* v.5#6 (Sep./Oct. 1998).

48. Author interview with L.J. Delsa, September 5, 2000.

49. Davy 164

50. Ibid.

51. Ibid 165

52. DiEugenio, James. "The Sins of Robert Blakey." *Probe* v.5#6 (Sep./Oct. 1998). The *Select* in Select Committee on Assassinations means that the Committee was not a standing Committee of the House and had to be reconstituted when the 94th Congress ended and the 95th began. This vote came on March 31, 1977, only a few hours after Oswald associate George DeMorenschildt had committed suicide.

53. Ibid.

54. Ibid.

55. DiEugenio, James. "The Probe Interview: Bob Tanenbaum." *Probe* v.3#5 (Jul./Aug. 1996)

56. DiEugenio 271

57. Lambert 243

58. Ibid 241

Chapter Eight

1. 10 HSCA 125
2. 1976 Affidavit of Kerry Thornley, NARA# 180-10109-10087.
3. Scott 3
4. Lopez Report, 138.
5. Scott 4
6. Pease, Lisa. "James Jesus Angleton & the Kennedy Assassination, Part II." *Probe* v.7#6 (Sep./Oct. 2000).
7. Scott 4
8. Ibid.
9. Ibid 17
10. Ibid 5
11. Ibid.
12. WCD 347
13. Scott 10
14. Azcue: 3 HSCA 136, Duran: 3 HSCA 69-70.
15. Fonzi 294
16. Scott 9
17. Ibid.
18. Ibid 17
19. Ibid.
20. Ibid 18
21. Ibid.
22. Riechmann, Deb. "Tape: Call on JFK Wasn't Oswald." *Associated Press* (November 21, 1999).
23. Ibid.
24. Ibid.
25. Memo from Nicholas deB. Katzenbach, Deputy Attorney General to Mr. Moyers, November 25, 1963.
26. For a good overview of the creation and history of the Warren Commission, see Brown, Walt. *The Warren Omission: A Micro-Study of the*

Methods and Failures of the Warren Commission (New Castle, Delaware: Delmax, 1996).

27. Davy 130
28. Ibid.
29. Garrison 274 n.
30. Ibid 294
31. Davy 197
32. Ibid 197-198
33. Ibid 198-199
34. Ibid.
35. Ibid 199-200
36. Ibid 95
37. Ibid 95-97
38. DiEugenio 209-211
39. Davy 96-97
40. Ibid 98
41. Ibid 100
42. Ibid 98
43. Lambert 203-204
44. Lambert video, *False Witness* History Channel Special
45. Davy 100
46. Orleans Parish Grand Jury Testimony of Regis Kennedy, May 17, 1967.
47. April 27, 1967 CIA Memo on Clay Shaw, NARA# 104-10013-10308.
48. Davy, William. "File Update: Notes on Some Recent Releases." *Probe* v.7#2 (Jan./Feb. 2000).
49. Ibid.
50. Davy 196. For info on the Mullen Co., see Harris, Bob. "Deep Throat: A few more thoughts about Watergate." *Sonoma County Independent* (July 3, 1997).
51. Ibid.
52. Davy 196

53. Ibid 195-196

54. Ibid 77

55. Ibid 294 n.16

56. Ibid 182

57. Ibid 146

58. Ibid 78-79

59. Ibid 79-80

60. Turner, William. "The Garrison Commission on the Assassination of President Kennedy." *Ramparts* (January 1968).

61. Davy 200

62. Ibid 88

63. May 8, 1967 CIA memorandum, NARA# 104-10013-10319.

64. Davy 88, 297 n.24

65. Davy, William. "File Update: Notes on Some Recent Releases." *Probe* v.7#2 (Jan./Feb. 2000).

66. Davy 88-89

67. Qtd. in Ibid 89

68. HSCA Executive Session interview with "John Scelso," [pseudonym for Whitten] May 16, 1978, hereinafter cited as Scelso deposition.

69. Ibid.

70. Ibid.

71. Davy 204

72. Ibid 85

73. Pease, Lisa. "David Atlee Phillips, Clay Shaw and Freeport Sulphur." *Probe* v.3#3 (Mar./Apr. 1996).

74. Ibid.

75. Ibid.

76. Davy 85-86

77. Ibid.

78. Pease, Lisa. "David Atlee Phillips, Clay Shaw and Freeport Sulphur." *Probe* v.3#3 (Mar./Apr. 1996).

79. Davy 93-94

80. Ibid 303 n.13

81. CIA memo "Garrison and the Kennedy Assassination: Cubans and other Latin Americans Allegedly Involved," March 7, 1968.

82. Davy 156

83. Ibid 153-154

84. Ibid 156

85. Davy and DiEugenio, "False Witness: Aptly Titled." *Probe* v.6#4 (May/Jun. 1999).

86. ARRB Testimony of Robert Tanenbaum, September 17, 1996.

87. Author interview with Robert Groden, September 16, 2000.

88. DiEugenio, James. "The Probe Interview: Bob Tanenbaum." *Probe* v.3#5 (Jul./Aug. 1996). Oswald was also seen, with Ferrie and numerous Cubans, at a "military training maneuver" near Lake Pontchartrain in early September 1963. This was near Bedico Creek, not the McLaney camp. (Kurtz 203)

89. Author interview with Robert Groden, September 16, 2000.

90. Author interview with L.J. Delsa, September 5, 2000.

91. DiEugenio, James. "The Probe Interview: Bob Tanenbaum." *Probe* v.3#5 (Jul./Aug. 1996).

92. Memo from S. Jonathan Blackmer to G. Robert Blakey, September 1, 1977. NARA# 180-10100-10054.

93. ARRB Deposition of Dr. J. Thornton Boswell, February 26, 1996.

94. Aguilar, Gary. "The Justice Department and medical military authorities protect Clay Shaw, interfere with MLK." *JFK Deep Politics Quarterly* v.7#1 (October 2001).

95. Davy 143-145

96. Ibid 173

97. Harold Weisberg memo to Jim Garrison, April 9, 1968. NARA# 1801007610190.

98. Ibid.

99. Ibid.

100. Summers 296-299

101. Ibid.

102. Ibid.

103. HSCR 138

104. Summers 300

105. A.J. Weberman website–Data Base Nodule 13 "Hemming's Activities: Loran Hall–Hemming Patsy–September 1963." http://www.weberman.com/htdocs/13/

106. FBI memo from Jerome K. Crowe, November 23, 1963. Located on-line at http://www.weberman.com/htdocs/13/

107. A.J. Weberman website–Data Base Nodule 13 "Hemming's Activities: Loran Hall–Hemming Patsy–September 1963." http://www.weberman.com/htdocs/13/

108. A.J. Weberman website–Data Base Nodule 13 "Hemming's Activities: Loran Hall–Hemming Patsy–September 1963." http://www.weberman.com/htdocs/13/13-5.htm

109. A.J. Weberman website–Data Base Nodule 13 "Hemming's Activities: Loran Hall–Hemming Patsy–September 1963." http://www.weberman.com/htdocs/13/13-6.htm

110. A.J. Weberman website–Data Base Nodule 13 "Hemming's Activities: Loran Hall–Hemming Patsy–September 1963." http://www.weberman.com/htdocs/13/13-7.htm

111. Ibid.

112. Art Kevin interview of Jim Garrison, December 29, 1967.

113. Harold Weisberg interview with Loran Hall, published in *National Enquirer*, September 1, 1968.

114. A recording of Hall's questioning can be found on-line at http://www.vegasradio.com/jfk3.html

115. Summers 301

116. Griffith, Michael. "Extra Bullets and Missed Shots in Dealey Plaza." On-line at http://ourworld.cs.com/mikegriffith1/id139.htm

117. alt.assassination.jfk post by Jerry P. Shinley, archived at http://reitzes.www4.50megs.com/jpssmrteb.html

118. Author interview with L.J. Delsa, September 5, 2000.

119. L.J. Delsa interview of Thomas E. Beckham, October 9, 1977.

120. FBI# 62-109060-4407.

121. L.J. Delsa interview of Thomas E. Beckham, October 9, 1977.

122. Ibid.

123. The Easy Papers. Information on the history of the Easy Papers from James DiEugenio e-mail to author, date unknown.

124. Jim Garrison memo to Jonathan Blackmer, July 18, 1977.

125. HSCR 91

126. Ibid 607 n.181

127. Author interview with L.J. Delsa, September 5, 2000.

128. DiEugenio, James. "The Sins of Robert Blakey, Part II." *Probe* v.6#1 (Nov./Dec. 1998).

129. Dave Reitzes e-mail to author, date unknown.

130. L.J. Delsa interview with Thomas E. Beckham, October 9, 1977.

131. Larry Hancock e-mail to author, March 18, 2001.

132. Pease, Lisa. "James Jesus Angleton & the Kennedy Assassination, Part I." *Probe* v.7#5 (Jul./Aug. 2000).

133. Ibid.

134. Ibid.

135. Ibid.

136. Ibid.

137. Ibid.

138. Ibid.

139. Ibid.

140. Ibid.

141. Ibid.

142. Pease, Lisa. "James Jesus Angleton & the Kennedy Assassination, Part II." *Probe* v.7#6 (Sep./Oct. 2000).

143. Pease, Lisa. "James Jesus Angleton & the Kennedy Assassination, Part I." *Probe* v.7#5 (Jul./Aug. 2000).

144. Pease, Lisa. "James Jesus Angleton & the Kennedy Assassination, Part II." *Probe* v.7#6 (Sep./Oct. 2000).

145. Ibid.

146. Scelso deposition.

147. Lane 312

148. Ibid 313

149. Pease, Lisa. "James Jesus Angleton & the Kennedy Assassination, Part II." *Probe* v.7#6 (Sep./Oct. 2000).

150. Ibid.

151. Ibid.

152. Lane 313

153. Scelso deposition.

154. Pease, Lisa. "James Jesus Angleton & the Kennedy Assassination, Part II." *Probe* v.7#6 (Sep./Oct. 2000).

155. Lane 171

156. For a full treatment of the problems with Lorenz's credibility, see Fonzi, Gaeton. *The Last Investigation* (New York: Thunder's Mouth Press, 1993).

157. Lane 135

158. Ibid 167

159. Pease, Lisa. "James Jesus Angleton & the Kennedy Assassination, Part II." *Probe* v.7#6 (Sep./Oct. 2000).

160. Ibid.

161. Lane 218

Bibliography

Government Documents

Report of the President's Commission on the Assassination of President John F. Kennedy (the Warren Report) (Washington: U.S. Government Printing Office, 1964), with accompanying 26 volumes of exhibits and testimony.

State of Louisiana v. Clay L. SHAW, Criminal District Court, Parish of Orleans (the Shaw trial transcripts) (Proceedings in open court from February 6 to March 1, 1969). Available on CD-ROM from L.M.P. Systems and in print from the Assassination Archives and Research Center (AARC).

Opinion of United States District Court for the Eastern District of Louisiana, New Orleans Division in the case of *Clay L. SHAW v. Jim GARRISON*, individually and as District Attorney for the Parish of Orleans, State of Louisiana (the Herbert Christenberry decision) (1971).

U.S. House, Select Committee on Assassinations, *Report*, with twelve accompanying volumes of hearings and appendices (material on Kennedy case as opposed to Martin Luther King, Jr., case) (Washington: U.S. Government Printing Office, 1979), 95th Congress, 2nd Session, 1979, H. Rpt. 1828.

Books

Brown, Walt. *The Warren Omission* (Wilmington, Delaware: Delmax, 1996).

Davy, William. *Let Justice Be Done* (Reston, Virginia: Jordan Publishing, 1999).

DiEugenio, James. *Destiny Betrayed* (New York: Sheridan Square Press, 1992).

Fensterwald, Bernard, Jr. *Coincidence or Conspiracy* (New York: Zebra Books, 1977).

Fonzi, Gaeton. *The Last Investigation* (New York: Thunder's Mouth Press, 1993).

Garrison, Jim. *A Heritage of Stone* (New York: Berkley Publishing Corp., 1970).

—-. *On the Trail of the Assassins* (New York: Sheridan Square Press, 1988).

Griffith, Michael. *Compelling Evidence* (Grand Prairie, Texas: JFK Lancer Productions and Publications, 1996).

Groden, Robert and Livingstone, Harrison Edward. *High Treason* (Baltimore: The Conservatory Press, 1989).

James, Rosemary and Wardlaw, Jack. *Plot or Politics?* (New Orleans: Pelican Publishing House, 1967).

Kirkwood, James. *American Grotesque* (New York: Simon and Schuster, 1970).

Kurtz, Michael L. *Crime of the Century* (Knoxville: University of Tennessee Press, 1993).

Lambert, Patricia. *False Witness* (New York: M. Evans and Company, 1998).

Lane, Mark. *Plausible Denial* (New York: Thunder's Mouth Press, 1991).

Livingstone, Harrison Edward. *High Treason 2* (New York: Carroll & Graf Publishers, 1992).

—-. *Killing The Truth* (New York: Carroll & Graf Publishers, 1993).

Marrs, Jim. *Crossfire* (New York: Carroll & Graf Publishers, 1989).

Martin, David. *Wilderness of Mirrors* (New York: Harper & Row Publishers, 1980).

Scott, Peter Dale. *Deep Politics II* (Grand Prairie, Texas: JFK Lancer Productions and Publications, 1996).

Sklar, Zachary and Stone, Oliver. *JFK: The Documented Screenplay* (New York: Applause Books, 1992).

Stroud, Henry. *The Best Suspect* (Mineral Wells, Texas: Stroud Publishing, 2001).

Summers, Anthony. *Not in Your Lifetime* (New York: Marlowe & Company, 1998).

Turner, William W. *Rearview Mirror* (Granite Bay, California: Penmarin Books, 2001).

Vea, Peter. *The Peter Vea Index: Chronology and Summaries of Files from the Garrison Investigation* (Sylmar, California: Citizens for Truth About the Kennedy Assassination, 1995).

Weisberg, Harold. *Oswald in New Orleans* (New York: Canyon Books, 1967).

Index

and Ferrie, 3-6, 24, 28, 30-40, 44-46, 63, 70-74, 76, 78, 80-82, 84, 88, 92-93, 107, 112-113, 117, 119-120, 122-125, 147-150, 156-158, 163, 169-173, 200-201, 204, 207-209, 215, 218, 227

and Grand Jury, 31, 40, 42, 49, 51, 63-64, 66, 68, 86, 90-92, 121, 127, 139, 142-143, 156, 209, 215, 217-218, 222, 225

and Gurvich, 41, 49, 68, 121, 153, 210

and *Heritage of Stone,* 125, 150, 215, 221, 232

investigation, 7, 22, 24, 31-33, 46-48, 52-53, 55, 60, 67-68, 79, 86-89, 91, 94, 101, 106, 108, 122, 125, 128-132, 135, 139, 149, 153-154, 156-159, 161, 164-165, 173, 179, 230, 232-233

and Leemans, 49, 211

and media, 3, 11, 37, 39, 46-47, 64, 66, 69, 120-123, 130-131, 133, 142, 153, 156, 173-174, 200

and *New Orleans Magazine,* 128, 149

and Novel, 8, 30-32, 36, 48, 63-64, 145, 153, 207

and Phelan, 43-47, 83, 112-113, 210

and Rault, 2, 7

and Sciambra, 29, 33-35, 37-39, 43-46, 56-59, 63, 66, 80, 83, 85, 112, 114, 142, 148, 196, 207-210, 213

and Shaw case, 43, 50-51, 86, 123, 127, 153, 219

trial of, 42, 53, 70, 105, 117, 129

Gaudet, William, 145, 204

Gerdes, Vernon, 204

Gervais, Pershing, 126

Goldsmith, Bernard, 57, 196

Goldsmith, Michael, 147, 160

Gonzales, Ernesto, 29

Graf, Allen D., 15

Grand Jury, 31, 40, 42, 49, 51, 63-64, 66, 68, 86, 90-92, 121, 127, 139, 142-143, 156, 209, 215, 217-218, 222, 225

Gurvich, William H., 41, 49, 68, 121, 151, 208

Phelan, James, 43, 83, 112
Phillips, David Atlee, 30, 145-146, 150, 163, 226-227
Plotkin, Stephen, 32, 153, 204
prostitution, 2

Quinn, Rosaleen, 16, 136
Quigley, John, 7
Quiroga, Carlos, 24, 204-205

Ray, Lloyd, 99
Registrar of Voters, 74, 76
Reid, Barbara, 57, 64, 67, 153, 193, 212
Reitzes, Dave, 52, 95, 97, 99, 158, 174, 204-205, 212, 221, 229
Reynolds, Warwick, 68
Roberts, Delphine, 3, 204
Rocca, Ray, 165
Roussel, Henry J., 15
Ruby, Jack, 72
Russell, Dick, 155, 167
Russo, Perry, 36, 39, 43, 48, 74, 80, 96, 106, 112, 117, 120, 122, 125, 132, 169, 171, 222

San Francisco, 29, 71-73, 113, 143, 172, 215
    International Trade Mart, 28-29, 57, 75, 107, 113, 141, 144-145, 194, 218
    Shaw's trip to, 72-73
Saturday Evening Post, 43-44, 46
Scalia, Sal, 148
Schact, Hjalmar, 141
Schiller, Lawrence, 71
Sciambra, Andrew, 29, 33, 37, 43, 46, 56, 63, 83, 85, 142, 148
    and Parrott, 89

Spicer, Henry C., 219

Spiesel, Charles I., 78, 80

Sprague, Richard A., 129

Stevens, Marguerite D., 143

Stone, Oliver, 35, 85, 131

Sullivan, J. Monroe, 29, 143, 172

Summers, Anthony, 52, 204

Tadin, Mr. & Mrs., 113

Texas, 4, 7, 34, 55, 72, 84, 113, 129, 155, 159, 179, 232

Thornley, Kerry, 8, 11, 22, 53, 56-57, 59-60, 62, 67-68, 89, 126, 132, 134, 139, 177, 193, 195-196, 224

and Andrews, 25-28, 30, 35, 40-41, 48, 51-53, 61-62, 73, 86-87, 90, 94-95, 149, 153, 206-207, 211, 214

and Banister, 2-3, 5, 23-24, 30-31, 63, 80, 83, 89-90, 112, 139, 148-150, 153, 158, 204-205

and Campbell, 63, 204, 214-215

and Deageano, 56-57, 64, 193-194, 212

and Dowell, 59

and Goldsmith, Bernard, 57, 196

and Grand Jury, 31, 40, 42, 49, 51, 63-64, 66, 68, 86, 90-92, 121, 127, 139, 142-143, 156, 209, 215, 217-218, 222, 225

and Cliff Hall, 59, 67, 213

and LaSavia, 61, 67

and Lifton, 53-56, 67, 212, 214

and McAuliffe, 89

and Oswald, 3-26, 29-30, 35, 37-38, 40-42, 44, 51-65, 67, 70-79, 82, 89-90, 106-107, 113, 117, 119-120, 123, 131, 134-139, 148, 150, 154, 158-160, 162-164, 169-173, 176, 181, 194-196, 199-202, 204-206, 209, 214-215, 223-224, 227, 233

and perjury, 41, 46, 51-54, 66, 113, 119-120, 123-126, 130, 211-212, 214-215

and Reid, 57, 64, 66-67, 153, 193, 212

and Spencer, 58-59

0-595-22455-5

Printed in the United States
4773

9 780595 224555